I0752948

This diary belongs to

____

____

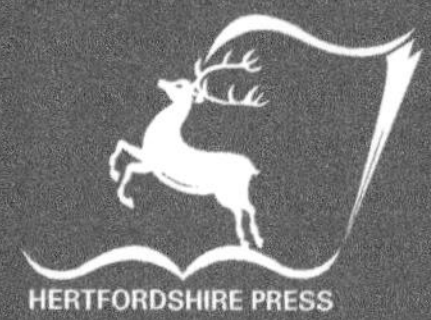

HERTFORDSHIRE PRESS (UK)
In conjunction with
the Eurasian Creative Guild (London)
https://www.1.eurasiancreativeguild.uk/
First published by Hertfordshire Press 2023

VOICES OF FRIENDS
POETRY & ART ALMANAC 2023

Translator Jonathan Campion, Timur Akhmedjanov
Project manager Anna Nikolaeva, Taina Kaunis
Design Alexandra Rey

A CIP catalogue record for this book is available in the British Library

ISBN 978-1-913356-59-0

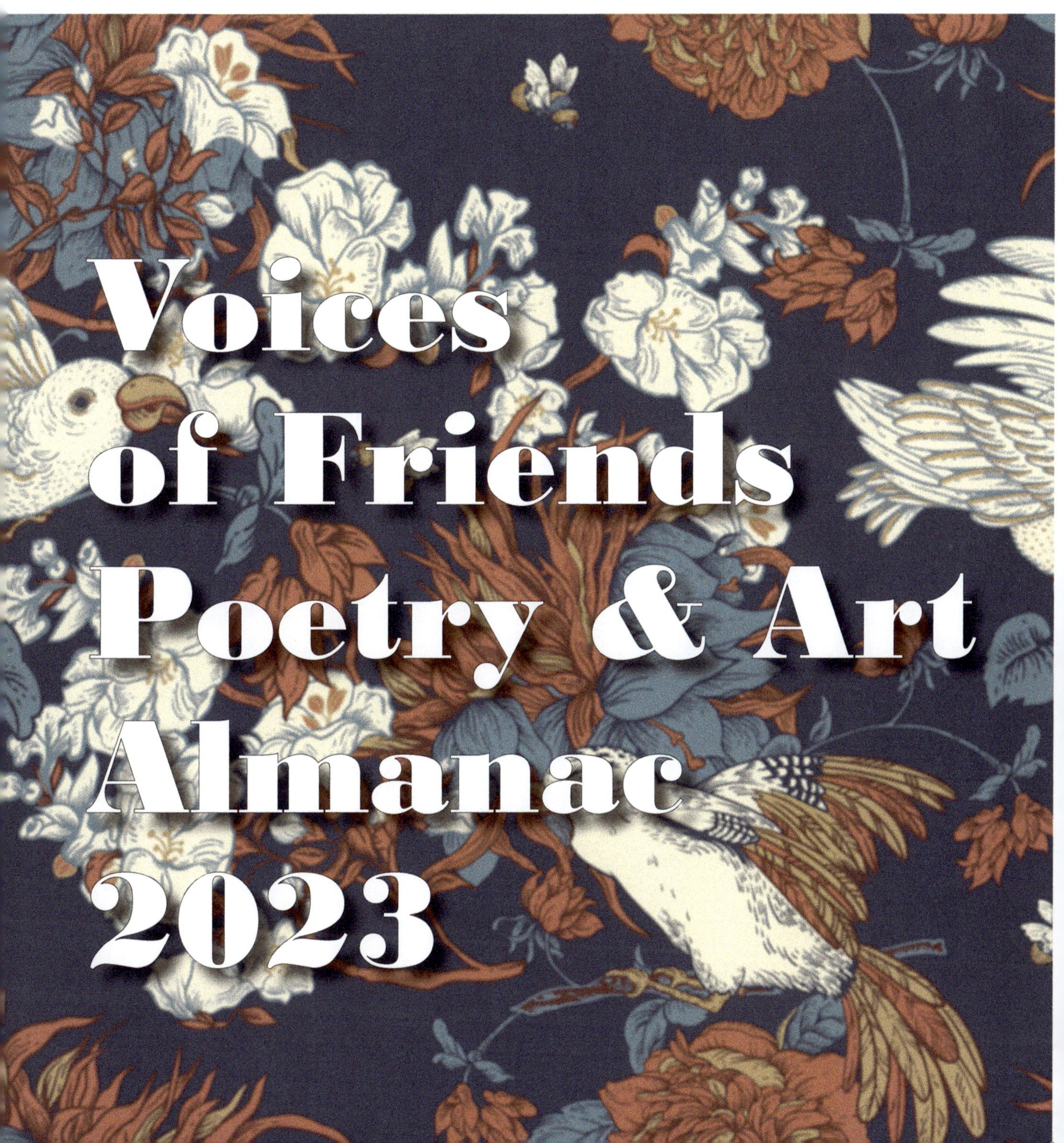
Voices
of Friends
Poetry & Art
Almanac
2023

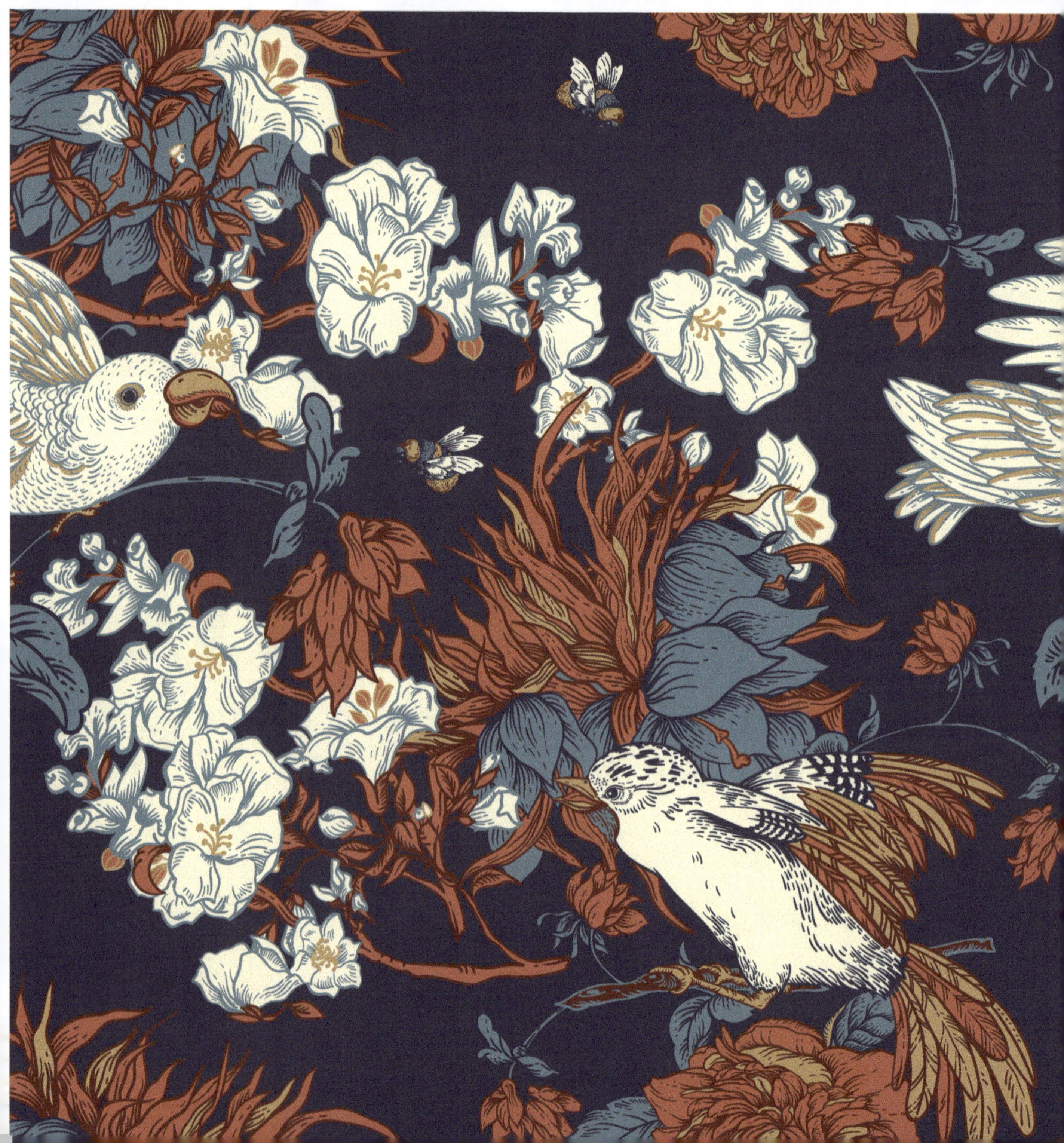

WELCOME TO OUR CIRCLE OF POETRY AND FRIENDSHIP!

I'm very pleased to introduce the 2023 edition of the Eurasian Creative Guild's almanac Voices of Friends. This year's collection of poetry and art may be our most complete and diverse ever. We are proud to include works from students and pensioners; poems about nature and cities, about love and about war; submissions from Moldova to Tajikistan – and masses of creativity from everyone and everywhere in between, proudly representing the Eurasian space in Great Britain.

The varied nature of these poems and artworks could have made for a disjointed book. But they all blend harmoniously together, thanks to what I think is a common theme: kindness.

Whether the subject matter is heartbreaking or playful – and there is plenty of both within these pages – each artist has created something that is, above all, genuine and kind.

But this should be no surprise: the Eurasian Creative Guild is such a kind group of people that everything we make always comes from the heart. As 2023 begins it feels like our parts of the world are in need of kindness now more than ever before. So if these works inspire you to contribute something to next year's Voices of Friends, let's see if we can fill it with even more love.

Happy reading,

Jonathan Campion
Translator and editor,
Eurasian Creative Guild
jonathancampion.com

CALENDAR 2023

January

S	M	T	W	T	F	S
1	2	3	4	5	6	7
8	9	10	11	12	13	14
15	16	17	18	19	20	21
22	23	24	25	26	27	28
29	30	31				

February

S	M	T	W	T	F	S
			1	2	3	4
5	6	7	8	9	10	11
12	13	14	15	16	17	18
19	20	21	22	23	24	25
26	27	28				

March

S	M	T	W	T	F	S
			1	2	3	4
5	6	7	8	9	10	11
12	13	14	15	16	17	18
19	20	21	22	23	24	25
26	27	28	29	30	31	

April

S	M	T	W	T	F	S
						1
2	3	4	5	6	7	8
9	10	11	12	13	14	15
16	17	18	19	20	21	22
23	24	25	26	27	28	29
30						

May

S	M	T	W	T	F	S
	1	2	3	4	5	6
7	8	9	10	11	12	13
14	15	16	17	18	19	20
21	22	23	24	25	26	27
28	29	30	31			

June

S	M	T	W	T	F	S
				1	2	3
4	5	6	7	8	9	10
11	12	13	14	15	16	17
18	19	20	21	22	23	24
25	26	27	28	29	30	

July

S	M	T	W	T	F	S
						1
2	3	4	5	6	7	8
9	10	11	12	13	14	15
16	17	18	19	20	21	22
23	24	25	26	27	28	29
30	31					

August

S	M	T	W	T	F	S
		1	2	3	4	5
6	7	8	9	10	11	12
13	14	15	16	17	18	19
20	21	22	23	24	25	26
27	28	29	30	31		

September

S	M	T	W	T	F	S
					1	2
3	4	5	6	7	8	9
10	11	12	13	14	15	16
17	18	19	20	21	22	23
24	25	26	27	28	29	30

October

S	M	T	W	T	F	S
1	2	3	4	5	6	7
8	9	10	11	12	13	14
15	16	17	18	19	20	21
22	23	24	25	26	27	28
29	30	31				

November

S	M	T	W	T	F	S
			1	2	3	4
5	6	7	8	9	10	11
12	13	14	15	16	17	18
19	20	21	22	23	24	25
26	27	28	29	30		

December

S	M	T	W	T	F	S
					1	2
3	4	5	6	7	8	9
10	11	12	13	14	15	16
17	18	19	20	21	22	23
24	25	26	27	28	29	30
31						

ALMAZBEK ATAMBAEV (KYRGYZSTAN)

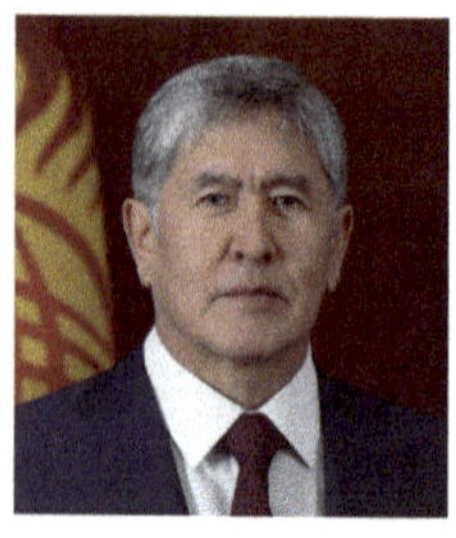

New Year

The day has come to close up my desk calendar
The last page of the calendar
The last day

I leave behind only remnants of memories to stay
For the last hour of this year is running out
Walking off like a kind old friend
He has decided to leave us forever
It's a shame I couldn't shake his strong hands in the end
Or reminisce on joy and sorrow we shared that you had to dissever

I'm sorry I didn't do everything the right way
And fully appreciate the kindness you had given us
For our bustling lives can sometimes be a useless, silly fuss
And so I've lost so many of your precious days
Alas, it's time to say goodbye, old friend
Can you please ask the New Year to be kind
So that we can have many more joyful days
And so that his reaching hand of hope will keep us safe and well

Our old year gifted us happiness and a melancholic dawn
And I will miss him everyday he is gone
The day has come to close up my desk calendar
And thank you for every precious day you gave to us

01

JANUARY

26 MONDAY

27 TUESDAY

28 WEDNESDAY

29 THURSDAY

30 FRIDAY

31 SATURDAY

01 SUNDAY

EDGAR ALLAN POE (USA)

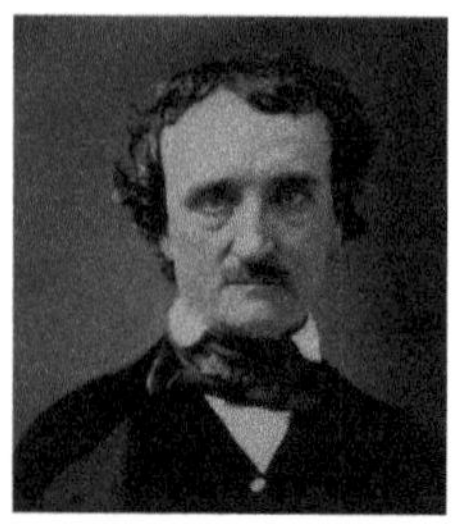

The Happiest Day

The happiest day – the happiest hour
My sear'd and blighted heart hath known,
The highest hope of pride and power,
I feel hath flown.

Of power! said I? yes! such I ween;
But they have vanish'd long, alas!
The visions of my youth have been-
But let them pass.

And, pride, what have I now with thee?
Another brow may even inherit
The venom thou hast pour'd on me
Be still, my spirit!

The happiest day – the happiest hour
Mine eyes shall see – have ever seen,
The brightest glance of pride and power,
I feel- have been:

But were that hope of pride and power
Now offer'd with the pain
Even then I felt– that brightest hour
I would not live again:

For on its wing was dark alloy,
And, as it flutter'd – fell
An essence – powerful to destroy
A soul that knew it well.

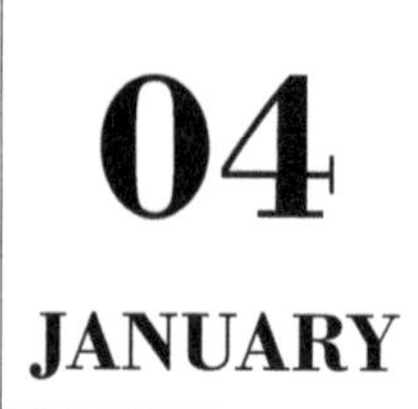

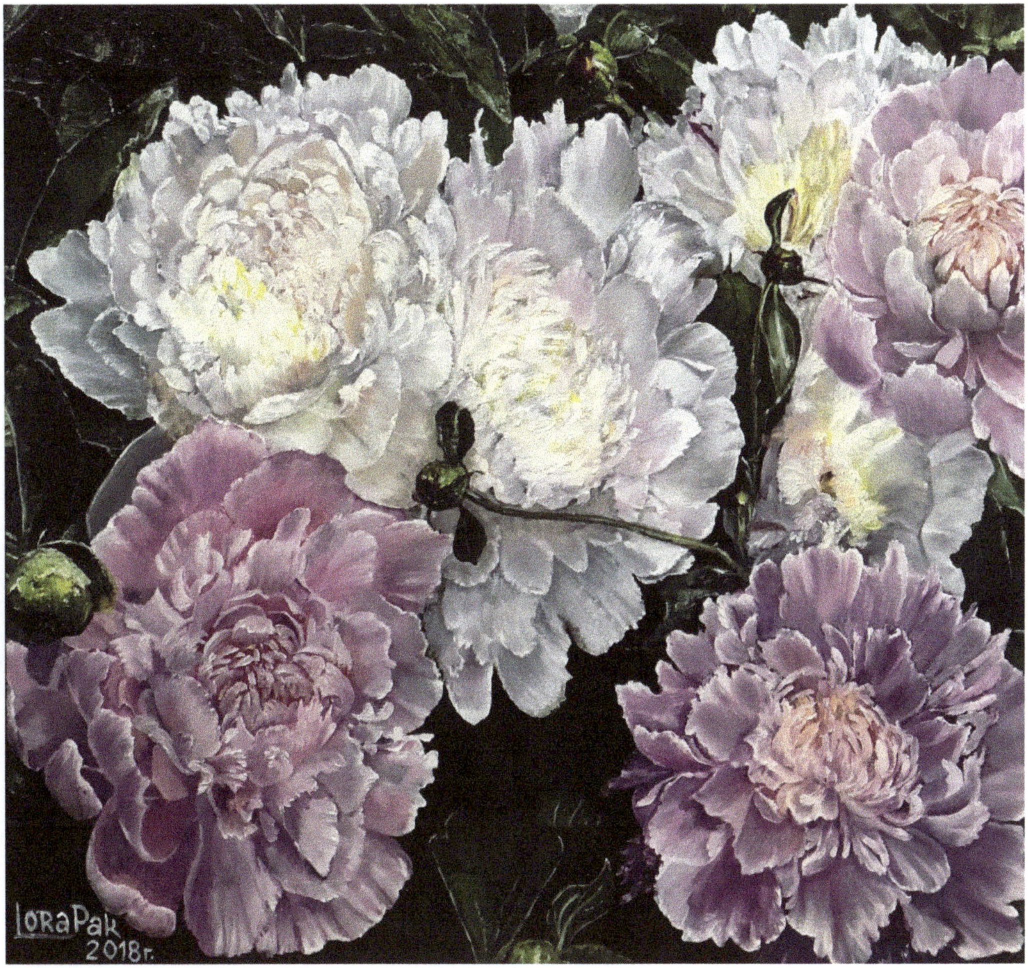

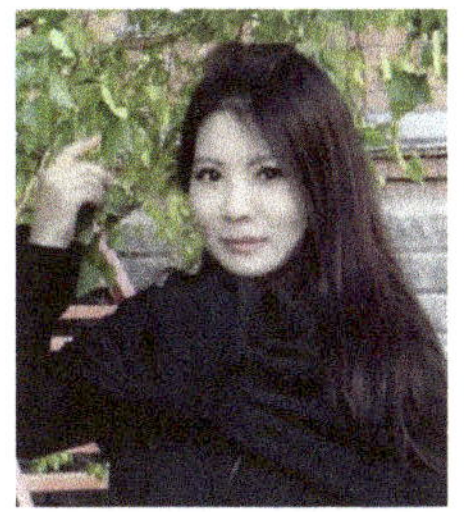

“Peonies” 2018,
canvas/oil, 50/60

In the picture “Peonies” I painted some of my favorite flowers. I wanted to convey all the beauty, texture of petals and leaves. So that the viewer looking at the picture could remember and feel the scent of these beautiful flowers.

05

JANUARY

INDIRA LAKTAEVA (UZBEKISTAN)

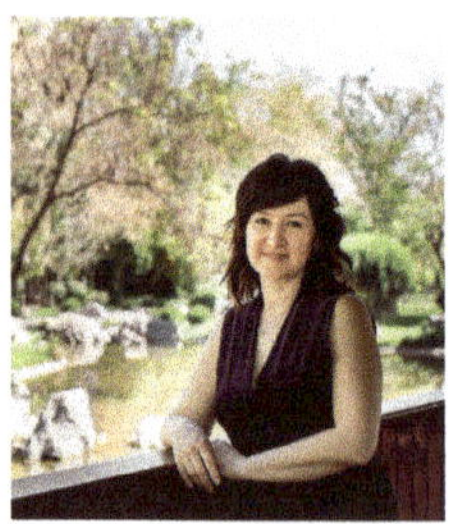

I Will Draw a Fairy Tale for New Year

I will draw a fairy tale for New Year,
I'll wrap it up on Christmas Eve,
I'll add bright snowflakes,
And I'll dress your house with rays of light.

I'll cover the night with a magic blanket,
Of stars, corals, fishes and more.
I'll ask the stargazers to beautifully shower
Our world with stardust.

I'll give a fairy tale for New Year,
About sparkling sunlight, peace and love.
I will invite you for New Year as a new great day
To greet the sunrise.

Sunrise, that'll show us the road
That calls us miles, very far.
I'll wave to you and me for our journey
I'll bring us a lot of luck!

25th of December, 2018

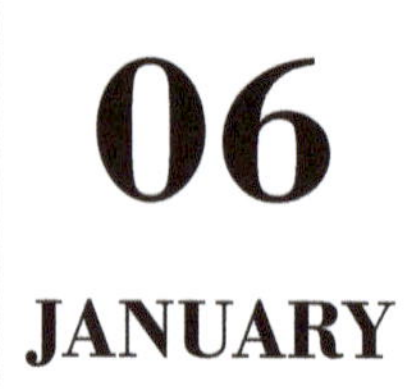

Под Новый Год я нарисую сказку

Под Новый Год я нарисую сказку.
Укутаю ее я Рождеством.
Снежинок я добавлю ярких
И в лучик света облачу ваш дом.

Укрою ночь волшебным одеялом
Из звезд, кораллов, рыб морских.
И звездочета, попрошу красиво
Осыпать пылью звездною наш мир.

Под Новый год я подарю вам сказку
Про мир, любовь, искристый солнца свет.
И в Новый год, как в новый день прекрасный
Я приглашу вас всех встречать рассвет.

Рассвет, что путь нам наш укажет,
Что вдаль с собою позовет.
В дорогу нам с тобой помашет.
Удачу нам он принесет!

25 Декабря 2018 года

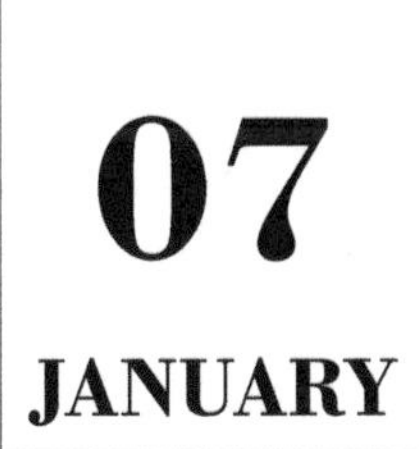

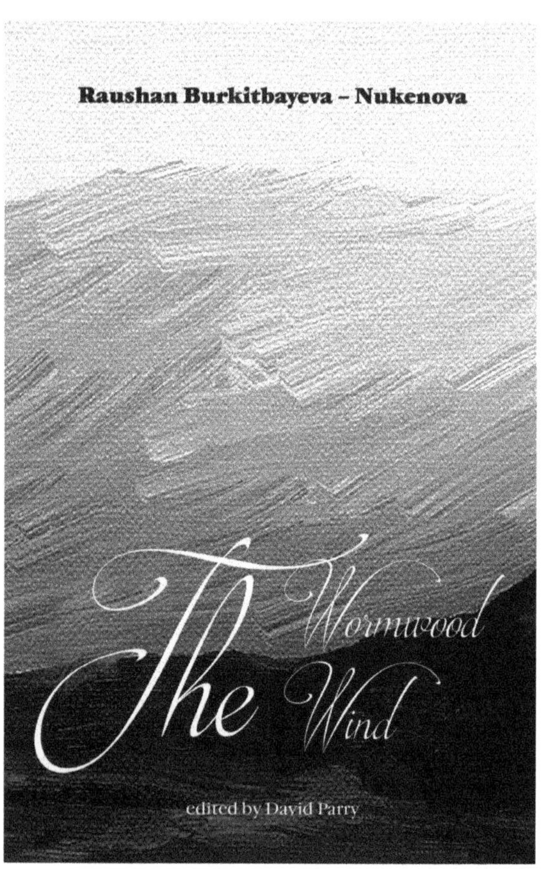

This candid poetry collection is clearly the literary outpouring of a planetary citizen. A woman equally at home on the Steppes of Central Asia as much as the Capital cities of Europe. To my mind, a far from trivial verity once we recognise the innate femininity of her versification. Similarly to Sappho (5th Century BC), Nukenova allows everyone access into a woman's world, wherein seductive complexities of thought becomes manifest through wit and rhetoric. Admittedly, her images are often sharp-carefully elaborated for their own jovial sake.

ISBN: 978-1-910886-12-0
RRP: £14.95

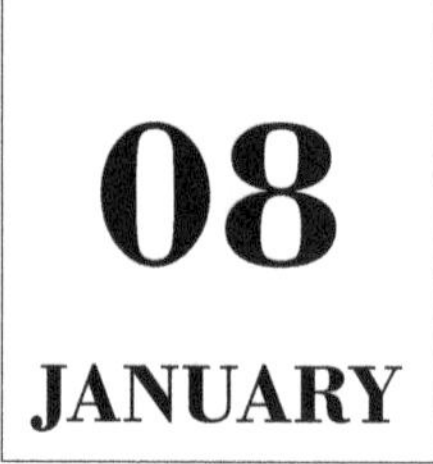

02 MONDAY

03 TUESDAY

04 WEDNESDAY

05 THURSDAY

06 FRIDAY

07 SATURDAY

08 SUNDAY

ELENA KERN (RUSSIA)

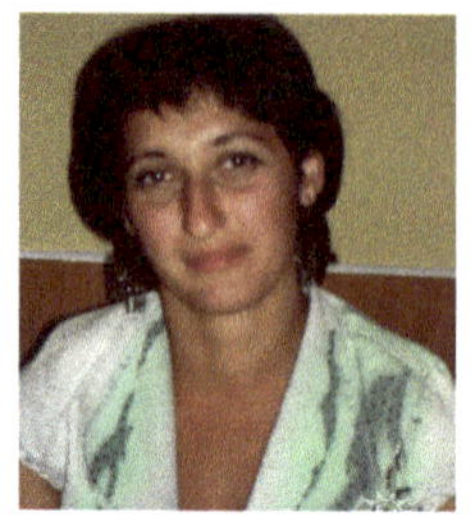

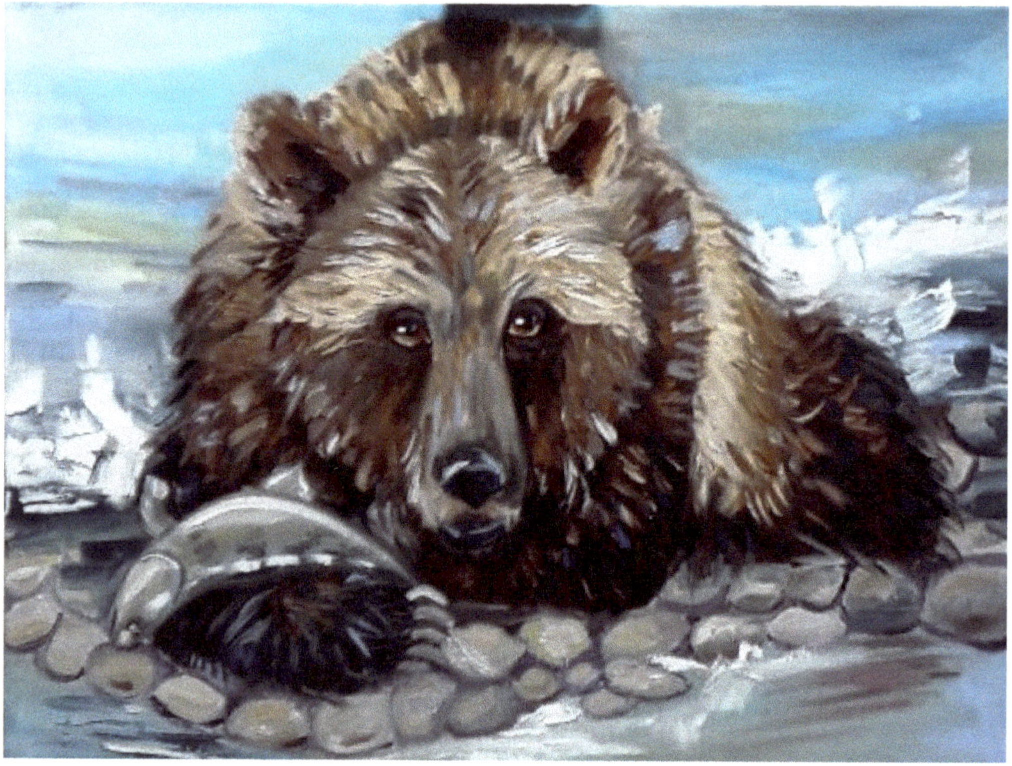

“The Bear”
Bear is a symbol of wisdom and power.

09

JANUARY

A Mother's Prayer

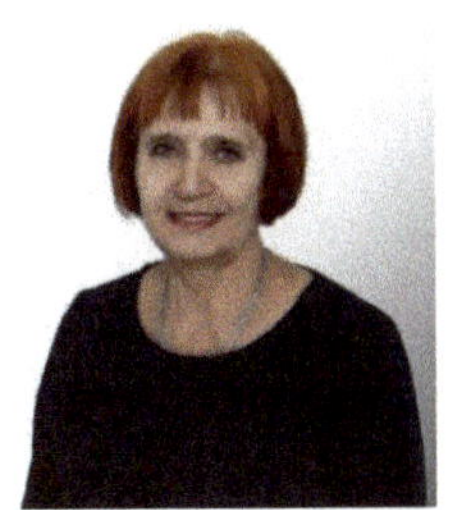

Our mother's prayer saves us.
Her soul's supplication to God,
That you and I may never know sorrow,
To live our life without tears.
She secretly keeps in her heart a prayer for our happiness.
A mother's heart begs for ever
In winter, in summer, in spring, in autumn...
In spring, so that the fragile sprouts
Are not destroyed by rain, or by a sudden wind.
In winter, for the frost not to be cruel and
Knock us down, freeze our heart.
For the summer's heat
Not to burn us with rays of falsehood.
In autumn, for there to be a harvest to marvel at.
A mother's prayer has power,
She leads the dark path
Through hell, where life is frozen,
She brings us back to the path of sinlessness.
A mother's heart in prayer
Day and night, every night.
She wants to keep us on the right path,
And for her soul to be free of torment.

14

JANUARY

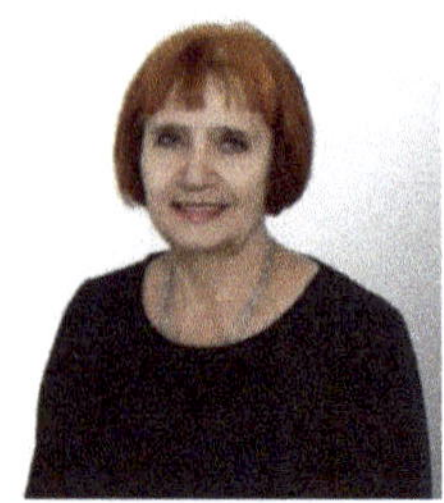

Малітва маці

Ратуе нас малітва маці –
Душы яе прашэнне Богу,
Каб нам з табой бяды не знаці,
Прайсці без слёз сваю дарогу.
Яна пад сэрцам патаемна
Мальбу аб шчасці нашым носіць.
Матулі сэрца просіць вечна:
Узімку, летам, весну, восень…
Вясной, каб кволыя прароскі
Не знішчыў дождж, раптоўны вецер,
Зімой мароз, каб не так жорстка
Студзіў, марозіў наша сэрца…
Улетку спёка не згубіла,
Не апяклі хлусні прамені.
Па восені - ўраджай на дзіва,
Каб без пакут і гонар мелі.
Малітва маці мае сілу,
Яна праводзіць цёмнай сцежкай
Праз пекла, дзе жыццё застыла,
Вяртае нас на шлях бязгрэшны.
Матулі сэрцайка ў малітве
І днём, і ноччу, кожны вечар.
З дарогі зычыць нам не збіцца,
Душу сваю не акалечыць…

15

JANUARY

09 MONDAY

10 TUESDAY

11 WEDNESDAY

12 THURSDAY

13 FRIDAY

14 SATURDAY

15 SUNDAY

LARISA PAK (KYRGYZSTAN)

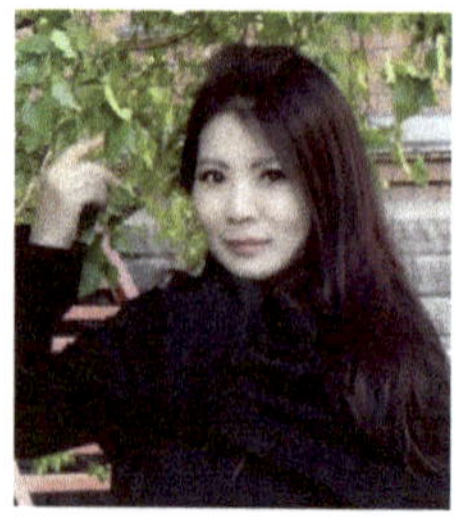

I will fill up my heart with more love

I will fill up my heart with more love,
So the blood quickens up through my veins,
And I'll wrap up my soul in new patience,
So that happiness comes in the end.
At my hardships I won't ever grumble,
To my pains I will just close my eyes,
And I'll tell myself what I've discovered –
It's my fate to be given this life.
I won't cry – no, and I shan't complain:
I keep only good thoughts in my mind,
So I'll pick myself up once again,
And write only of happier times.

18

JANUARY

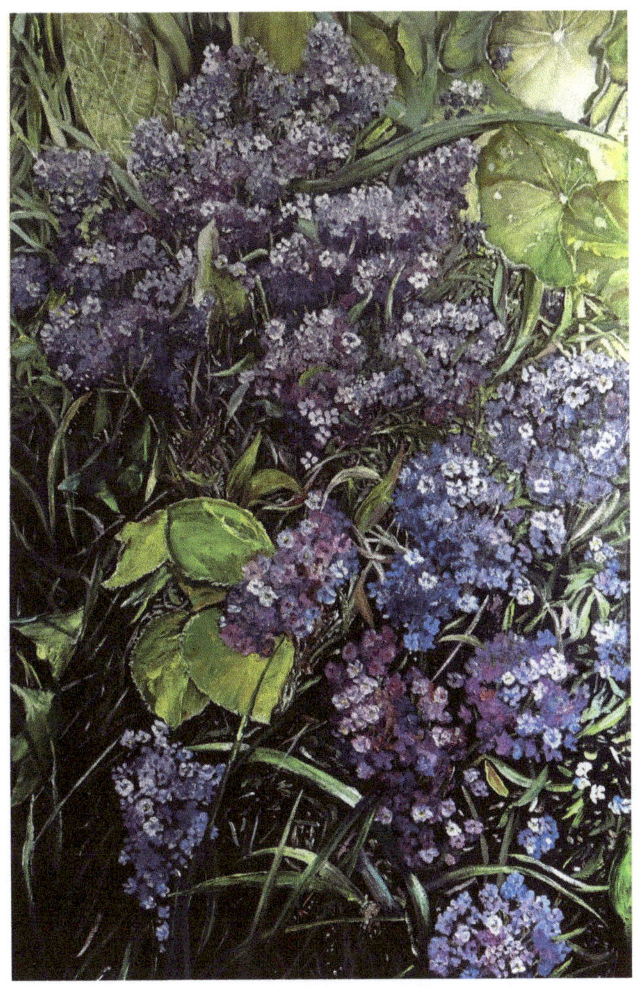

"Autumn alyssum", 2020
canvas/oil, 100/57

The painting depicts a fragment of the fall colors of alyssum. Buds, collected from small flowers from lilac to pink, drown among other plants of different shapes and greens.

19

JANUARY

LARISA PAK (KYRGYZSTAN)

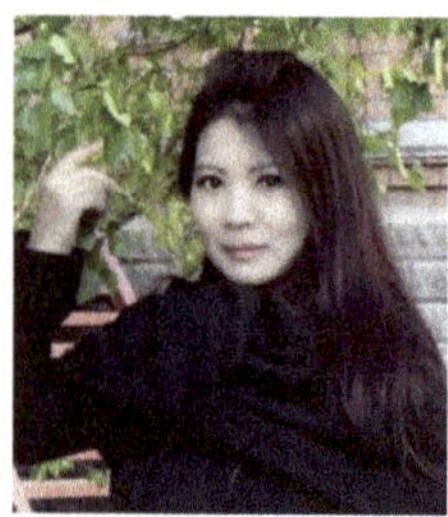

I am thankful

I am thankful for everything –
For what my life came to be.
I was born at night, to muted joy:
If only I had been a boy…
I am thankful for laughter,
And sorrow, and my peaceful heart,
And that, right from the very start,
My guardian angels have kept me safe,
Protected me and given comfort.
I am thankful for my children,
And for their children, and for all my friends.
I'm thankful that I love the life I have;
That I can talk to you today, to hear your thoughtful words,
And be considerate myself, and feel that I am heard.
For the kindness of hearts, and for the roof above my head.
For choosing not to be callous, but compassionate instead.
For the man who sleeps in the room next door,
Whose snoring keeps me awake at night.
He lets me know that I am alive; and
He won't let me die with no-one by my side.
I'm thankful for each gentle word, and every selfless act.
For knowing that my peace of mind has always been intact.
I am thankful. It's true that I'm thankful.
For every day and morning.

20

JANUARY

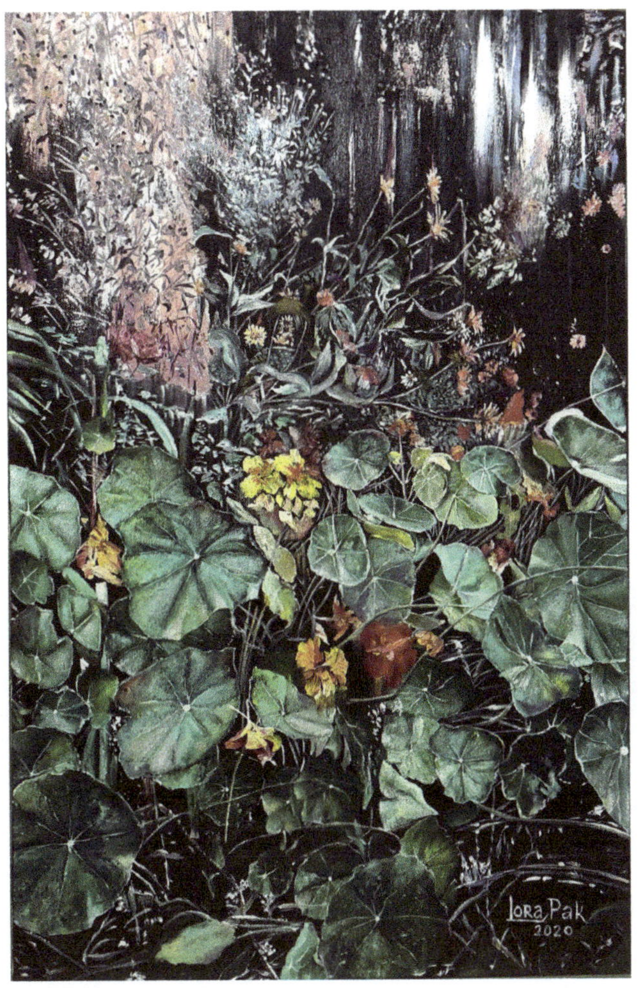

"Nasturtium (Tropaeolum)", 2020
canvas/oil, 100/65

In the picture "Nasturtia" it was originally planned to convey the festive mood, despite the outgoing blooming season. Bright, fiery shades of nasturtium with rounded leaves, against the background of salute in the form of small flowers in pastel colors, give a contrast in color and shape.

21

JANUARY

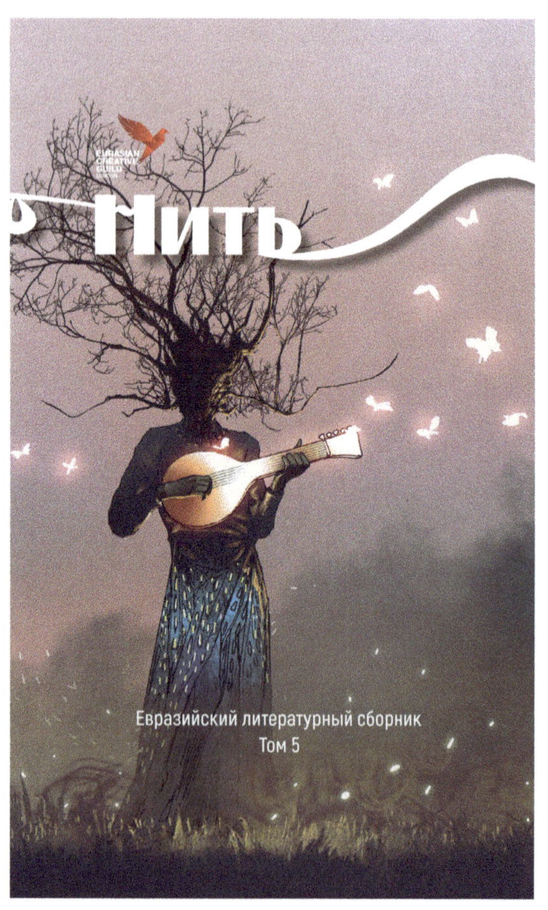

This edition is the fifth in a series of European literary collections Thread.

During its existence, the collection has brought together the works of seventy-nine authors from nineteen countries aged 12 to 94 years. The authors of the project express the hope that the collection conveys the common spirit of the peoples of Eurasia and contributes to the cultural mutual enrichment of writers and forms respect for the history and present of other countries, connects the thoughts and feelings of different generations.

This year, many winners and finalists of the international literary competition Open Eurasia, held annually by the Eurasian Creative Guild, decided to take the opportunity to find their way to their readers through this collection. In addition, all the authors are members of the Guild, active participants in its projects and advice, and, undoubtedly, remarkable masters of the artistic word.

ISBN: 978-1913356385
RRP: £17.50

22

JANUARY

16 MONDAY

17 TUESDAY

18 WEDNESDAY

19 THURSDAY

20 FRIDAY

21 SATURDAY

22 SUNDAY

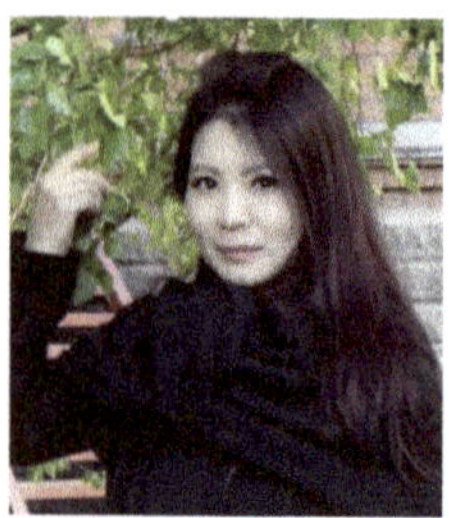

May God spare you

May God spare you from travails like these,
From thoughts of cruelty and sadness,
So that your soul can feel at ease –
Be pure, and full of joy, and humble.
When you ruminate on negatives,
Don't be so quick to take offence: be patient.
Accept the gifts that each day gives,
Pour some cold water over your flames.
And every night, gaze up on high,
Where stars shine sumptuously in cloudless skies,
And tell the moon and stars your dreams,
Send them brightly through the galaxies.
May all of your wishes be heard,
And may they grow wings and soon take flight,
So that your most genuine phrases and words
Will be the kindling that sets your dreams alight.
With new lightness, without the stone in your heart,
Forgive and forget, let go of pain.
So that when you turn to a fresh new page
You can smile and begin your life again.

24

JANUARY

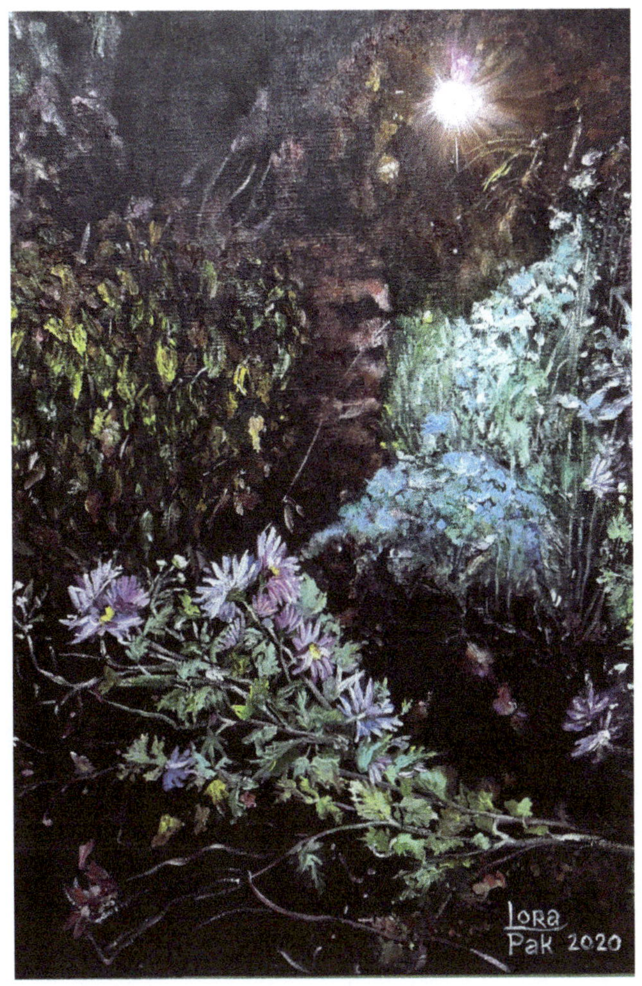

"Autumn night", 2020
canvas/oil, 74/53

The picture "Autumn Night" in the foreground shows a branch of aster with slightly yellowed leaves, which ducked to the ground. In the background rarely dried flowers, and shrubs with yellowed foliage presented in the light - this is the mood of the night landscape. Cool, quiet night.

25

JANUARY

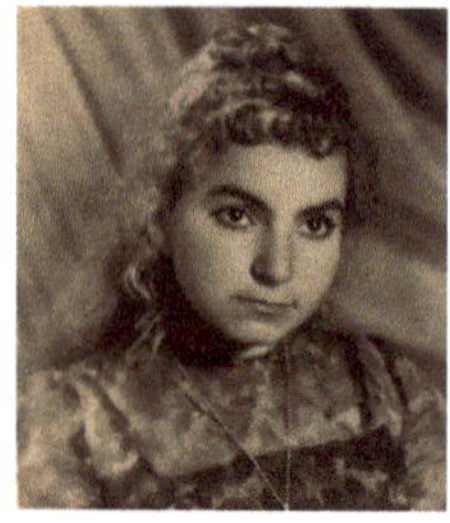

Hello, morning!

Hello, morning,
Young morning!
In the glare of the sun, in the petals of the dawn
You blossom with roses, and it's as if
In the blue of the sky you soar with freshness.
You light up your feelings, your thoughts,
Full of life, of joy, of wonder.
You lift up a lush ear in the field
And you dive and catch the splash of the river.
You caress every worm.
The mighty forest of green.
Like the first creature of clay
You send a message to the world!
In the spectrum of happiness I'm dissolving again
And I strive towards you
Truth is the basis of all wisdom
I behold the youth within me.
The colours of the morning stir my heart
I'm a bird in the air.
I want to embrace my dear, dear Belarus
I want to take my wings in my arms again!
And my deeds, my accomplishments call me...
Oceans deep, stars of the far away light,
And love and the search for abandon
It's all as it was in the past, in my twenties.

26

JANUARY

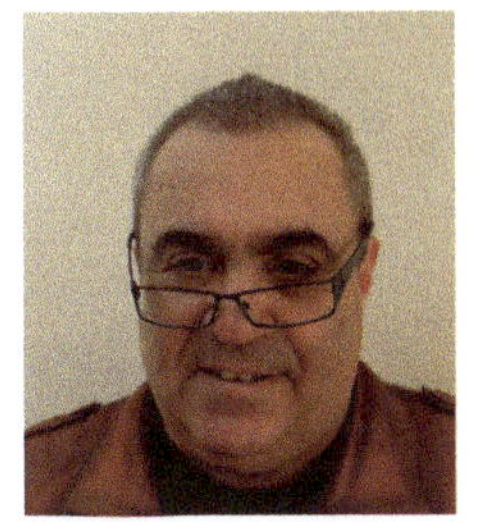

The Old Man

On a Saturday night in May, in the dark,
At a table covered with a tablecloth,
On an old viola with a broken deco,
An old man in a soldier's uniform was playing.

He's lost his touch with the strings and bows,
And the old man's hands trembled,
And, from the first notes,
there was the semblance of a jolt
But the sound was heard when it came.

But then the sounds, suddenly,
soared from the ground
with a power never before heard,
And Jewish tears flowed in them
And dripped on their graves.

And the souls of their daughters listened to them,
That became cold ashes in Sobibor,
The young sons of the destroyer's foremen,
Drowned in the Barents Sea.

He survived, it seems, in spite of all death,
And triumphed, like Judas Maccabeus,
And he was sure that he was saved
by the intervention of the Almighty –
not by a miracle.

All the same: Medals, decorations,
A kippah instead of a faded cap,
And his eyes searched for Hebrew letters,
And the names of our ancestors came to life.
And remembered the homes that were taken,
The blood stained on the enemy's throat,
And the fates he had saved.
It was the month of May.
The old man had come home from the war.

27
JANUARY

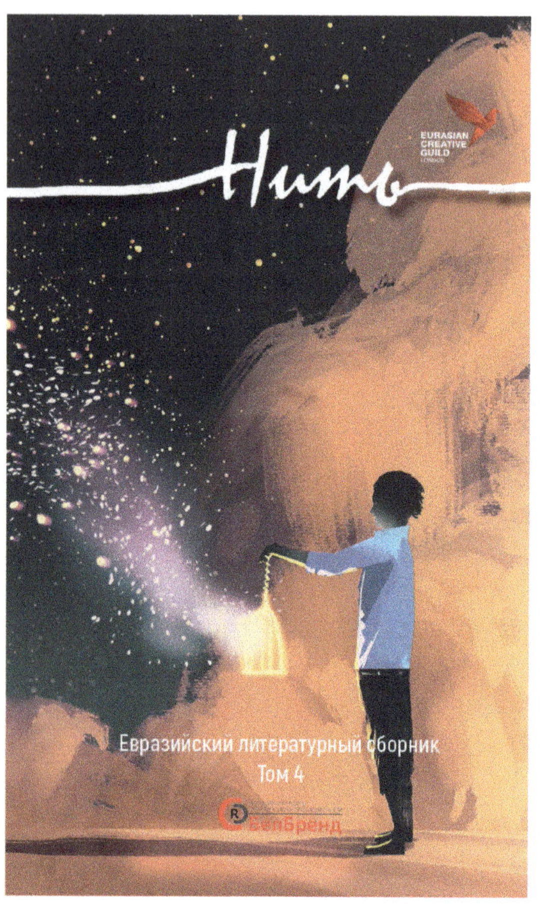

This edition is the fourth in a series of Eurasian literary collections Thread.

More than sixty authors from fourteen countries have taken part in this project since 2018 and wove their wonderful works into this thread of generations and peoples, once united by one common cultural space - the countries of the former Soviet Union.

The authors share their thoughts, wisdom, their own philosophy with readers, give ground for reflection and fantasies. Someone will find here something new for themselves, something worth thinking about, someone will understand themselves better, and someone may even find meaning in their own life and actions. Someone will laugh, someone will be sad, someone, perhaps, the lines will be touched to tears, and someone will remember their loved ones ....

ISBN: 978-1913356200
RRP: £17.50

28

JANUARY

23 MONDAY

24 TUESDAY

25 WEDNESDAY

26 THURSDAY

27 FRIDAY

28 SATURDAY

29 SUNDAY

INDIRA LAKTAEVA (UZBEKISTAN)

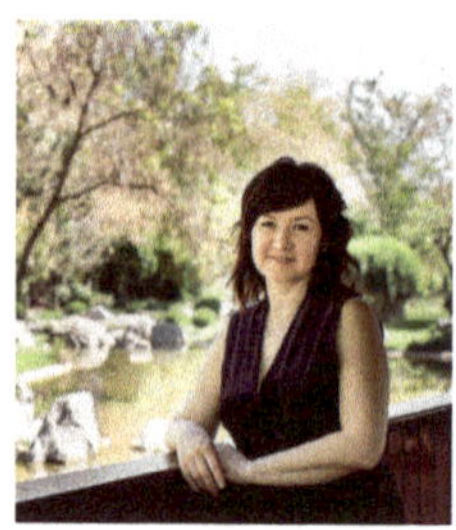

Manhattan

The city of people,
The town of courage,
The beautiful morning
For us every day.

The sun shining and
Greeting our future achievements
For people for challenges
As natural day.

Be ready for movements
For career growth
Desires and wishes
To dream up on high.

I wish you to be happy
I wish you to be honest
Be grateful for living
And follow your way!

January 30th 2020

30

JANUARY

The book reveals the versatility of the soul of the poet and artist Marina Shkrobova-Vernalis. The author is a philosopher who views the magic ball of life through the prism of poetry and painting! Hence the interest in various subjects in painting - landscapes, still lifes, flower compositions and portraits, painted exclusively with the love of the heart.

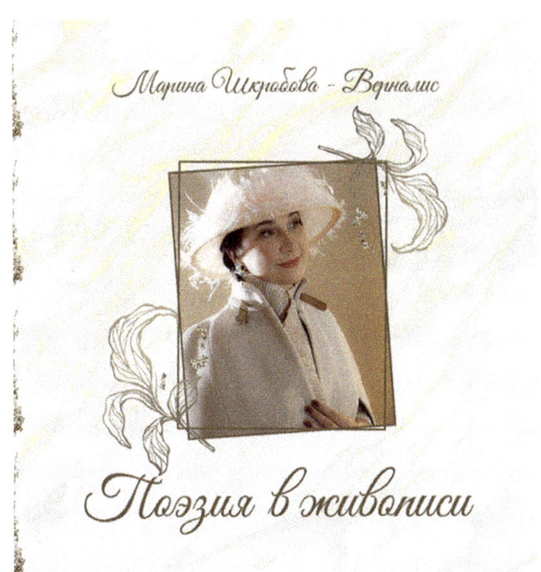

The deep interconnection of meanings and images is interesting in the image of the autumn alley, the wisdom of solitude lives, the insomniac soul is embodied in the image of a young maiden, and in portraits even the background color is a mystery!

Spirituality lives here! And the author addresses everyone as a soul, which he knows and feels for a long time as kindred!

This is a unique conversation with those who are ready to recognize themselves and reflect the world with the beauty of their thoughts!

RUSSIAN
ISBN: 978-1913356538
RRP: £17.50

31

JANUARY

IGOR KHENTOV (ISRAEL)

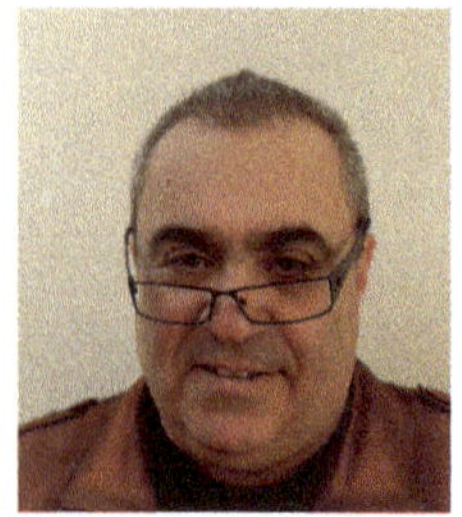

A Mendelssohn Concerto

And Mendelssohn was writing a concerto
For violin in E minor.
He must have known the recipe for happiness
Since he was young and without sin.

In harmony with a tight string
The bow in the soul sang,
And, without disturbing the string,
God's voice was in the violin.

And the instruments' voices,
In the heat of earthly passions,
Melted into the heavens
And into the blue of the seas.

And the echoes of wars are hushed,
Even if only for a moment.
And the world had a wonderful dream
And the world was blissfully peaceful.

And the ghosts of countless troubles
Froze at the gates,
And the crescendo was invisible through the years.
The coming crescendo.

And Buchenwald did not loom,
Where, by the pounding of the heart,
Through the blood-soaked Inferno,
Mendelssohn's grandson walked.

03

FEBRUARY

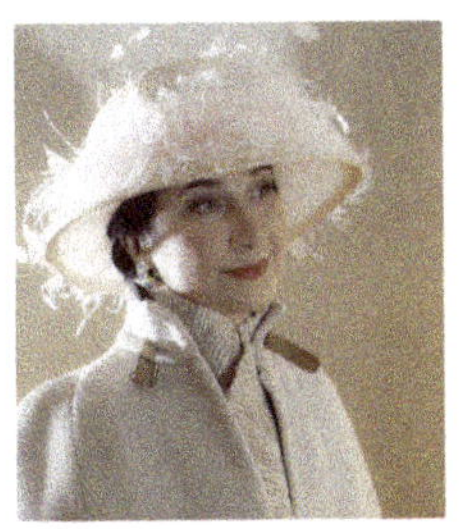

The World Is Made of Me

The sun rises in my soul every morning,
It passes through me into the dawn.
And, following the life-maker's plan,
The day rises out of me every tiME!

A new world is eMErging.
And this MEans I change too.
And everyone is changing in the saME way.
I am born again every day with new strength
That's why my spirit is so important.

The world is made of ME, of everyone, of many!
And how lovely it is depends
On how careful and strong
We will be when creating our own world!

The world is made of ME!.

04

FEBRUARY

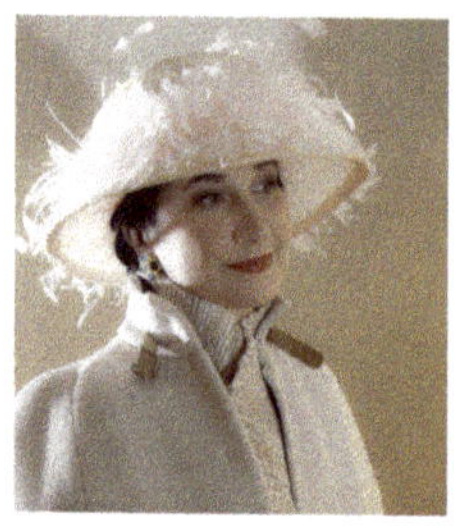

Мир из меня

С утра в моей душе восходит солнце,
Через меня в рассвет переходя.
И, следуя задумке жизнетворца,
День всякий раз восходит из МЕНЯ!

И изМЕНЯет мир. И я МЕНЯюсь.
И каждый изМЕНЯется со мной!
Я с новой силой каждый день рождаюсь -
Вот почему так важен мой настрой.

Мир из МЕНЯ, из каждого, из многих!
И качество зависит от того,
Насколько будем бережны и строги
Мы к сотворенью мира своего!

Мир из МЕНЯ!..

05

FEBRUARY

30 MONDAY

31 TUESDAY

01 WEDNESDAY

02 THURSDAY

03 FRIDAY

04 SATURDAY

05 SUNDAY

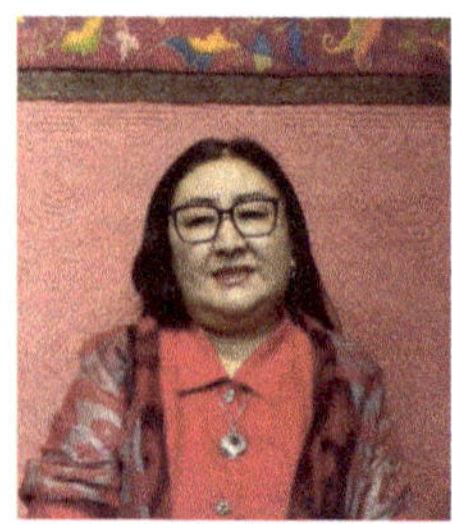

***

A dead tree
A lifeless sky
Crackling of broken glass,
A whining bullet and a cry
A bleeding foam on the face
That is not true!
Fire in the brain, in a flawed mind
That is not true!
That is a war in dreams
A tree in blossom
A waterfall
A bird stands still in flight
That is not true!
That is a dream –
He, She and Child

07

FEBRUARY

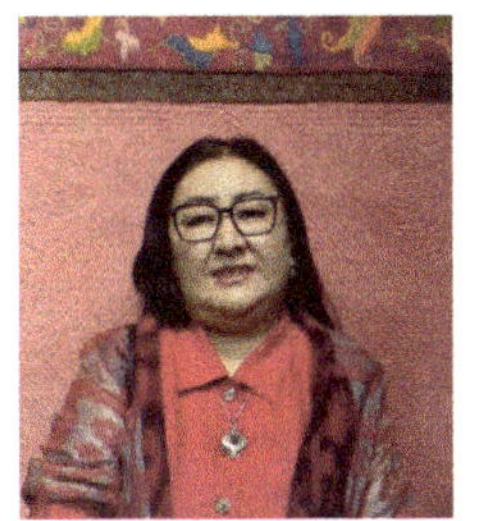

***

Time is magic
It cures wounds
So mortal!
That denying God.
But you keep living
As if in dreams
Time revives as years come
You face another fate.
Oh Time, Time!
So elusive
All not reversed
It is impossible to stop you – Time
My life you otherwise can stop.
We worship years as we live
But what are the years?
What are they?
They are just time.
Like a clock that has pressed the years
As your insight appears on the face.

08

FEBRUARY

LAZZAT SAMRAT (KAZAKHSTAN)

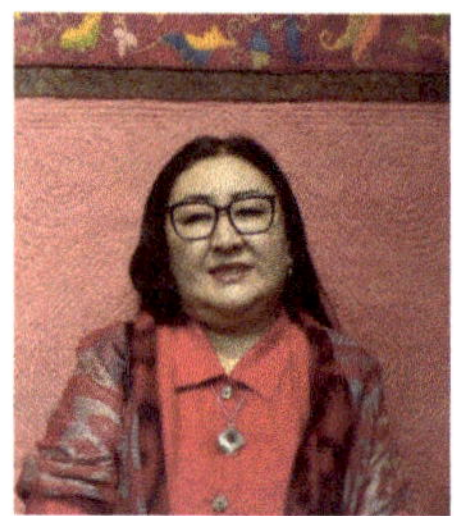

***

One person alone is not weird
It's like the norm
No one betrays you
You live alone without age, ethnicity and gender
You have some food, some clothes and shoes
You have some love – one loves you.
You live alone with your own rules.
No paradigm, no compromise
Syntagma – you live alone
One plus one – that is the rule
It's like the norm
You will be alone
I will be alone
We will be then alike
Surplus when we are two
System when there are two
One plus one – that's paradigm
But all in all
In evening late
In autumn
A soul becomes a clot
You have no drug
To stand this pain
To understand
You are alone on the rock.

09

FEBRUARY

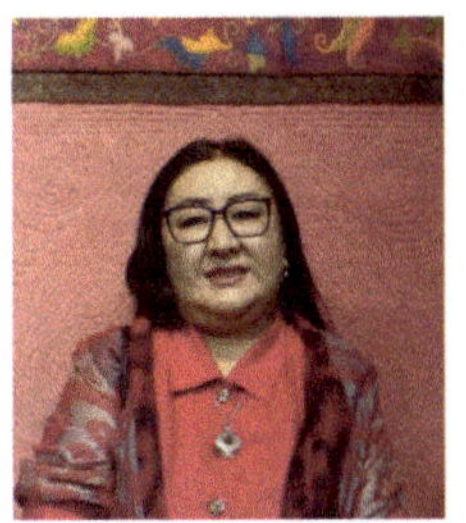

***

Who are you?
Who is your mother?
She-wolf, she-dog?
Who fed you?
You hold all of Russia
So where they are
These Pushkins, Lermontovs and Chekhovs?
What are you doing?
You're killing these mums
You're killing these dads
You're killing these kids
Ukraine on fire
Ukraine in smoke
Who is your father?
Who the hell are you?

10

FEBRUARY

LAZZAT SAMRAT (KAZAKHSTAN)

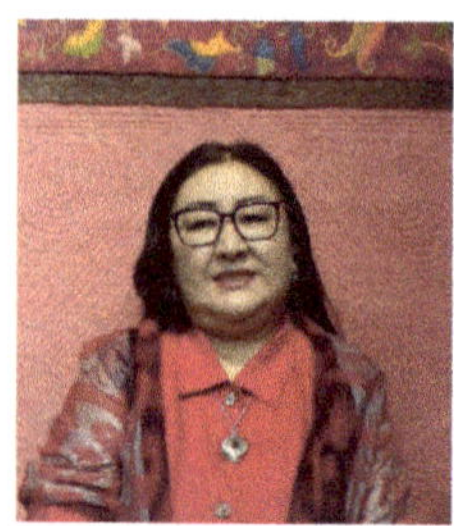

***

My heart is love insatiable
To you, my land, my Qazaqstan
Nowhere is more beautiful
Nowhere is warmer
With dombra vibes, with steppe winds
Nowhere else is tipsy kumys
Nowhere else is tasty shubat
Nowhere else is the flying horse
It's endless sky
That calls to head for space
The peaky mountains uplift you with their dreams.
My son is my heart
My Qazaqstan is to become so strong
When everyone makes a proud wall
For Justice, Honour and Law
When forces newly born
When massive storms
Demolish the steady stance
When all the best
That stay with me and you
That come for ages
Will finally revive us.

11

FEBRUARY

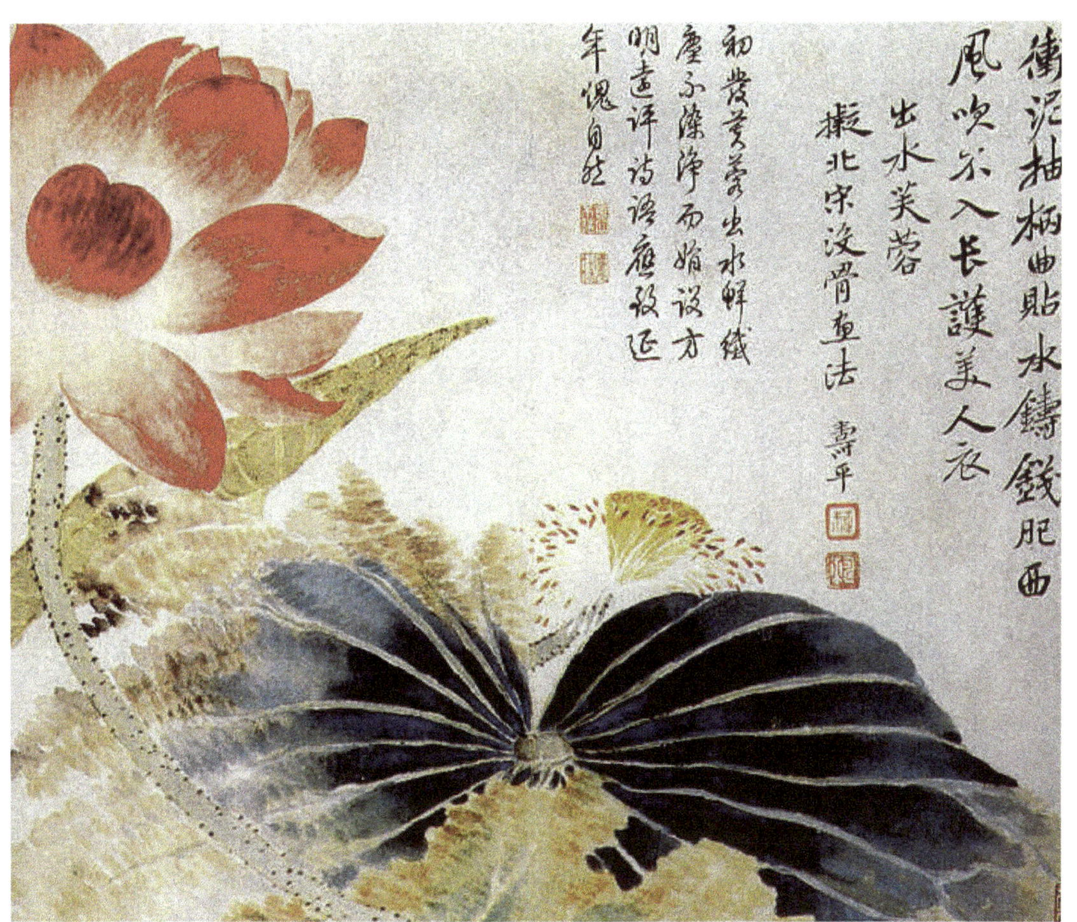

"Lotus Flower Breaking the Surface",
17th century, Qing Dynasty

12

FEBRUARY

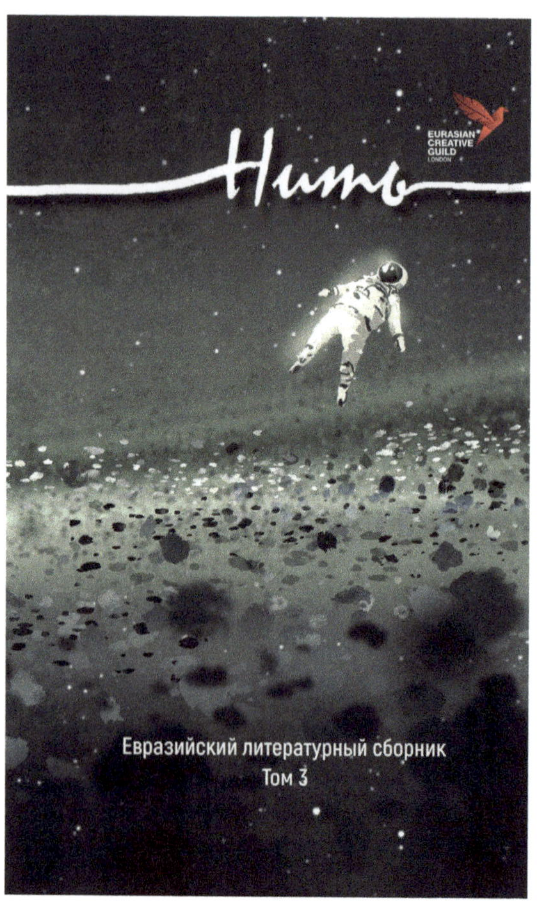

This edition is the third book in the series of Eurasian literary collections "Thread". Since 2018, the collection has included works by more than fifty authors from eleven countries.

In this book, authors from Belarus, Great Britain, Israel, Kazakhstan, Russia, Uzbekistan, Ukraine share their feelings and memories, perception of reality and fairy tales with the reader.

The Eurasian Creative Guild supports creativity in all its manifestations. In this collection, the reader will find both prose and poetry, and lyrics, and a scientific approach to preserving the world and the environment, and even the active citizenship of the author. Such different in style and character works of the authors - members of the Guild, presented in this book, unite love for the native land and nature, their own philosophy of perception of the surrounding reality.

ISBN: 978-1913356064
RRP: £17.50

06 MONDAY

07 TUESDAY

08 WEDNESDAY

09 THURSDAY

10 FRIDAY

11 SATURDAY

12 SUNDAY

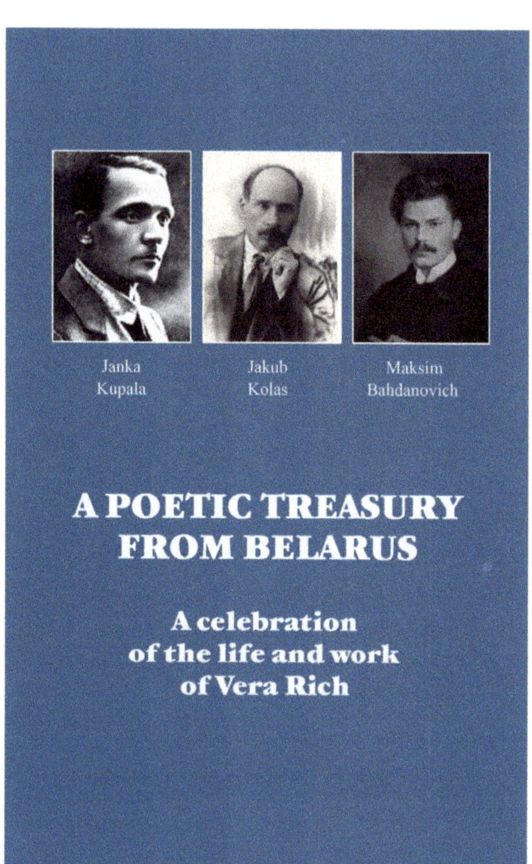

In this adventurous poetic treasury, three remarkable wordsmiths from Belarus are further introduced to specialists and general anglophone readers alike. A feat only realisable, possibly, through the outstanding vision and almost legendry skills of translator, journalist, songsmith and cultural historian, Vera Rich. Indeed, her insightful, pioneering, work on the potent and stirring verses of Janka Kupala - the bard and prophet of Belarusian letters, is herein accompanied by subtle interpretations of Jakub Kolas as the wry observer of Belarusian customs, along with Maksim Bahdanovich as its experimental, sophisticated and lyrical literary moderniser. Each fearless poet, in turn, constructing the very foundations upon which contemporary Belarusian literature is built. And as such, this proud collection of captivating poetry from a uniquely gifted nation truly celebrates the achievements of an astonishing lady.

ISBN: 978-1-913356-04-0
RRP: £14.95

13

FEBRUARY

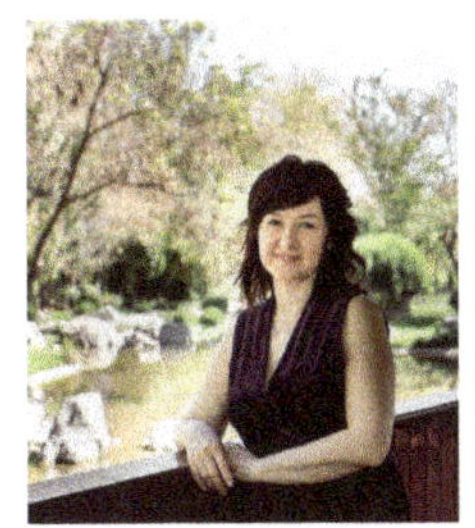

There Is No Love, There Is a Beauty of Soul

Voices, beauty and love,
I have lost myself in them all.
To the gates, clouds, on the steam
To nowhere I flew.

Talk, come – run to me
Visit, dedicate evenings to yourself,
Don't dream about love
There is none.

There is freedom of love, the flight,
Breathlessly beautiful.
Help, take it with you
To a world of love, full of dreams.

Talk about it, don't be silent,
There's no happiness, there's due
On the foliage until dawn
There is dawn.

By your beauty befuddle
My life, flight of birds
Noise of wind and love
That inside burning – calling with itself.

May 7th 2022

14

FEBRUARY

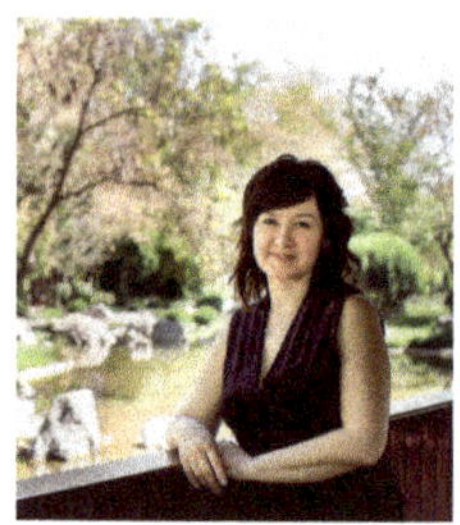

Нет любви, есть красота души

Голоса, красота, любовь.
Потеряла себя совсем.
В ворота, в облаках, на парах
Улетела я в никуда.

Говори, прибегай ко мне,
Навещай, посвяти вечера себе
О любви не мечтай
Её нет.

Есть свобода любви, полет,
Красота взахлёб.
Помоги, забери с собой
В мир любви, полный грёз.

О любви говори, не молчи,
Счастья нет, есть роса
На листве до зари
Есть рассвет.

Красотою своей опьяни
Жизнь моя, птиц полет
Ветра шум и любовь,
Что внутри обжигает – с собой зовет.

7 мая 2022 года

15

FEBRUARY

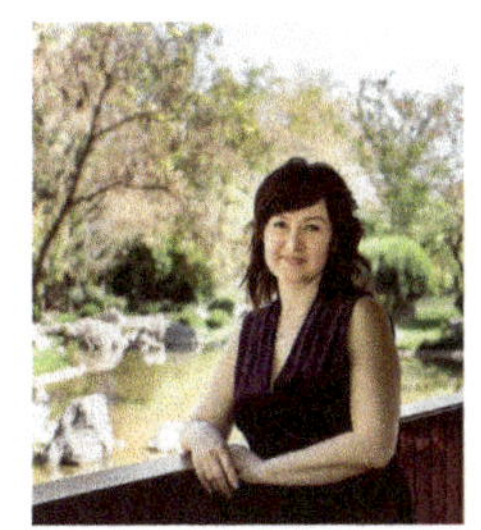

I Want To Be Who I Was Yesterday

I want to be who I was yesterday,
Without any mask and gloves, in a serpentine,
With a cutie smile and lights in my eyes
Like dolphins jumping in the sunshine.

I want you to be who you were yesterday!
With the eyes of a one-year-old child,
Looking at me with trust
So open, tender, caring, kind.

Today I can only realize
The gifts I hadn't noticed before.
I can forgive, know, and accept you
As myself, not to seem as not enough.

Today I go and buy flowers,
I will see the sun and dream
My life is full of miracles and beauty
I don't need someone else's life!

So, step by step and every day
I will fulfill my dreams.
Let's have some tea for now
With lemon, ginger, and with the whole Universe!

February 2nd 2021

16
FEBRUARY

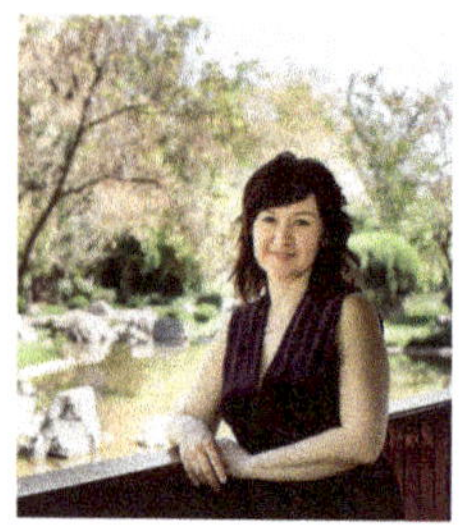

Хочу вернуть вчерашнюю себя

Хочу вернуть вчерашнюю себя,
Без маски и перчаток, в серпантине.
С улыбкой озорною и в глазах
Светящегося лучиком дельфинов.

Хочу вернуть вчерашнего тебя,
С глазами годовалого ребенка,
С доверием смотрящим на меня
Открытым, нежным, чутким, добрым.

Могу сегодня только осознать
Подарки, что я раньше не внимала.
Могу тебя понять, простить, принять,
Как и себя, чтоб не казалось мало.

Сегодня я пойду куплю цветов,
На солнышко взгляну и замечтаю
Жизнь чудную, красивую мою!
Мне больше не нужна она - чужая!

И так за шагом шаг и каждый день
Приду к своим мечтам я постепенно.
Ну, а пока давай мы выпьем чай
С лимоном, имбирем со всей Вселенной!

2 Февраля 2021 года

17

FEBRUARY

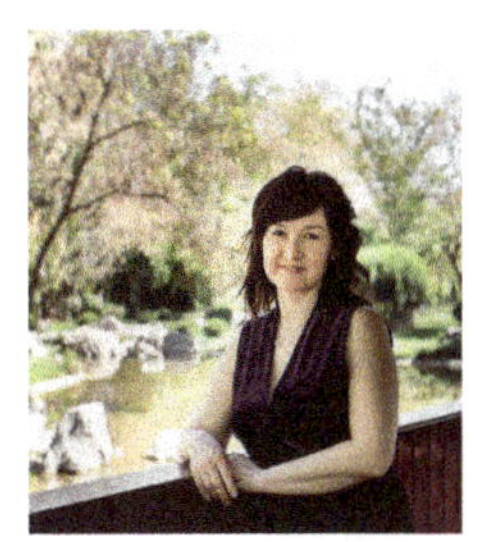

A Mother's Heart

A mother's heart cries for her child.
It tries but it cannot do it in any other way.
It wants to sing, dance, but it cannot.
Only a mother understands the worry.

If her son gets sick, or her daughter
Mother doesn't sleep and worries at night.
If her son forgot his hat in the fierce winter,
In his forties she still cares about him.

She cannot stop enjoying looking at happiness
That is shining in light brown eyes.
She will ask a hundred questions
And be fulfilled with a lot of joy.

Wish all mothers – happiness to their life!
Lots of gladness and joy!
Tasty spices and sweets!
Their heart only laughs and light up with the
love and warmth!

April 10th 2020

18

FEBRUARY

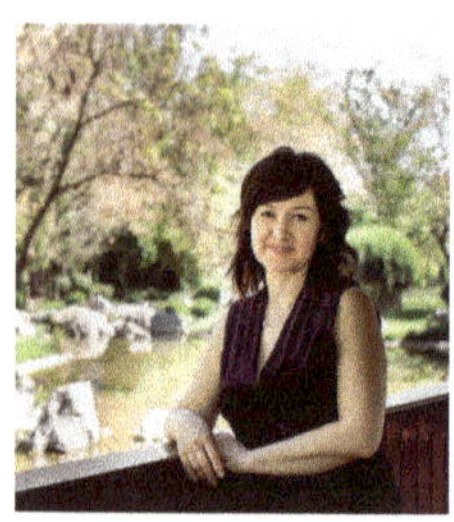

Сердце Матери

Сердце матери за ребенка плачет.
Оно старается, не может иначе.
Хочет петь, танцевать, но не можется -
Только мать понимает тревожицу.

Если сын заболел или доченька,
Мать не спит т ночами тревожится.
Если шапку забыл в зиму лютую
В его сорок, о нем она думает.

Нагладется не может на счатие,
Что лучится в глазах светлокариих.
Сто воппросов задаст с ожидания
И от радости переполняется.

Матерям – счастья в жизнь!
Много радости, удовольствия,
Пряностей, сладостей!
Чтобы сердце лишь только смеялося
И любовью, теплом озарялося!

10 апреля 2020 года

19

FEBRUARY

13 MONDAY

14 TUESDAY

15 WEDNESDAY

16 THURSDAY

17 FRIDAY

18 SATURDAY

19 SUNDAY

MARTA BRASSART (UK)

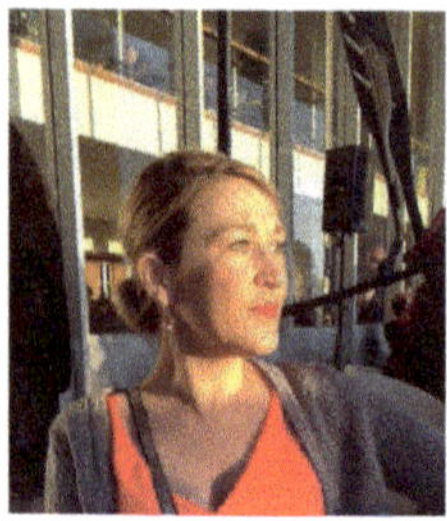

Grandfather

At the kitchen table facing the sun
Grandfather is in his chair
Cutting an apple into pieces,
Soaking bread in sugar,
And the water, so clear,
Strengthens his body before he leaves
To graze his flock.
Sheep wander like woollen clouds
On the succulent meadow,
Till the evening got the better of them with dew

At the kitchen window the chair is empty
Since he left for his flock.
The world has changed, its face to unpredictable,
Given reality of childhood bathed
In the taste of cherries and honey.
A gold coin – the shape of humble work
Lying on the kitchen counter
Invariably

Children's eyes can see.

Marta Brassart, 2014 from the book Caryatides

21

FEBRUARY

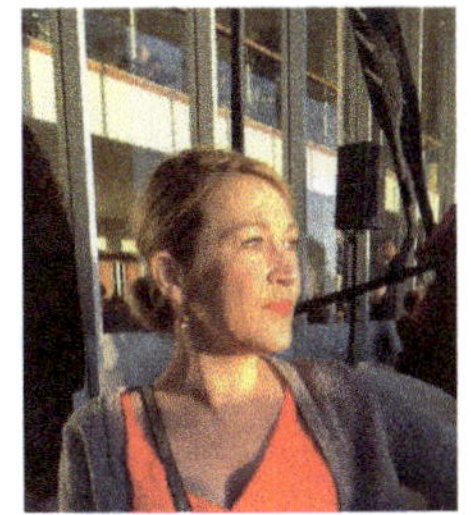

Dziadek

W kuchni przy stole twarzą do słońca
Dziadek na krześle
Kroi jabłko na cząstki
Chleb moczy w cukrze
I woda taka przezroczysta
Krzepi ciało zanim wyjdzie wypasać swe stado
Owce wełnianym obłokiem wędrują
Na soczystej łące
Aż po wieczór co je zmorzy rosą

W kuchni przy stole stoi krzesło
Od kiedy wyszedł do swego stada
Świat zmienił oblicze na nieobliczalne
Zastana rzeczywistość dzieciństwa skąpanego
W smaku czereśni i miodu
Moneta złota – kształt pokornej pracy
Leży na kuchennym blacie
Niezmiennie

Oczy dziecka widzą

22
FEBRUARY

MIRZA KADYM IREVANI (AZERBAIJAN)

"Portrait of sitting woman"
1870s

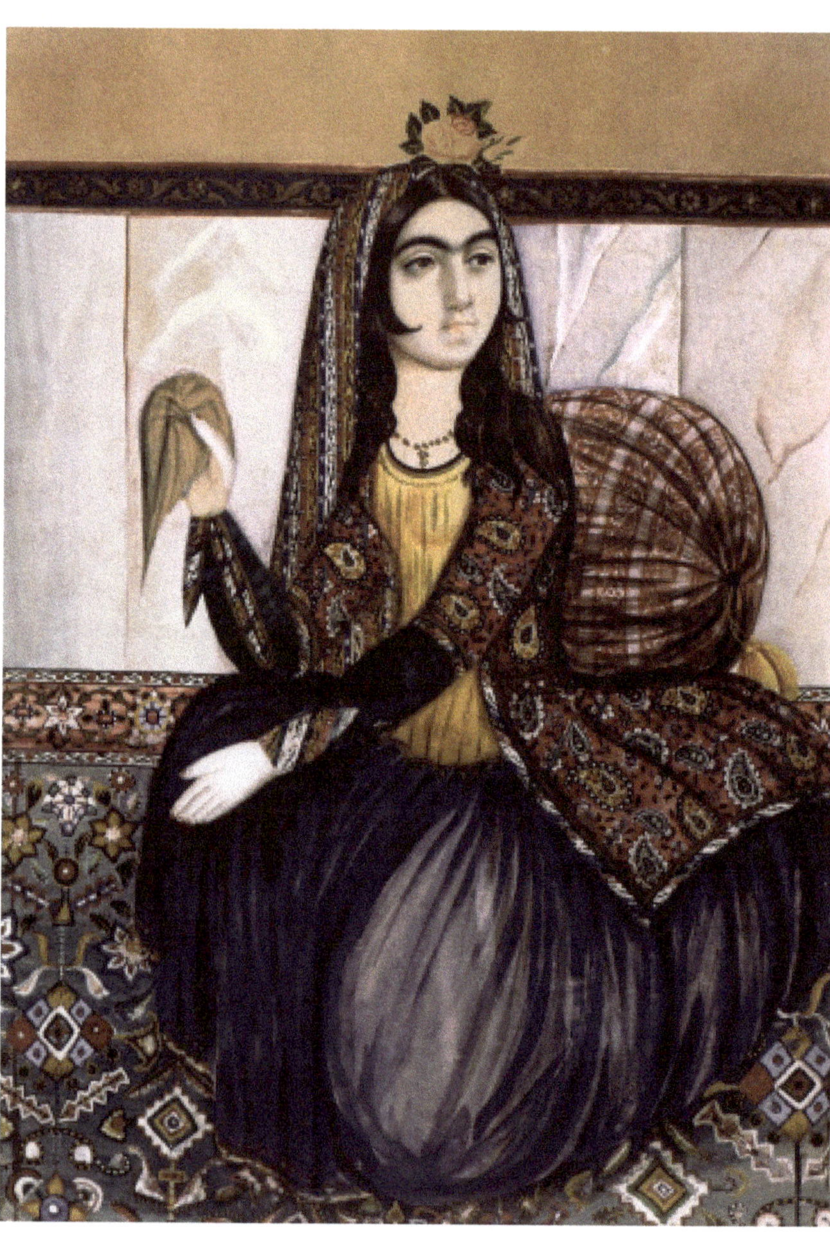

23
FEBRUARY

19 MONDAY

20 TUESDAY

21 WEDNESDAY

22 THURSDAY

23 FRIDAY

24 SATURDAY

25 SUNDAY

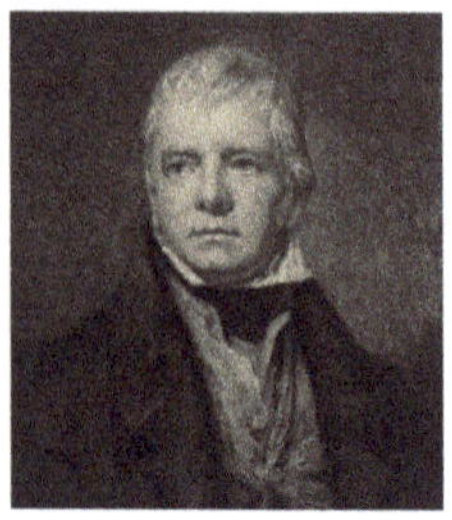

THE VIOLET

The violet in her greenwood bower,
Where birchen boughs with hazel mingle,
May boast itself the fairest flower
In glen, or copse, or forest dingle.

Though fair her gems of azure hue,
Beneath the dew-drop's weight reclining;
I've seen an eye of lovelier blue,
More sweet through wat'ry lustre shining.

The summer sun that dew shall dry,
Ere yet the day be past its morrow;
No longer in my false love's eye
Remain'd the tear of parting sorrow.

26

FEBRUARY

ФИАЛКА

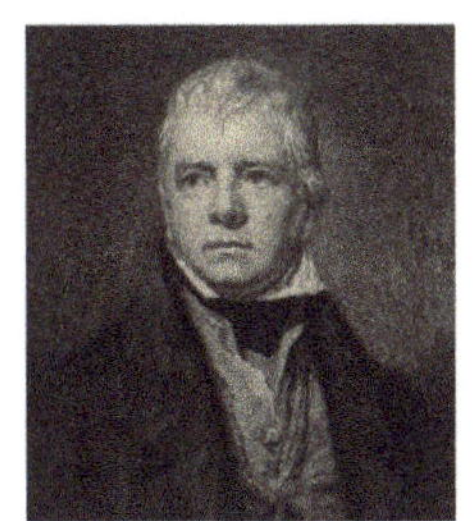

Где сучья берёзы с лощиной смешались,
Фиалка в тенистой беседке зелёной
Своей красотой неземною сверкает,
В лощине, в долине, в местах затаённых.

И, хоть лепестки её, словно сапфиры,
Лазурью горят под хрустальной росою,
Со взором прелестницы, глаз её синих,
Не сможет сравниться и чудо такое.

Вновь летнее солнце росу осушает,
Лишь скроется день за невидимой далью,
В очах дивных той, кто с любовью играет,
Слеза испарится прощальной печалью.

Поэтический перевод Михаила Ананова

27

FEBRUARY

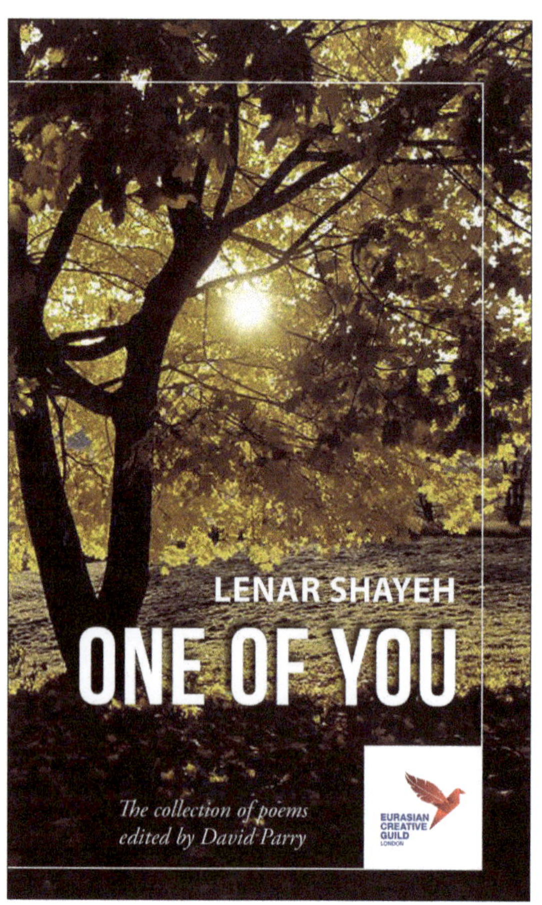

Overall, I am deeply suspicious of Impressionism. As a 19th-century movement in the Arts, it seems to be continually dominated by inconsequential compositions, with far too much emphasis on our ever-changing perspectives - exaggerated, as these occasionally are, by the effects of one's passage through time. This is not to say, of course, that only empirical facts should be the defining feature of aesthetic endeavour. Indeed, the predictably dreary and often bland productions of Soviet-style Social Realism perpetually stand as a grim reminder to this failing. However, "abstraction", in itself, obviously stretches beyond an insistence on arbitrary sensory adjustments, inordinately detailed atmospheres, or evocative environmental qualities. Truly, our world makes an impression upon the physical senses, but as part of a two-way process; whereby human exteriors struggle against an equal flood of sophisticated substances welling up from inside ourselves. So, editing a series of manifestly Impressionist poems by Lenar Shayeh in his collection *One of You* was, at first, something of a mixed blessing.

ISBN: 978-1-910886-47-2
RRP: £9.50

03

MARCH

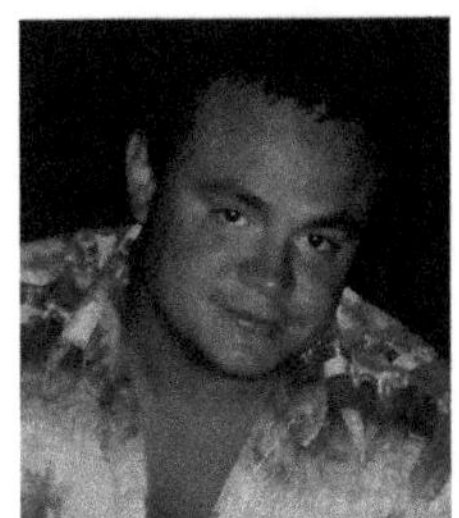

***

Here, driven by heaven,
Stretched over the crosses
And over mother's peace,
I'm flying where above you
Her kind words
The bright wind is calm

And a blind veil
soothed by me
Someone is rushing into the interfluve ...
I will spread my wings
After all, they are of such a cut -
Edge, forever red

From mute, salty blood.
Do not be silent ... come on, say -
What do you want? I have time,
I can do everything, except maybe
Land on the ferry
Between us to sing there.

I can do everything, I just know
That I will die ... sleep, dear,
I will stay.
I scatter - I guess
And I know who she is
Our old age.

***

Вот, гонимый небесами,
Распростёртый над крестами
И над маминым покоем,
Я лечу там, где над Вами
Её добрыми словами
Светлый ветер упокоен

И незрячей пеленою
Успокоенная мною
Кто-то мчится в междуречье...
Я крыла свои раскрою,
Ведь они такого кроя -
Края, красного навечно

От немой, солёной крови.
Не молчи... давай, промолви -
Что ты хочешь? Я успею,
Всё успею, может кроме
Приземлиться на пароме
Между нами, чтобы спеть там.

Всё успею, только знаю,
Что погибну... спи, родная,
Я останусь.
Раскидаю - погадаю
И узнаю, кто такая
Наша Старость.

2010

04
MARCH

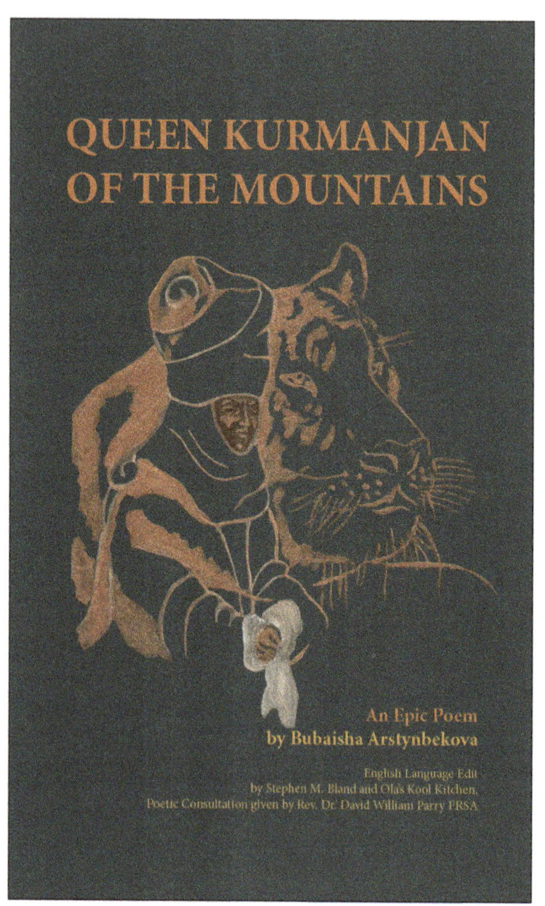

Bubaisha Arstynbekova's epic poem, *Queen Kurmanjan of the Mountains* tells the story of Kurmanjan Datka, 'The Tsaritsa of Alai,' a courageous and noble woman who was not afraid to break with tradition. An important politician, in the second half of the eighteen century, Kurmanjan ruled over the Alai region wisely, both seeking compromise and fighting for the rights of her people. A lyrical ode to the Queen, Arstynbekova's book also reveals the traditions and way of life of the Kyrgyz people in this period of intrigue and instability.

ISBN:978-1913356323
RRP: £ 24.95

26 MONDAY

27 TUESDAY

28 WEDNESDAY

01 THURSDAY

02 FRIDAY

03 SATURDAY

04 SUNDAY

ELENA BOSLER-GUSEVA (KYRGYZSTAN)

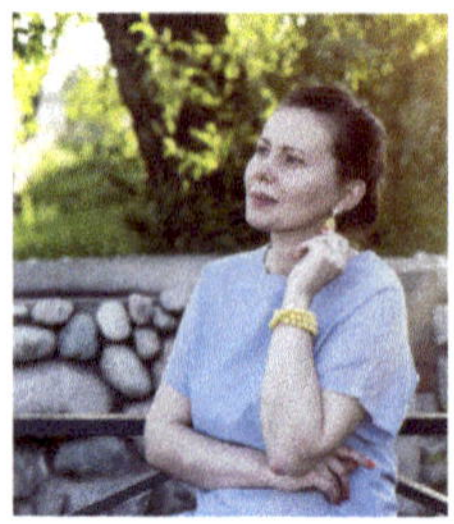

Artist: Elena Tarlykova
"Portrait"
A4, watercolour

This portrait was painted from a photograph of my friend Elena Tarlykova, who left this world two years ago. It is published in this Almanac on the day of her birth. Her memory lives on with her children, and in the hearts of her friends.

Marie Stricher, Sketcher.
Lyon, France
www.rendezvous-carnetdevoyage.com

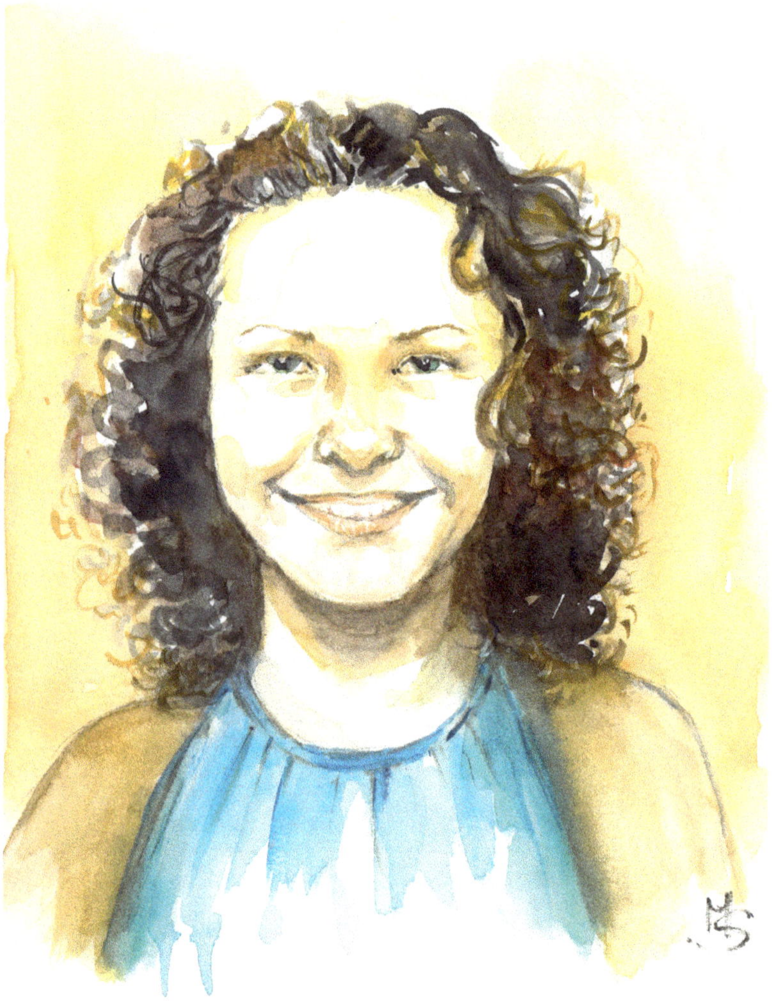

07

MARCH

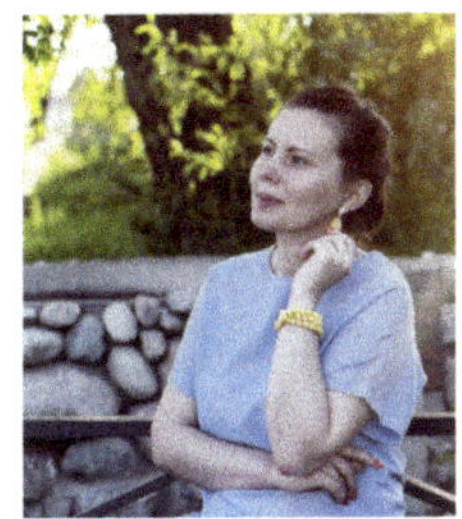

***

What do we know about Friendship? What is she like?
How do we feel if she appears in life?
What form does she have? Which colour, aroma?
O! There is nothing more beautiful, stronger!
She gives us warmth in the harshest of frosts,
And instantly calms us when we weep in floods.
She can cheer us up swiftly and scatter the sorrows,
And open the door to sentimental souls.
Significant is to know what is truth, and how we should use
Such beautiful, special moments,
Sitting near the magic lady's bright fire,
Enjoying the symphony of our heart's fibres.

***

Что мы знаем о Дружбе? Какая она?
Какая на вкус и чем пахнет она?
Какой формы и цвета? Чем важна, дорога?
О! Нет прекрасней и крепче её! Ведь она
Способна согреть нас в лютый мороз
И вмиг осушить поток горьких слёз.
Она может взбодрить, развеять печали
И двери души распахнуть,
Чтоб познали, что бренно, что вечно,
В чём истина есть, а что лишь пустое… Его бы отсечь!
Оставить что ценно, что дорого, важно,
Согревшись у яркого Дружбы костра,
Напомнить себе, что жизнь так прекрасна,
Если звучат в ней друзей голоса.

08

MARCH

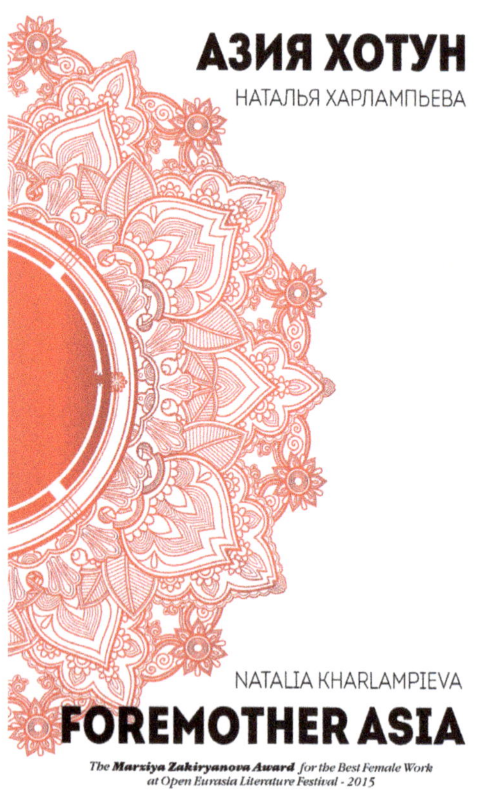

In this first ever collection of Sakha poems in our English language, the highly talented poet Natalia Kharlampieva weaves openly neo-Impressionistic threads of common heritage, communal faith and shared ethnicity, into an overall tapestry of cultural optimism. Indeed, to Kharlampieva's mind, the unique significance played by independent women (willing to endure every hardship) in these restorative endeavours clearly signals the spiritual strength of Central Asia. A lesson, moreover, she obliquely suggests the West itself still needs to learn. Of course, in Kharlampieva's case, these powerful declamations are set against the grinding impact of icy expanses on Sakha psyches. And as such, Kharlampieva invites the readers of Foremother Asia into a hardy, but delicate world: a narratorial sphere characterised by the need to survive against all odds. Indeed, once her reader's grasp that the capital city of the Sakha Republic is located a mere 450 kilometres south of the Arctic Circle, they will begin to accept the insights of this crisp and original volume as a singular contribution to Global Text. Unanimously applauded as an impassioned book revealing the delights of a recovered national identity, Kharlampieva also captures Natures savage beauty, as well as the harsh existential truths of life in the far North.

ISBN: 978-1910886229
RRP: £12.50

11

MARCH

05 MONDAY

06 TUESDAY

07 WEDNESDAY

08 THURSDAY

09 FRIDAY

10 SATURDAY

11 SUNDAY

ROBERT LOUIS STEVENSON (UK)

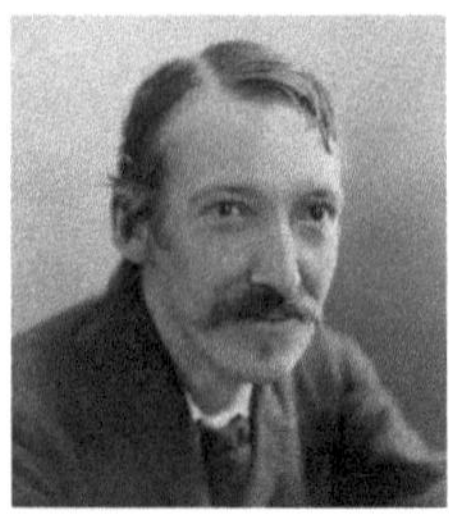

My Kingdom

Down by a shining water well
I found a very little dell,
No higher than my head.
The heather and the gorse about
In summer bloom were coming out,
Some yellow and some red.

I called the little pool a sea;
The little hills were big to me;
For I am very small.
I made a boat, I made a town,
I searched the caverns up and down,
And named them one and all.

And all about was mine, I said,
The little sparrows overhead,
The little minnows too.
This was the world and I was king;
For me the bees came by to sing,
For me the swallows flew.

I played there were no deeper seas,
Nor any wider plains than these,
Nor other kings than me.
At last I heard my mother call
Out from the house at evenfall,
To call me home to tea.

And I must rise and leave my dell,
And leave my dimpled water well,
And leave my heather blooms.
Alas! and as my home I neared,
How very big my nurse appeared.
How great and cool the rooms!

13

MARCH

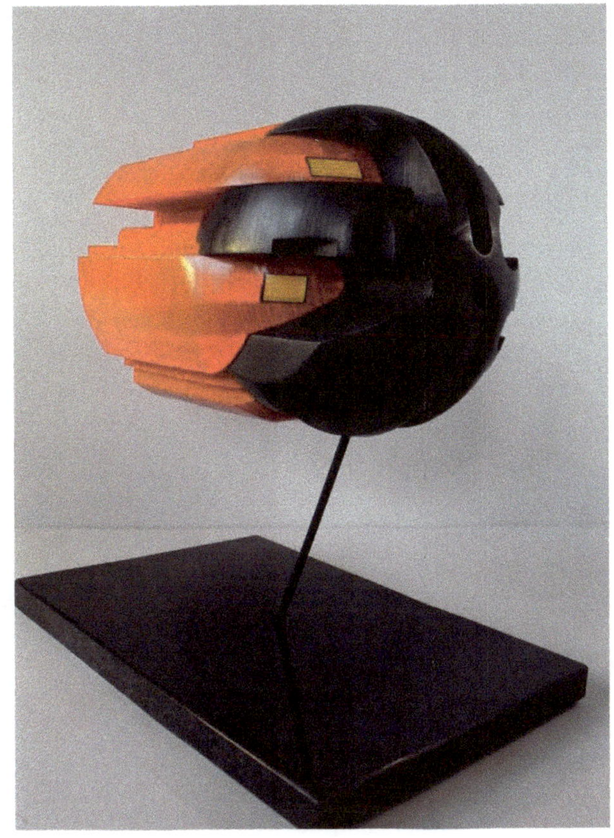

My work grew from my love of the Afrofuturist Music of Sun Ra and his 'Cosmic Philosophy', which was a result of his claimed alien abduction to Saturn.

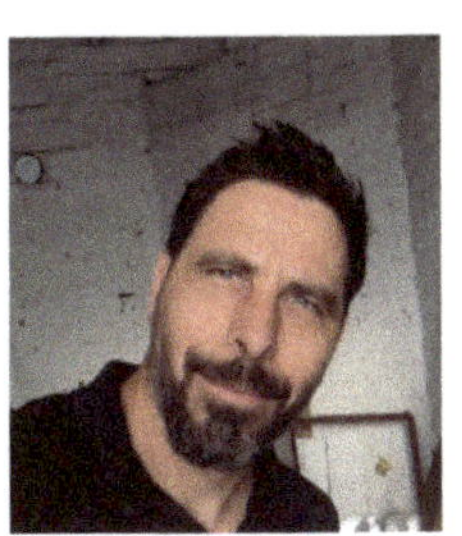

"Baraka"
acrylic, wood, marble
2019

Sun Ra's Cosmic Philosophy may have been an act of personal mythology, or the result of an artistic creation, but as a consequence he created some strangely beautiful music from beyond binding myths, the cosmos and all kinds of possible realities.

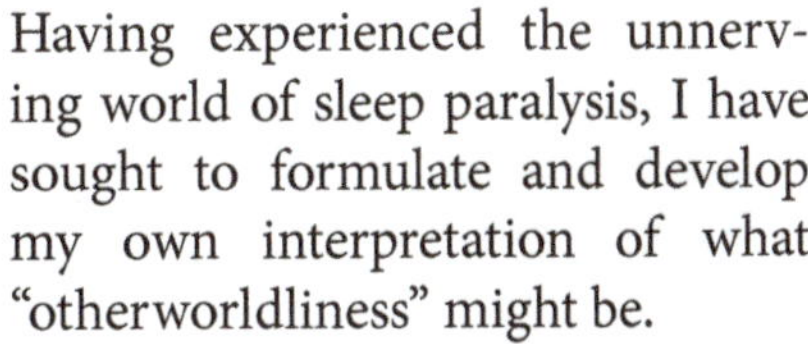

Having experienced the unnerving world of sleep paralysis, I have sought to formulate and develop my own interpretation of what "otherworldliness" might be.

I work with modular forms, by stretching and transforming material properties and attempt to make a unique building creation for this faux universe in art.

Many individual elements combine to create numerous building shapes, which are then tessellated to create a series of planetary forms.

I'm represented by The London Contemporary Art Gallery

14

MARCH

RICHARD SLEE (UK)

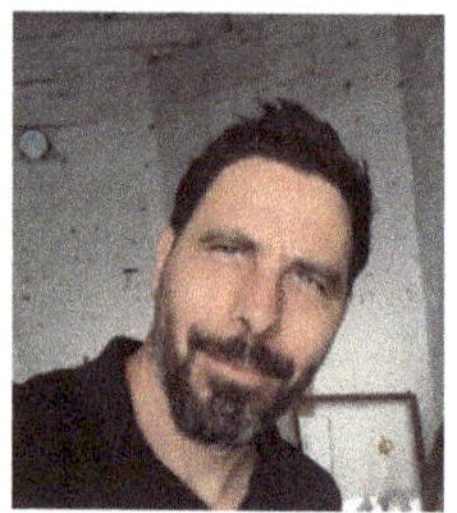

"Element 115"
2017

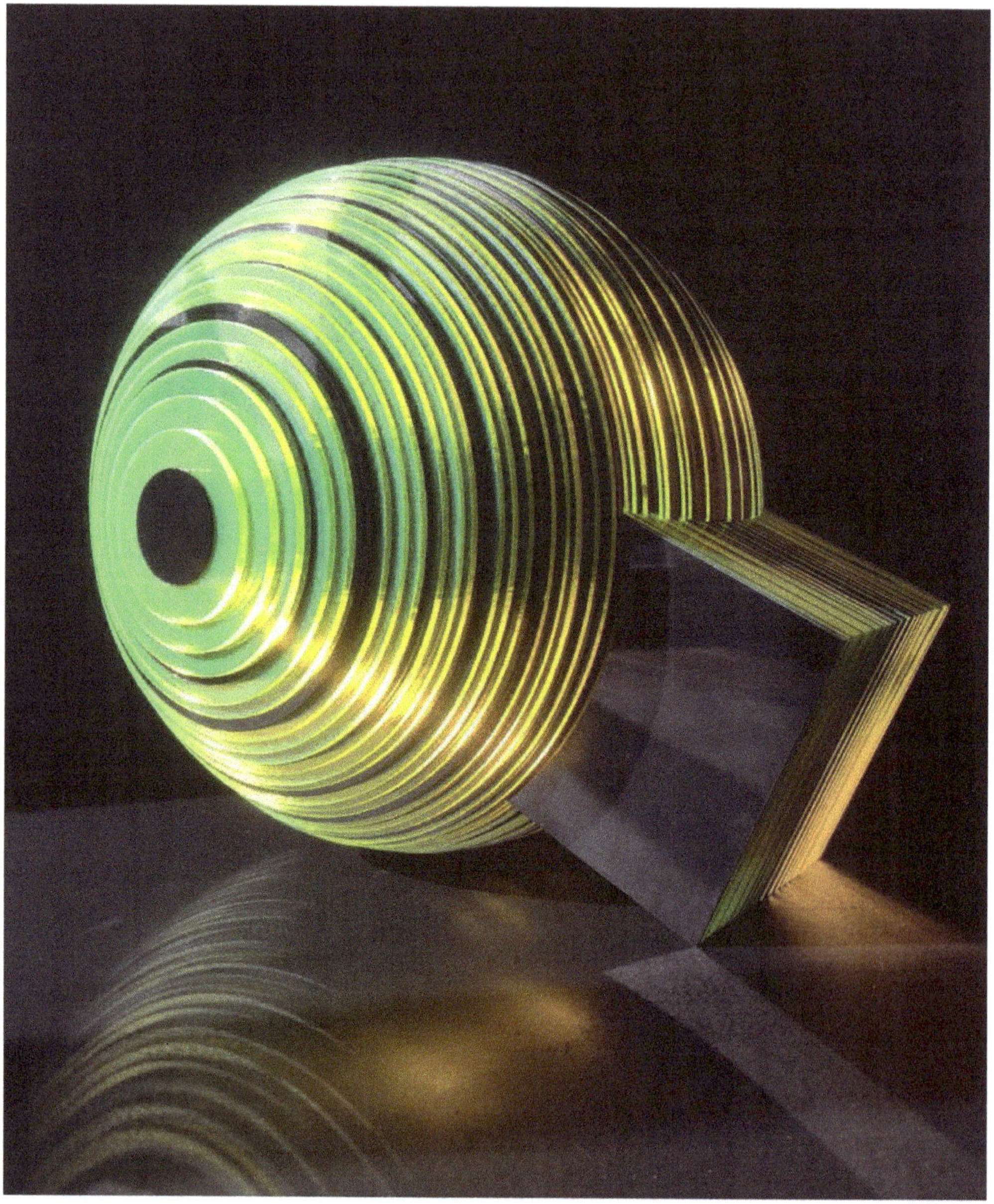

15

MARCH

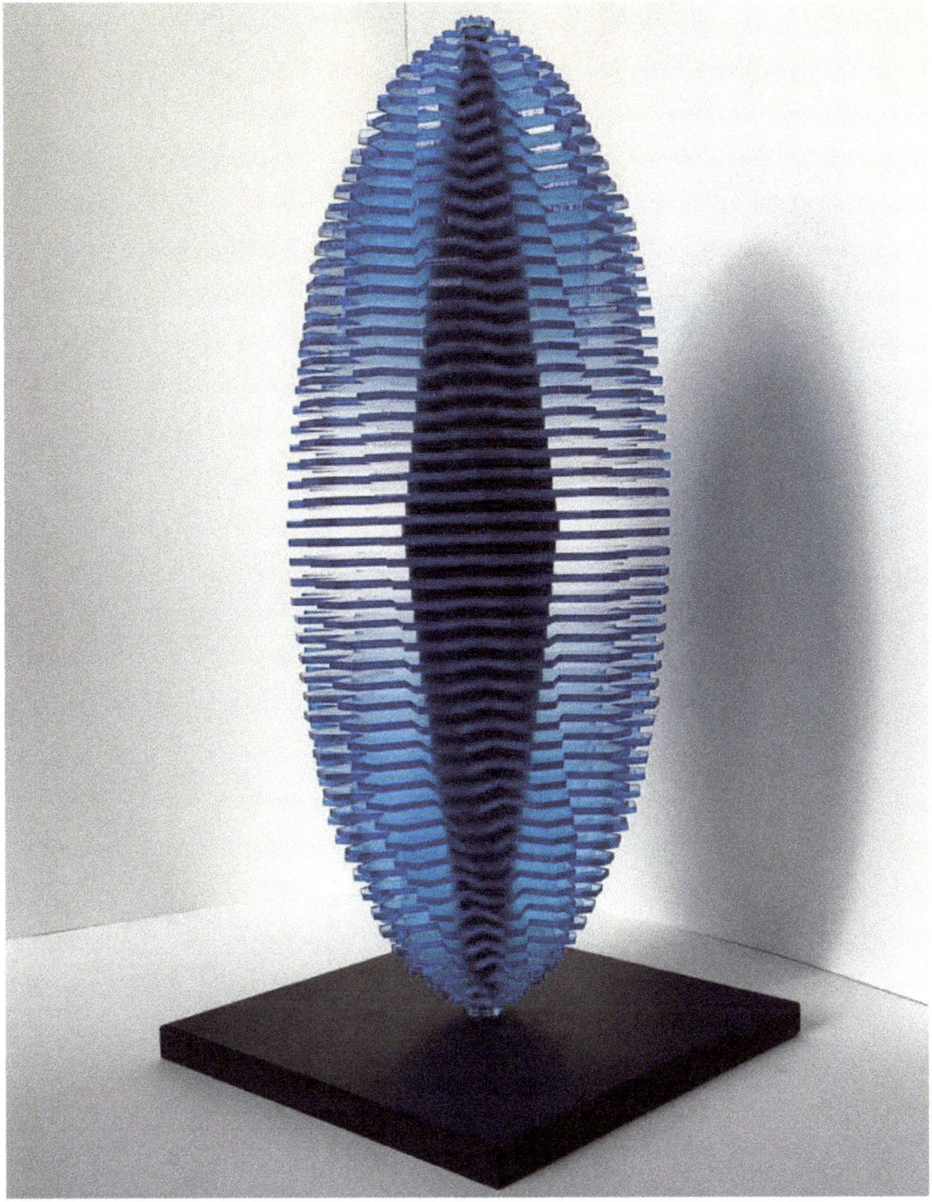

RICHARD SLEE (UK)

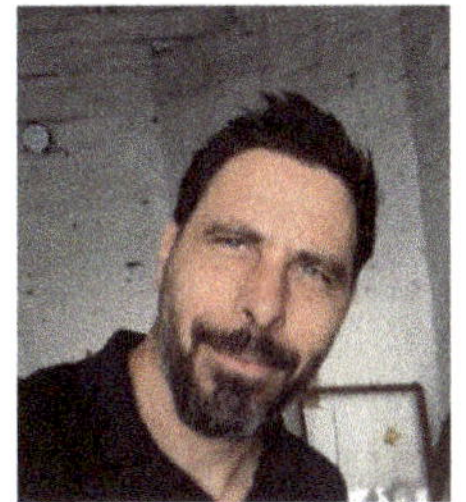

"Heliocentric worlds"
2018

16

MARCH

RICHARD SLEE (UK)

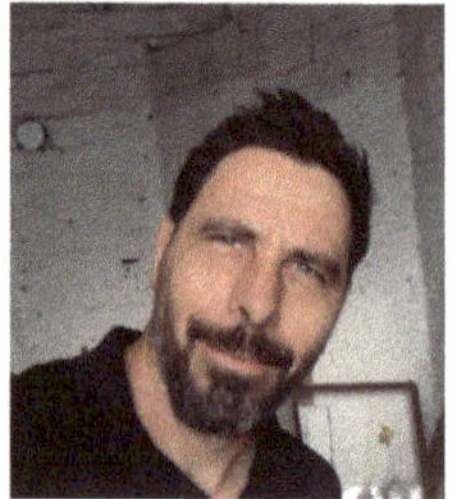

"Joyous union"
2019

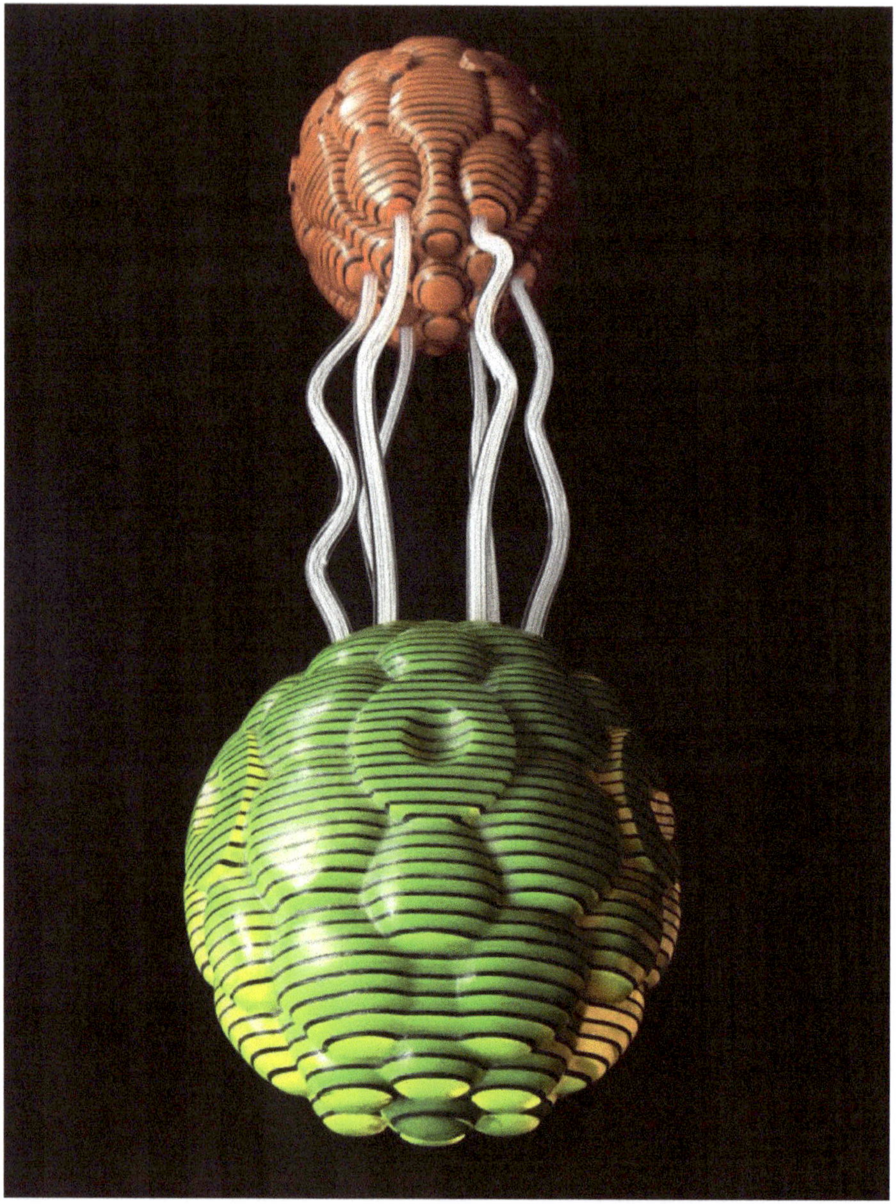

17

MARCH

12 MONDAY

13 TUESDAY

14 WEDNESDAY

15 THURSDAY

16 FRIDAY

17 SATURDAY

18 SUNDAY

ARNOLD BÖCKLIN (SWITZERLAND)

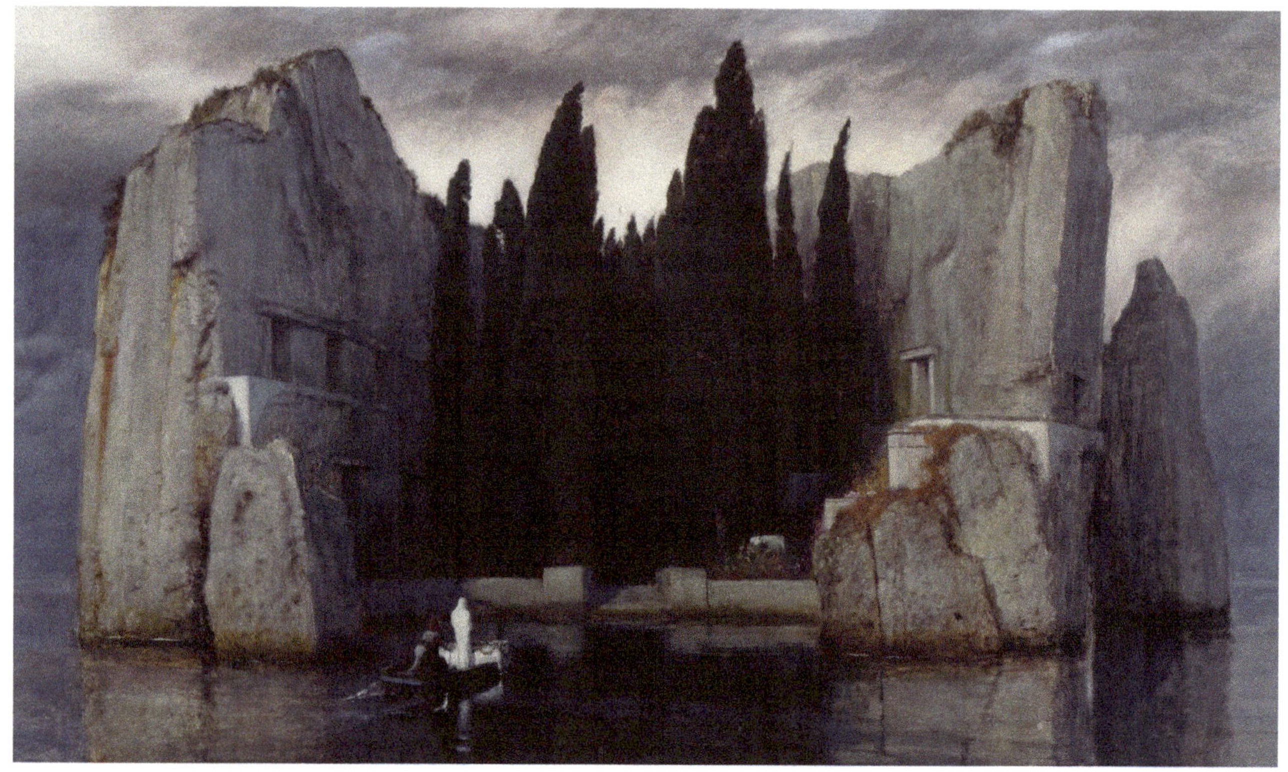

"Isle of the Dead" 3rd version
1883

19

MARCH

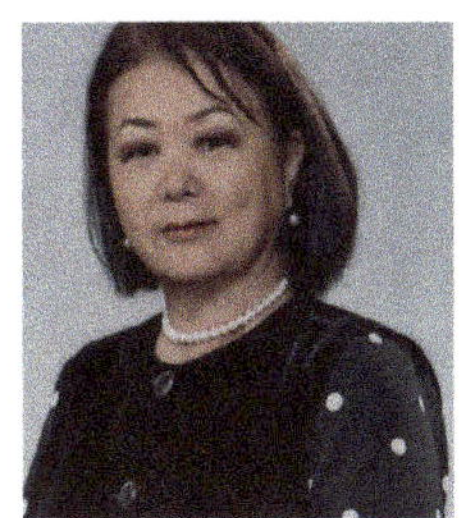

Care

Cares tie my hands,
No time for creativity, no time for poetry.
Business ends, sounds fade - A white sheet of clouds beckons.
A white sheet of paper beckons into the world of clouds.

And thoughts will fly in the open fields,
I'll swim without feeling the sea.
The universe is in me, all in my will,
I'll give my peace of mind to the songs.

Don't take away my time, my cares,
Don't say no to my verses.
Oh, life, go away in its circles,
Give up a little, don't follow my footsteps!

20

MARCH

JOHN MARTIN (UK)

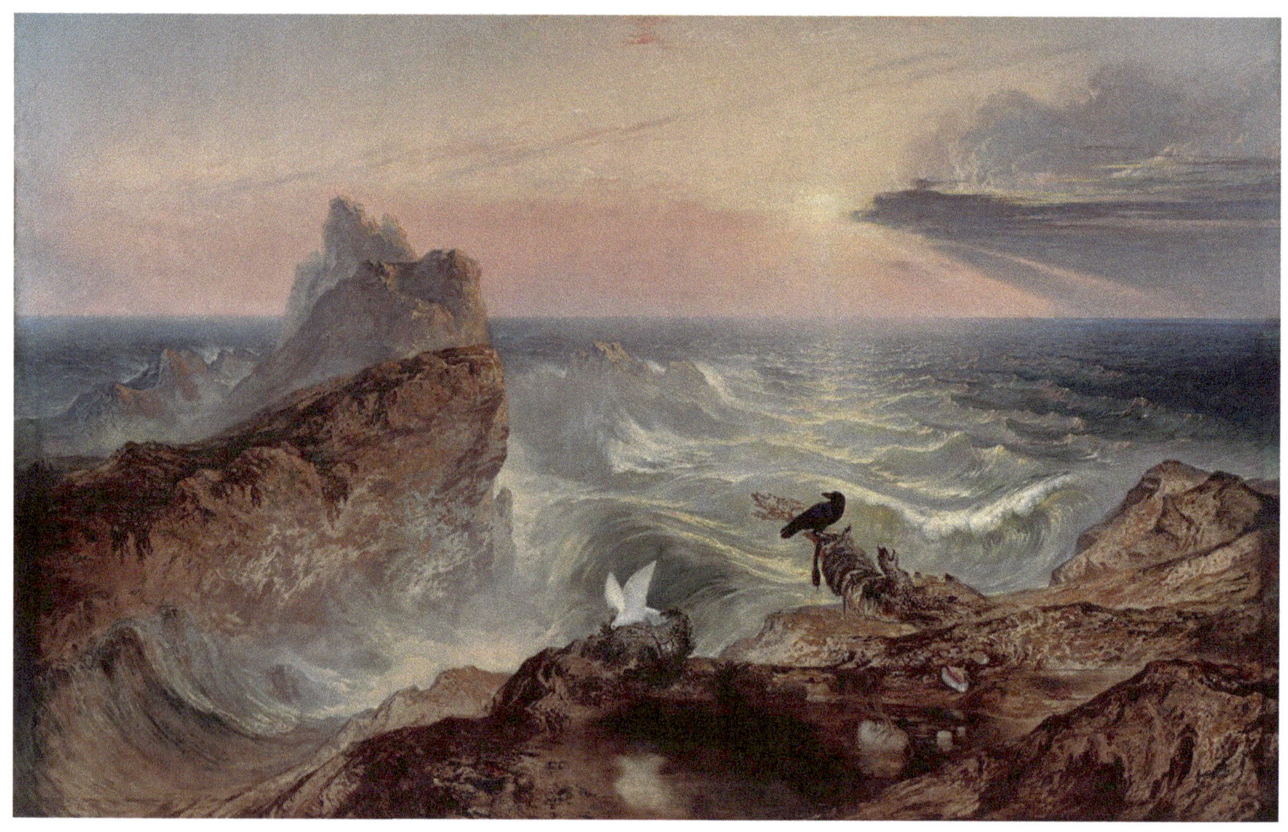

"The Assuaging of the Waters"
1840

21

MARCH

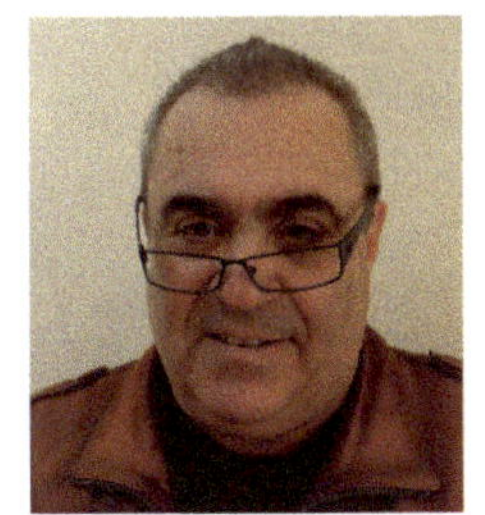

All Things Pass, And This Too Shall Pass

And in anticipation of troubled times,
Trouble lurks at the gates,
But Solomon once said:
All things pass, and this too shall pass."

And there was a great groaning in the land...
In a year that had been trampled by tempest,
But Solomon once said:
"All things pass, and this too shall pass."

The grief was announced by a flock of crows,
The passing of an age.
But Solomon once said:
"All things pass, and this too shall pass."

The spheres of the heavens ring out,
The long-awaited sun has risen,
For Solomon once said:
"All things pass..." and it has passed.

22
MARCH

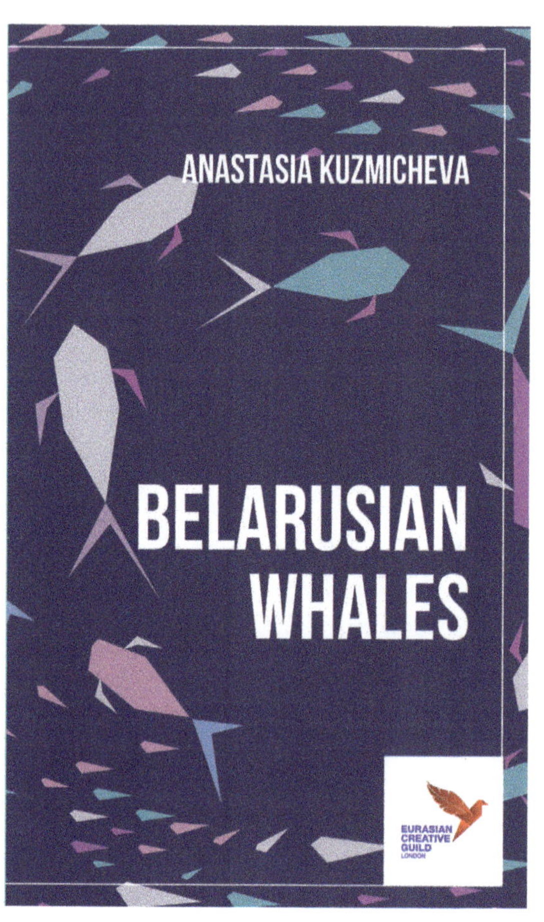

The title of Anastasiya Kuzmicheva's work *"Belarusian Whales"* invites readers into a world of contradictions and doubts. Indeed, while reading these verses one grasps the apparently conflicting depths of the author's own point of view - thanks to a wide and clever usage of poetic figures. As such, her sky is "always without make-up", while her brain "will wipe the dream like dust". Meanwhile, warmth, light, shame, and love, are created through the imagery surrounding a "white temple" ….. an antithesis to previous assertions. Overall, this poet's irony seems to be both subtle and comical, since one encounters lines like: "a whale escaped like all men" as a clear critique of average truth claims. Hence, those parts of the poem devoted to meaningful answers and pithy solutions remains the largest section of the entire composition. Albeit quickly followed by more questions. Curiously, neither "who", nor "what" the whales represent is ever outlined. Instead, a sense of intelligent mystery points to "the names of chapters" as our only clue. After all, we already know that " …everyone saw the whale…", which leaves each reader to make up his, or her, own mind in this regard.

— *Nadezhda Kolesnikova, writer*

25

MARCH

ISBN: 978-1-910886-45-8
RRP: £14.95

19 MONDAY

20 TUESDAY

21 WEDNESDAY

22 THURSDAY

23 FRIDAY

24 SATURDAY

25 SUNDAY

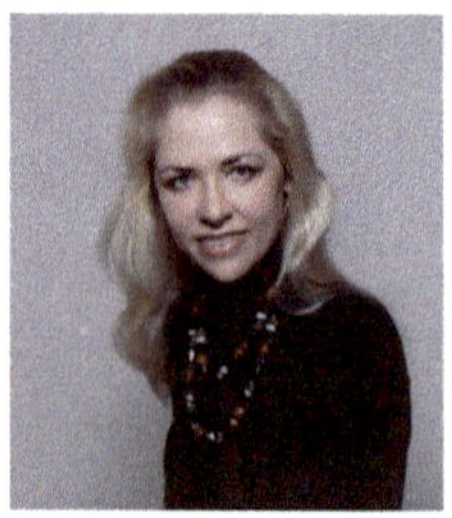

The Nocturnal Song (Lullaby)

When the twilight grasps the silence,
Then the world will bring us play.
When the Moon rejoices darkness,
Then we feel our pain allay.
We are creatures of no sorrow,
We are nameless in the morrow.
Come with us until it's over,
You'll become a fearless rover.

When you listen to the whisper,
You can hear us pitter-patter.
When we cover up a child,
This will make dreams so much better.
We shall dance upon the starlight,
We are floating in the blue night.
Step inside this glowing kingdom –
Rest your heart in newborn freedom.

When you find your soul is crying,
Then we'll heal it at a touch.
When your hopes are slowly dying,
We'll return them twice as much.
We are hiding in this aura,
We must vanish in Aurora.
Don't look back at all your fears,
Find your way when Sun appears!

29

MARCH

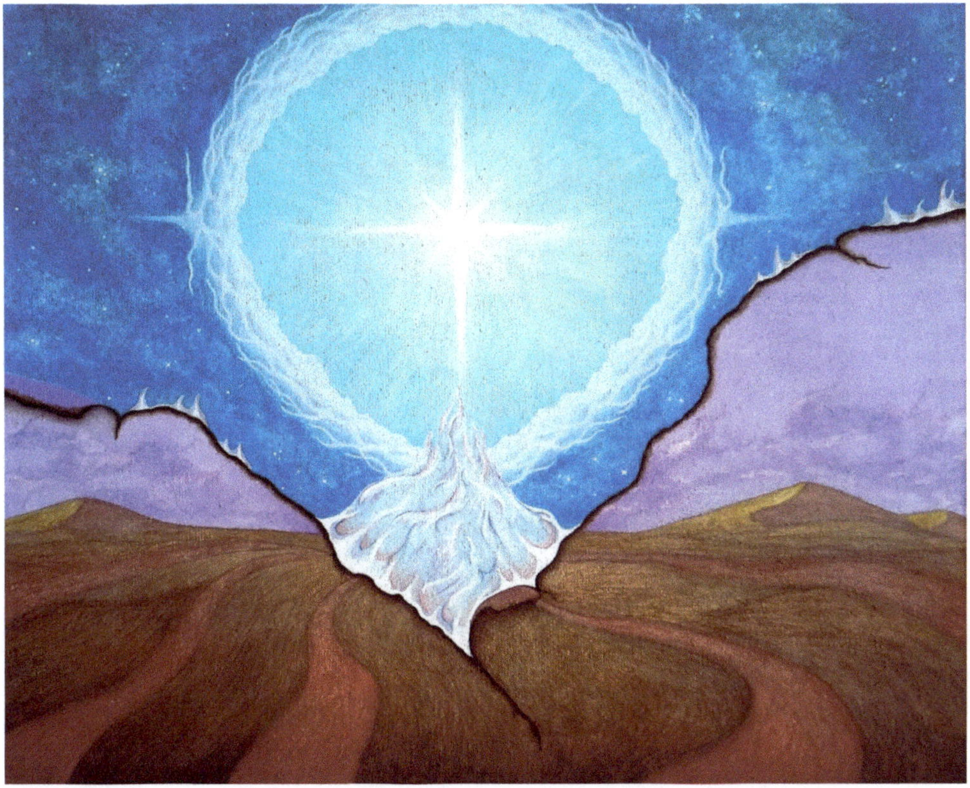

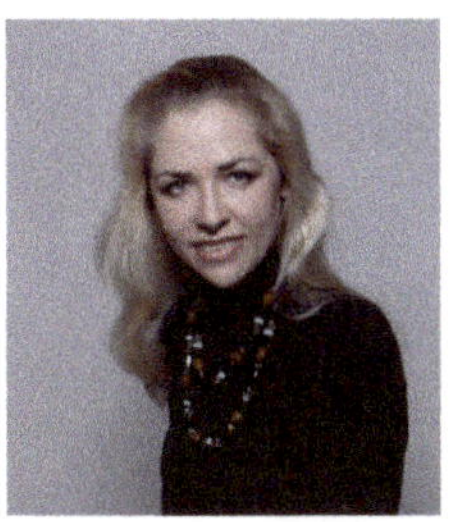

"The Last Horizon", 2007
acrylic paints on wood,
25"/19"

30

MARCH

DARYA ZALESSKAYA (KAZAKHSTAN)

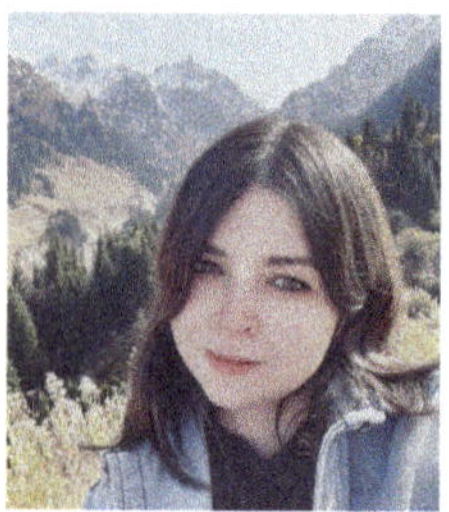

"On high", 2022

For every creature in the world, height is different.

Humans climb to the heights of a career, politics, religion, and even family.

Predators find themselves on a high when they surpass their prey for strength and speed.

For fish, being on high means swimming closer to the surface of the water, regardless of their fear of the unknown.

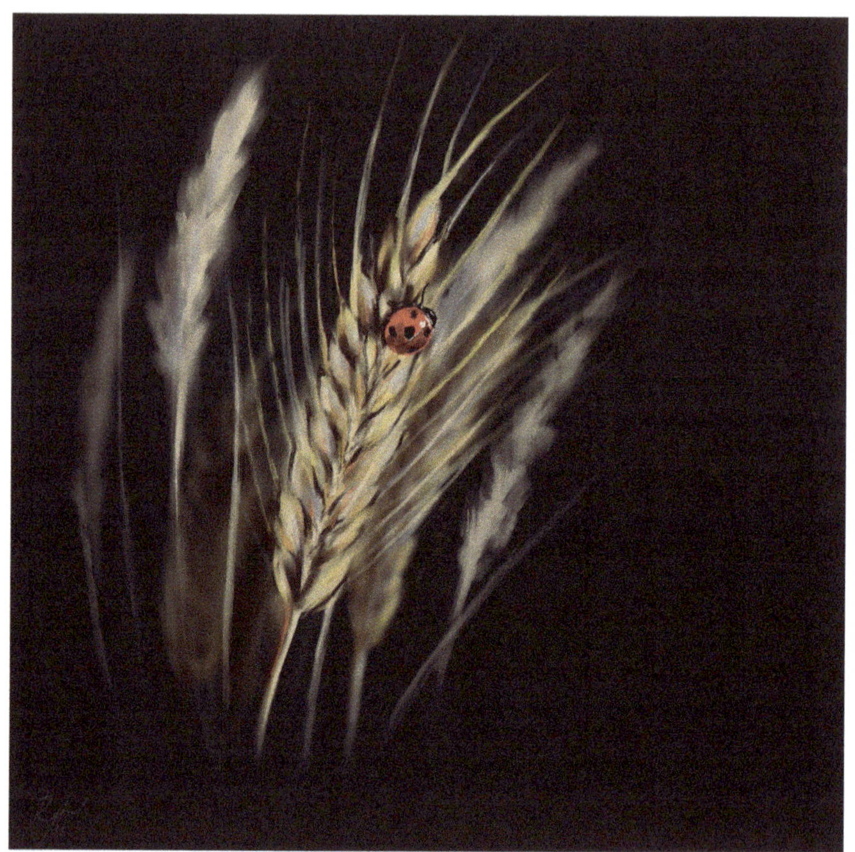

And for the ladybird, height is climbing to the top of a spike of wheat. Holding on to the wind with its small paws, it sees a field of wheat spreading out, and for a moment it feels great.

2022

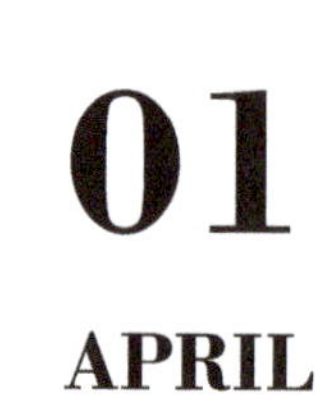

26 MONDAY

27 TUESDAY

28 WEDNESDAY

29 THURSDAY

30 FRIDAY

31 SATURDAY

01 SUNDAY

DARYA ZALESSKAYA (KAZAKHSTAN)

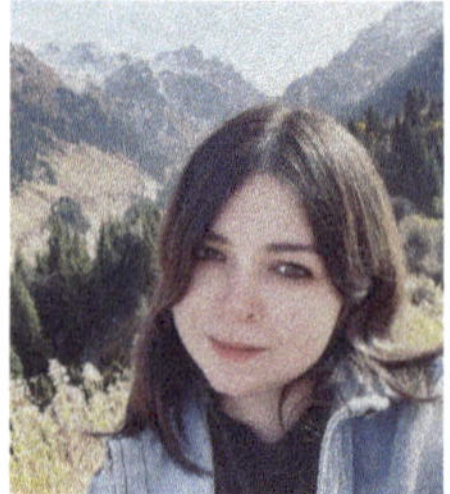

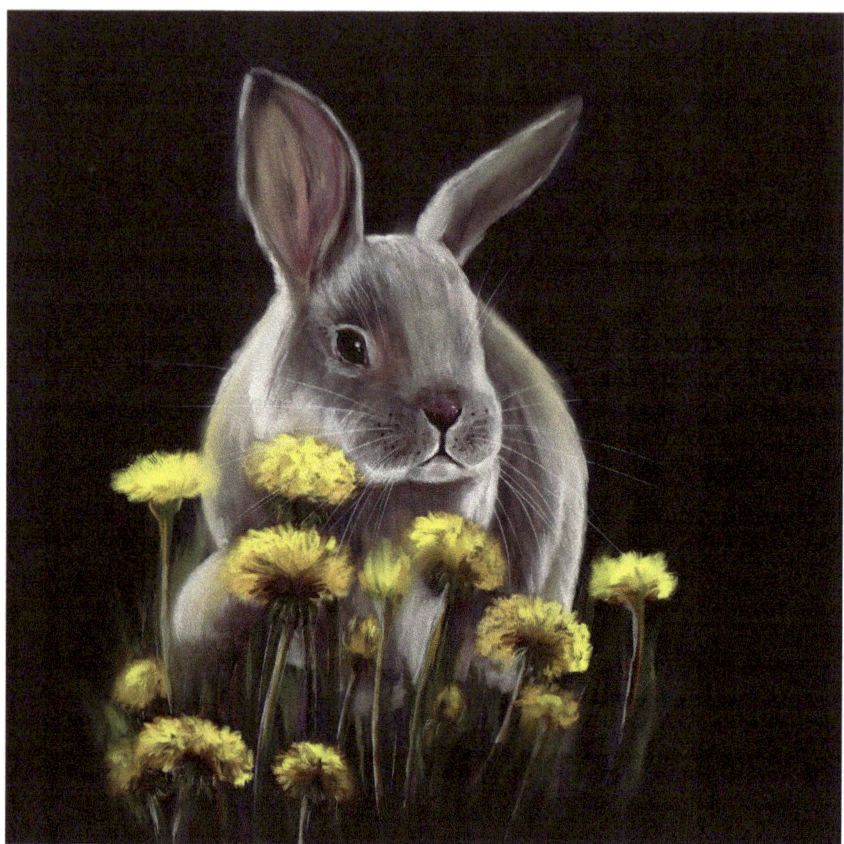

"In the dandelions", 2022

Rabbits are warmer in the spring. It's not so scary in springtime. They can hop through forests, fields and meadows, and look around almost without fear.

The world is brighter in the spring. You can burrow into a mound of dandelions and sit, enjoying the bright rays of the sun. As if you're in a yellow and fluffy sea and you don't want to swim out of it.

In spring you are inspired to be alive. And you want to live forever…

2022

02

APRIL

This was a Poet - - It is That

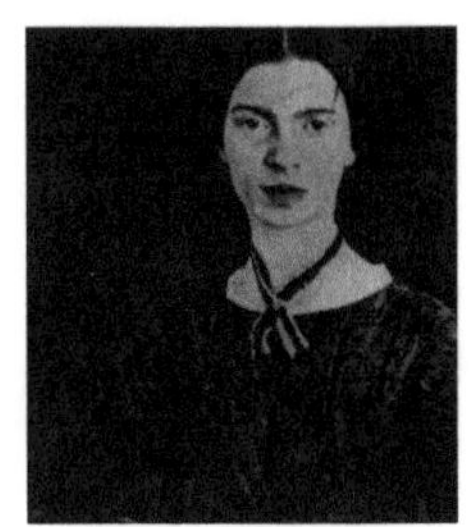

This was a Poet -- It is That
Distills amazing sense
From ordinary Meanings --
And Attar so immense

From the familiar species
That perished by the Door --
We wonder it was not Ourselves
Arrested it -- before --

Of Pictures, the Discloser --
The Poet -- it is He --
Entitles Us -- by Contrast --
To ceaseless Poverty --

Of portion -- so unconscious –
The Robbing -- could not harm --
Himself -- to Him -- a Fortune --
Exterior -- to Time –

03

APRIL

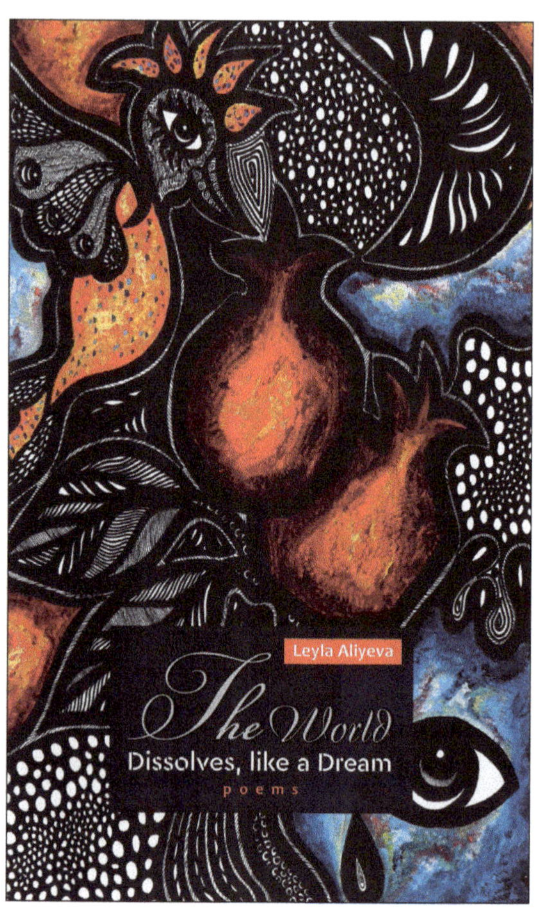

This collection of poetry is the first book in Azerbaijani written by the talented young poet Leyla Aliyeva, who is known in our iterary circles for moving poems, such as *"Don't Go, Mother"*, *"I will Go and Cry a Little"*, *"The Swan"*, *"The Butterfly"*, *"To Each Their Own End"* and "I am Blind". From her very first work, these poems have shown her own way of thinking and distinctive view of the world. They are like unfading flowers that retain sorrow, love, the warmth of the air, rain, drizzle and scent. For several years now Leyla Aliyeva has been earning the admiration of a wide, intellectual readership.

ISBN: 978-1-910886-76-2
RRP: £19.50

06

APRIL

The Wonder of Borovoe

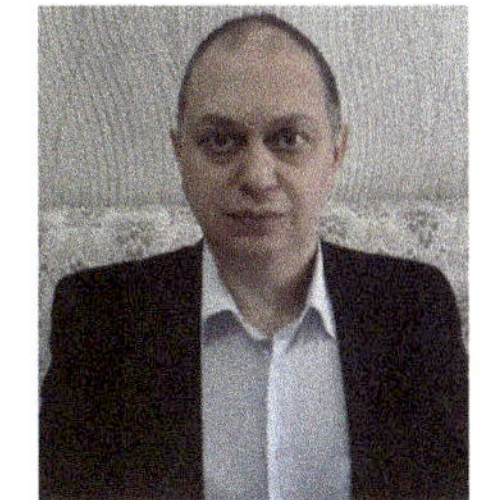

Nature welcomes us all here,
Wherever you cast your gaze,
In the pine forest, the slopes of the ancient mountains,
Here the heart is filled with inspiration.

From heaven itself a reward is sent down:
A meteor from space.
The progenitor of two great lakes,
And your thoughts grow wings and take flight.

Forests, caves, cliffs, clouds.
A light hand sculpts the landscape,
A spirit admiring the creative rush.

In this picturesque land in a corner of our planet,
This Festival of Friendship has gathered all our friends,
Burabay gives us its love.

07

APRIL

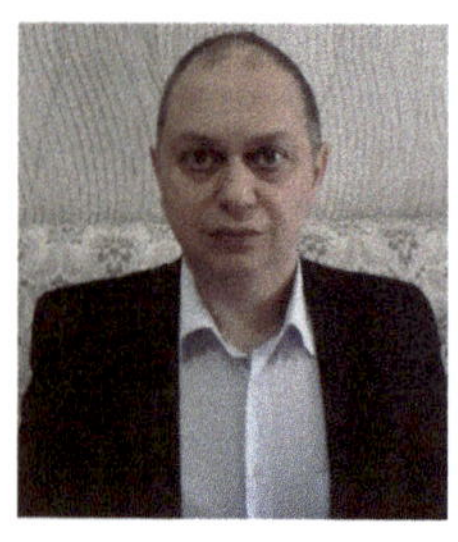

Чудо Боровое

Природа нас всех чествовать здесь рада,
Куда ни кинь ты свой пытливый взор,
В бору сосновом склоны древних гор,
Тут сердце вдохновением объято.

С самих небес ниспослана награда:
Из космоса упавший метеор, –
Родоначальник двух больших озёр,
И мысль твоя становится крылатой.

Леса, пещеры, скалы, облака, –
Пейзаж ваяет лёгкая рука,
Дух в творческом порыве восхищая.

Планеты нашей живописный край,
На Фестиваль друзей всех созывая,
Свою любовь нам дарит Бурабай.

08

APRIL

02 MONDAY

03 TUESDAY

04 WEDNESDAY

05 THURSDAY

06 FRIDAY

07 SATURDAY

08 SUNDAY

IRENE YAVCHUNOVSKY (ISRAEL)

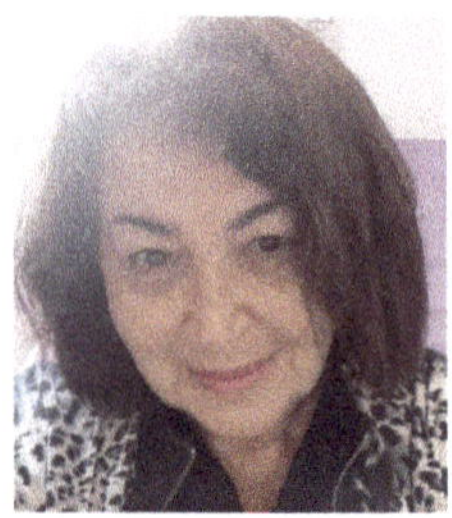

Spring Comes

Spring comes as if a magic dream,
A tender leaf of May.
It soon will spread its rainbow wing
And then will fly away.

Then cruel summer heats the world,
The air is hot and still.
The sky is red, the sand is gold,
The dry is daffodil.
But at the fragrant summer night
When nightingales sing,
It seems that spring began its flight
And spread a rainbow wing.

Then autumn brings sadness to the land.
Cold winds their music play,
And bare trees like old men bend,
The sky grows dull and grey.
But rainy droplets clear and light
Weave streaming-gleaming strings,
As if the spring began its flight
And spread rainbow wings.

Like rapid brooklet, time flows,
And winter steps inside
With stormy clouds, silver snows,
With cold and gloomy sight.
But crystal snowflakes in warm light
Dance and the branches swing.
As if the spring began its flight
And spread a rainbow wing.

09

APRIL

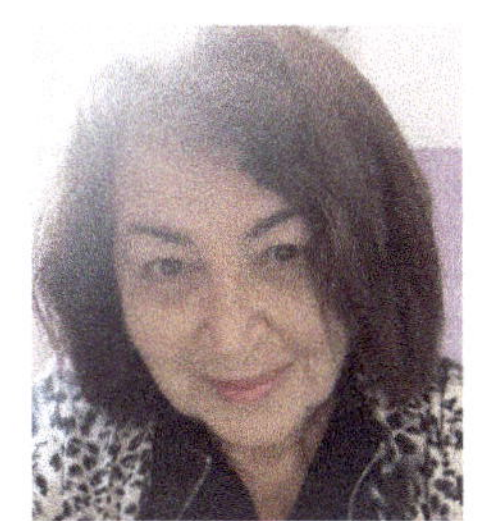

Desert

A road winds through the desert.
The landscape is dreary here.
A stupid camel is gazing
At Bedouins' shelters near.

Fresh winds here are like magic.
All dried up without rains.
I close my eyes and imagine
The flight of a flock of cranes.

Dust-cobweb is spinning, swaying,
And creeping along the roads.
And I think of valleys, plains,
And puddles with paper boats.

But poppies grow in the desert,
Emerging all of a sudden.
And now to my amazement
The desert becomes a garden.

My tedious weekdays go.
Life's path isn't always pleasant.

10

APRIL

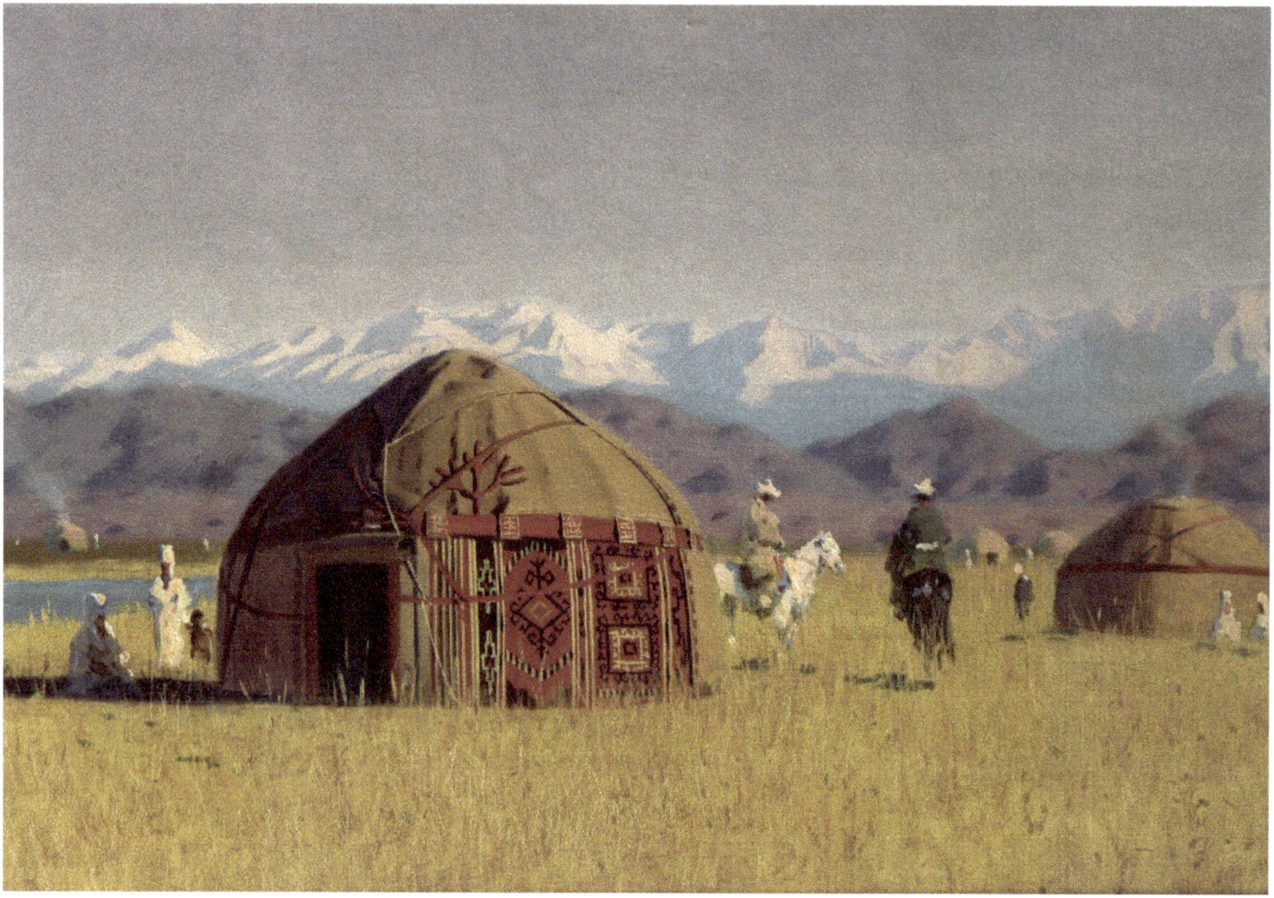

VASILY VERESHCHAGIN (RUSSIA)

"Kyrgyz cabins on the Chu River", 1869-1870

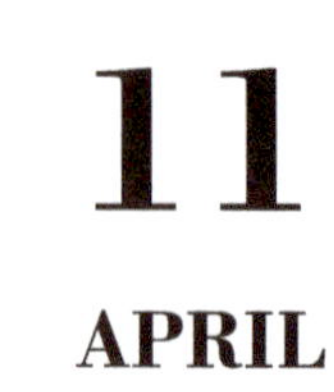

09 MONDAY

10 TUESDAY

11 WEDNESDAY

152THURSDAY

13 FRIDAY

14 SATURDAY

15 SUNDAY

ANTON RAFFAEL MENGS (GERMANY)

"The Dream of St. Joseph", between 1773 and 1774

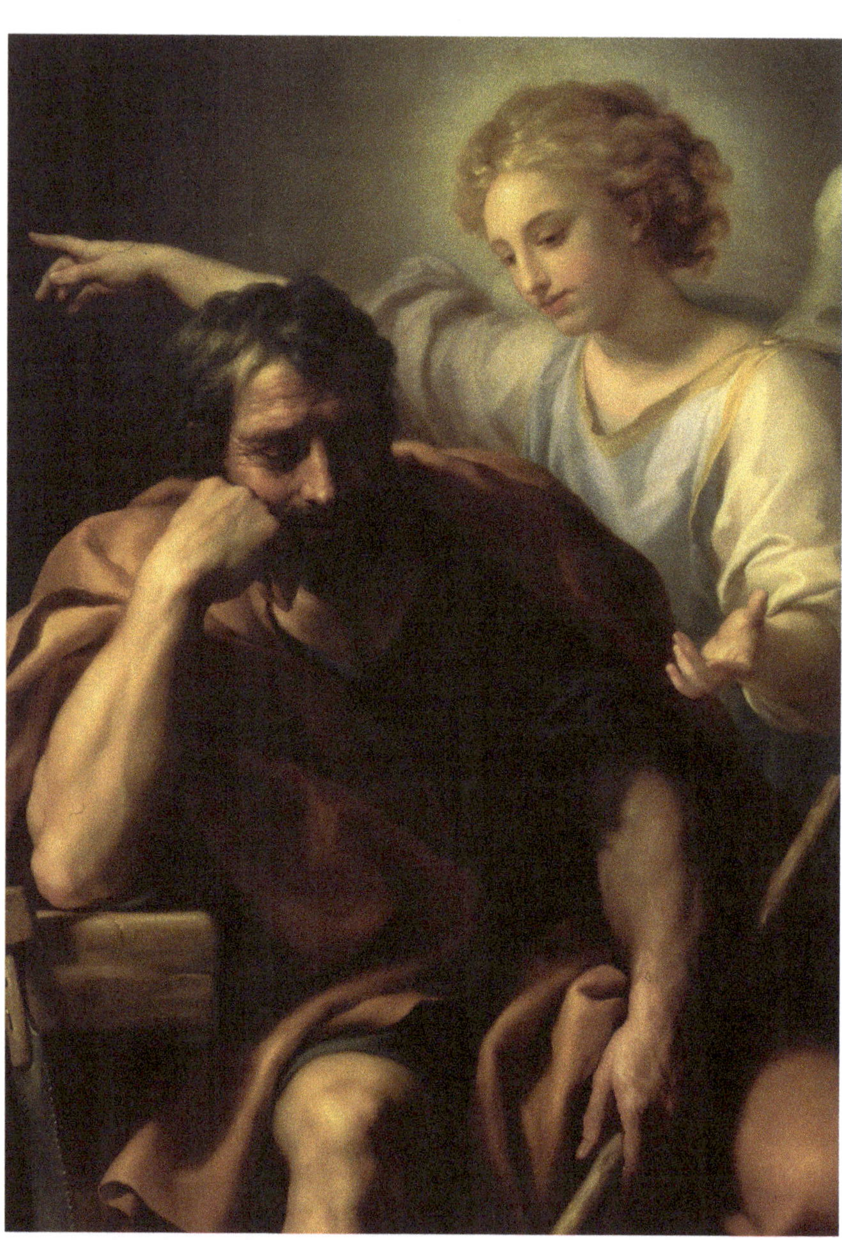

16

APRIL

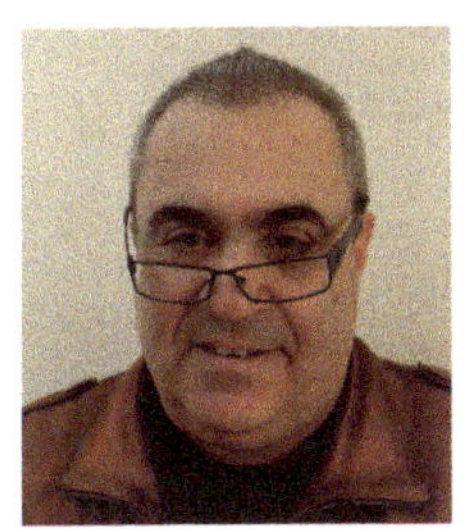

The Shoah

It is madness that became reality,
It is the recent form of Gehenna,
It is the last, wheezing words:
This is the Shoah.

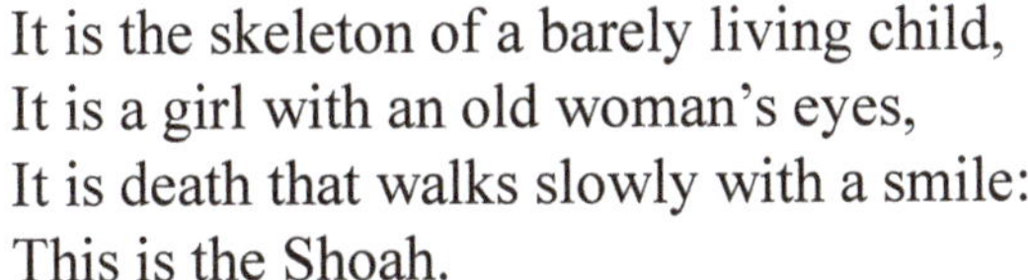

It is the skeleton of a barely living child,
It is a girl with an old woman's eyes,
It is death that walks slowly with a smile:
This is the Shoah.

It is a shoe, lying without a pair,
It is a bunk with no planks,
It is life under the merciless gaze of a knife:
This is the Shoah.

It is teeth and shards of crockery,
It is fragments of human bones,
It is a dead soul:
This is the Shoah.

It is killing people for pleasure,
It is violence, mutilation, confusion,
It is the rabbi's last song:
This is the Shoah, the Holocaust, the burnt offering.

17
APRIL

KONSTANTY GÓRSKI (POLAND)

"Krysia Świtezianka", 1933

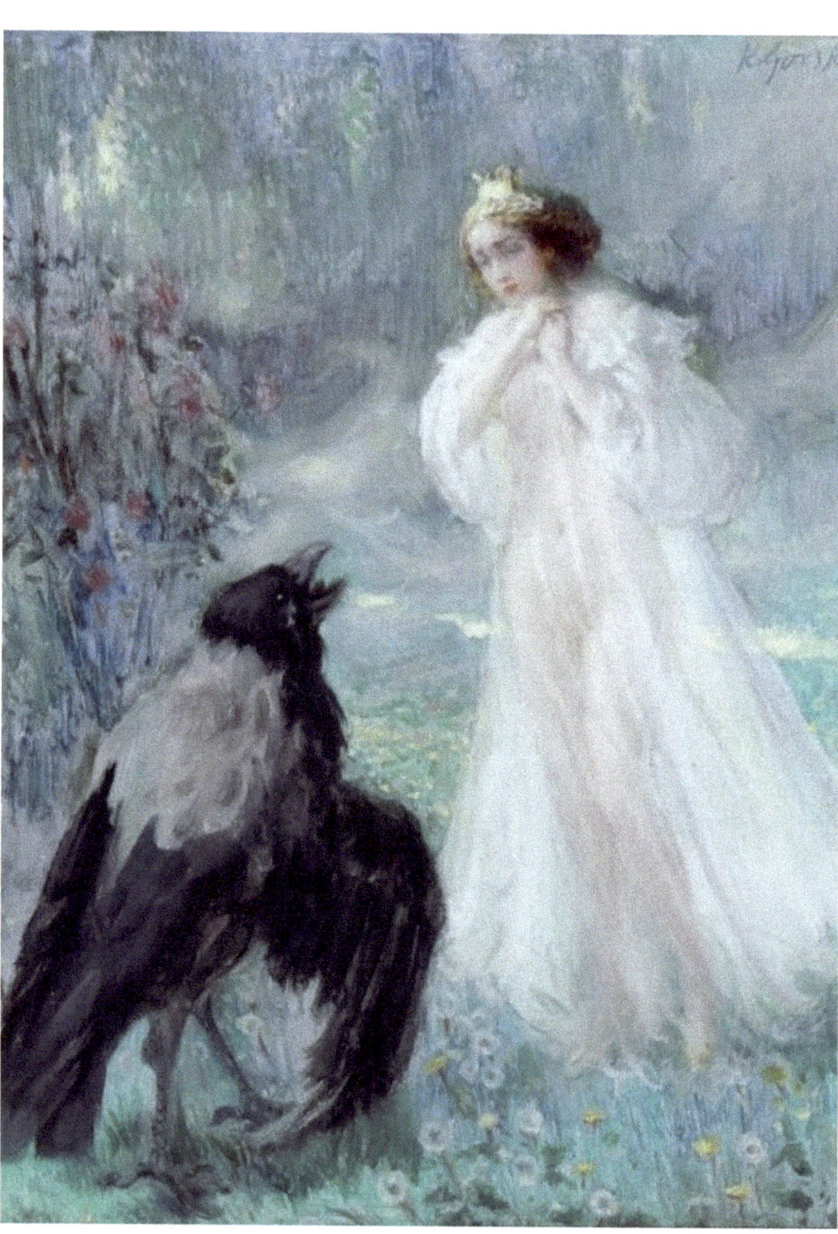

20

APRIL

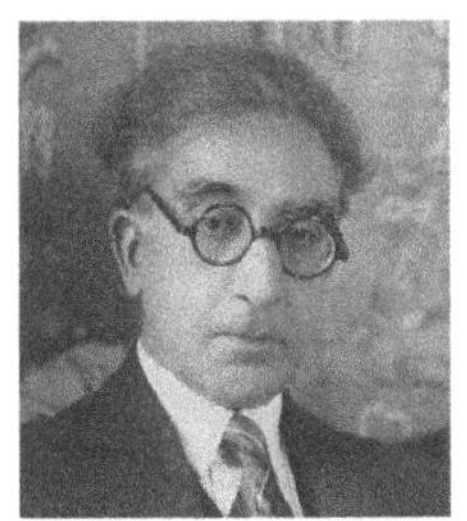

***

I remember your last words:
It's impossible not to love you.
Someone is bound to love you. Believe me, and you'll be happy!
When you said those words, you flew away.
It's been so long
Like it was yesterday
Perhaps you were Venus?
To me...
And now you've got a family
Beautiful children, and a husband
But your eyes are full of sadness
You want to smile, but...
But your eyes never lie
Maybe when it all started
You didn't need to confess?
But it's not your fault and nor is it mine
But I know who's to blame:
It's Petersburg's fault
It's the White Nights, the beauty
Where you and I
Talked till morning
Walking till morning...
Strange, strange it would be
Not to declare my love
In the City of Heroes
Strange that I still keep
All your letters
And I know
You keep mine, too...

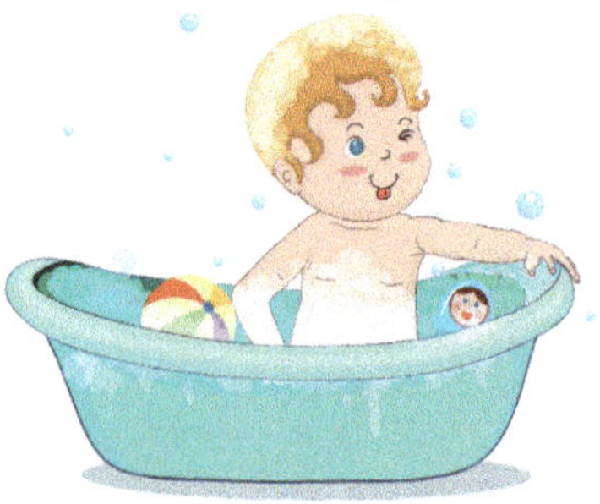

A prize-winning poem by Moldovan author, Ludmila Dubcovetcaia, Rhymes about Boys is a vibrant tour de force. Joyful and witty in equal measure, this engaging and fast-paced book is bound to captivate children. Can you find your name in there?

ISBN: 978-1-913356-03-3
RRP: £22.50

16 MONDAY

17 TUESDAY

18 WEDNESDAY

19 THURSDAY

20 FRIDAY

21 SATURDAY

22 SUNDAY

NADEGDA BOGOVICH (RUSSIA)

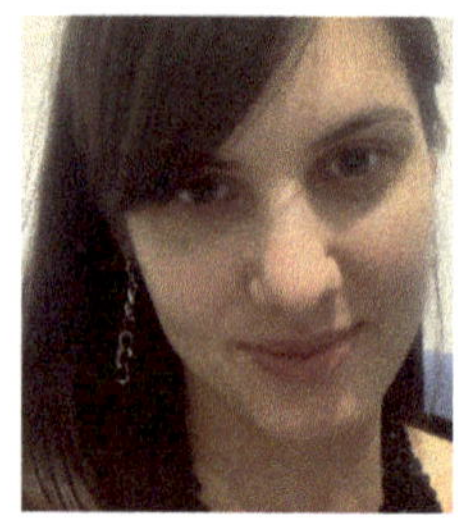

I'll Never Forget You...

I'll never forget you,
You're with me everywhere and everywhere
Every breath is filled with you...
In my mind you're always with me!

I'll never forget you
I'll remember you and me
I'll carry our feelings with me
I'll write them down and
I'll open them to you...

I'll never forget you
And I'll love you, I'll love you!
That love is equal to God's miracle
I trust fate - I'll be obedient to it
But I'll never forget you

Without you I feel an emptiness
I live, I love - I'm for real!
Every day I think of you
I hold your hand tenderly and then I let you go...

22

APRIL

I'll never forget you
It's like a miracle when we meet
It'll never be the same
I'll never forget you

I'll look for you in the moonlight
I'll talk to you about my passions
I'll never forget your jokes
And I'll listen to your stories!
Two pipes and a garage
I won't forget
And I'll always love you!

I'll talk to you as if I were you
As if I were you and back!
My darling, I won't forget you
My man, I'll be your wife!

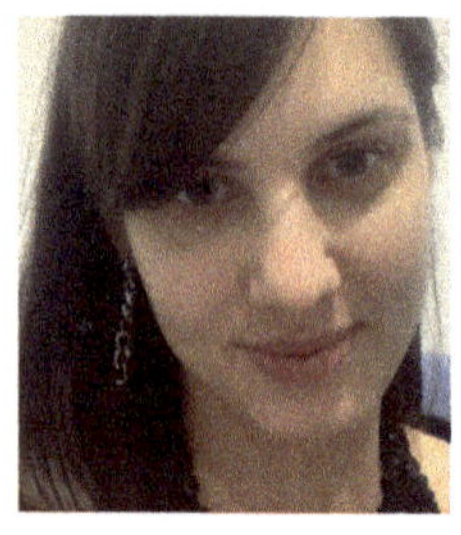

Я тебя никогда не забуду…

Я тебя никогда не забуду,
Ты со мною везде и повсюду!
Каждый вдох лишь наполнен тобою…
В моих мыслях всегда ты со мною!

Я тебя никогда не забуду,
Вспоминать о нас с тобой буду!
Пронесу наши чувства с собою,
Напишу и тебе их открою...

Я тебя никогда не забуду,
И любить, тебя лишь я буду!
Та любовь - равна Божьему чуду…
Доверяюсь судьбе - я покорной ей буду,
Но тебя никогда не забуду!

Без тебя пустоту ощущаю...
Я живу, я люблю - не играю!
Каждый день я тебя вспоминаю...
Руку нежно держу, а затем отпускаю...

23

APRIL

Я тебя никогда не забуду,
Наша встреча похожа на чудо!
И другой похожей не будет...
Я тебя никогда не забуду!

В лунном свете искать тебя буду...
О жарках говорить с тобой буду,
Твои шутки я не забуду!
И вслух сказки твои слушать буду!
Две трубы и гараж не забуду...
И любимой навеки я буду!

Говорить мне с тобой так приятно…
Словно я - это ты и обратно!
Мой любимый - тебя не забуду,
Мой мужчина - твоей женой буду!

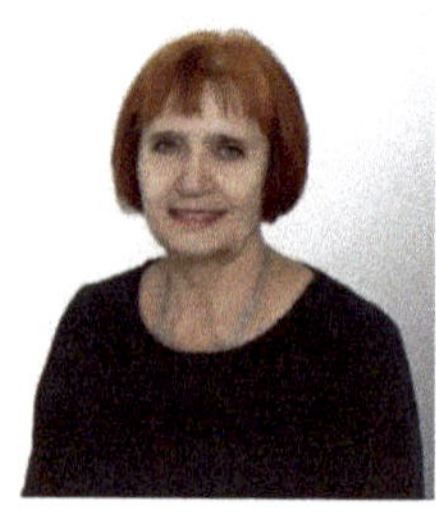

To Be Human

I ask my heart sincerely,
I always ask my soul with tenderness
Don't measure people by your own yardstick.
Don't depend on the weather...
To be strong in times of trouble,
To strive to understand, not to shame.
Patience can move mountains,
And in haste, you can cut deep.
To be tolerant of those you know,
But do not let yourself be offended.
Not to spin on the upswing
In the search for praise from critics.
The best reward is
To know that I was human;
For my family
To remember me with pride.

26

APRIL

Быць чалавекам

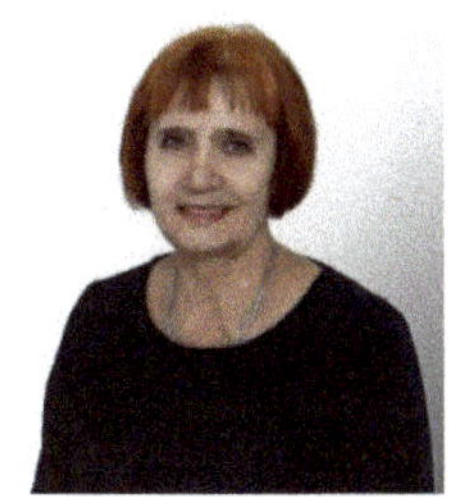

Прашу я шчыра сваё сэрца,
Заўжды душу прашу з лагодай
Сваёю меркаю людзей не мераць
Ды не залежаць ад пагоды…
Ў часіны кепскія быць дужым,
Імкнуцца зразумець, не зганьбіць.
Цярпеннем можна горы зрушыць,
А ў спешцы глыбака параніць…
Быць талерантным да знаёмых,
Але не даць сябе пакрыўдзіць.
Не закружыцца на пад`ёме
Ў спакусе ад хвалебных крытык.
Найлепшая узнагарода -
Пачуць, што быў я чалавекам,
Яшчэ, калі нашчадкі роду
Успомняць з гонарам славечкам…

27

APRIL

NADEGDA BOGOVICH (RUSSIA)

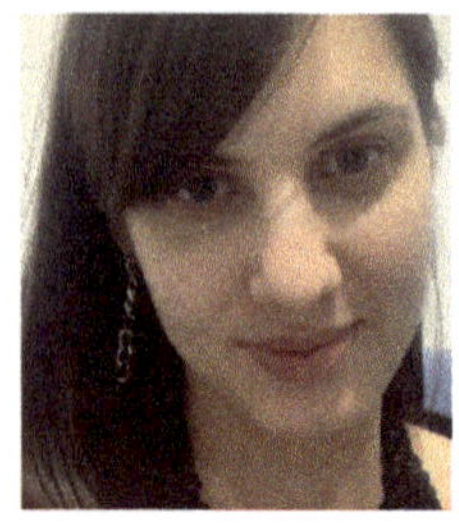

Not for Medals

It was not for medals that this feat was done,
Not for medals did men die.
Not for medals did they leave their families,
Not for medals, not for medals.

Not for medals did they go into battle,
But how many lives were lost?
They gave their lives to their Motherland,
But they didn't go forward for medals.

And we spilled blood on the ground,
And the enemy's bayonets were pierced through.
Friends, relatives, family...
Not for medals, not for medals.

They stayed awake day and night -
they drove the fascists away,
Starving and freezing,
And whether they would meet the dawn,
The soldiers of those times didn't know...

One thing warmed their hearts
That their loved ones were supporting them.
And they had no thoughts
Of mere medals.
And they didn't question anyone,
But went forward and defended.
And all who were there
They were so scared...
It was like going to hell.

28

APRIL

They tasted the earth
And the smoke of fire
But they never lost their spirit
With their backs to each other

Through the pain of war and death
They defended their country
through the pain of loss.
Not for the glitter of brass on their chest,
That's not what they wished for.

So how can we forget now?
The heroes of those days
That have long gone...

I wish we could appreciate the life
For which our grandfathers died.
Not for medals, not for medals.

The heroes of the whole country,
God grant that we do not forget.
And know their faces!
They gave their lives!

And now we must remember!
So we shall never meet this fate again!
All the pain of that cursed war
For the price of a single medal!

NADEGDA BOGOVICH (RUSSIA)

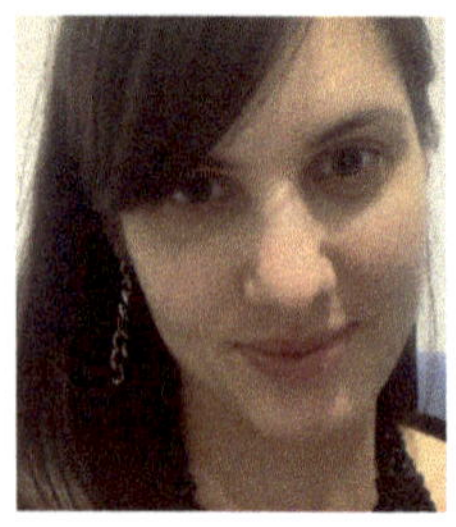

Не за медали

Не за медали подвиг совершали,
Не за медали люди умирали.
Не за медали семьи оставляли,
Не за медали, не за медали.

Не за медали шли в бои,
А сколько жизней потеряли?
Но Родине - свой долг так отдавали,
И шли вперед, не за медали.

И землю кровью поливали,
Врагов насквозь штыками протыкали.
Друзей, родных, семью спасали...
Не за медали, не за медали.

Не спали день и ночь - фашистов гнали,
И голодали, и замерзали,
И встретят ли рассвет,
Солдаты тех времен, тогда не знали…

Одно лишь грело сердце их,
Что их родные за спинами.
И мысли не было у них,
Чтоб думать о медали.

И никого не вопрошали,
А шли вперед и защищали.
И все кто были там
Им было страшно так…
Что словно в ад попали.

29

APRIL

Узнали вкус земли,
И дым огня,
Но силу духа не теряли,
Спиною друга закрывали.

Войну прошли сквозь боль потерь,
Страну свою, лишь защищали.
Не для того чтоб медь блестела на
груди,
Не этого желали.

Так что же нам забыть теперь?
Героев подвиг, давних дней,
Что шли и совершали…

Хочу, чтоб жизнь ценили мы!
Ради которой деды умирали.
Не за медали, не за медали.

Героев всей страны,
Дай Бог, чтоб мы не забывали.
А знали их в лицо!
Они ведь жизни отдавали!

И помнить мы теперь должны!
Чтоб никогда не повстречали,
Всю боль проклятой той войны,
Цену - одной медали!

If you believe in miracles small and large, then this book is undoubtedly for you. It is not so much about the journey as about the fact that the world is full of exciting, unpredictable, and sometimes dangerous, but fascinating moments. Interesting things are very close, you just have to believe and take the first step - and you will see how the wonderful world will step towards you. No, this book is not about magic, but about the great discoveries of a small creature. A creature of valor and loyalty, so devoted to embark on a dangerous journey for the sake of the dream of his beloved mistress. You will have to go through this difficult path together. If you agree, then what are we waiting for? Forward to adventure!

ISBN: 978-1913356330
RRP: £24.95

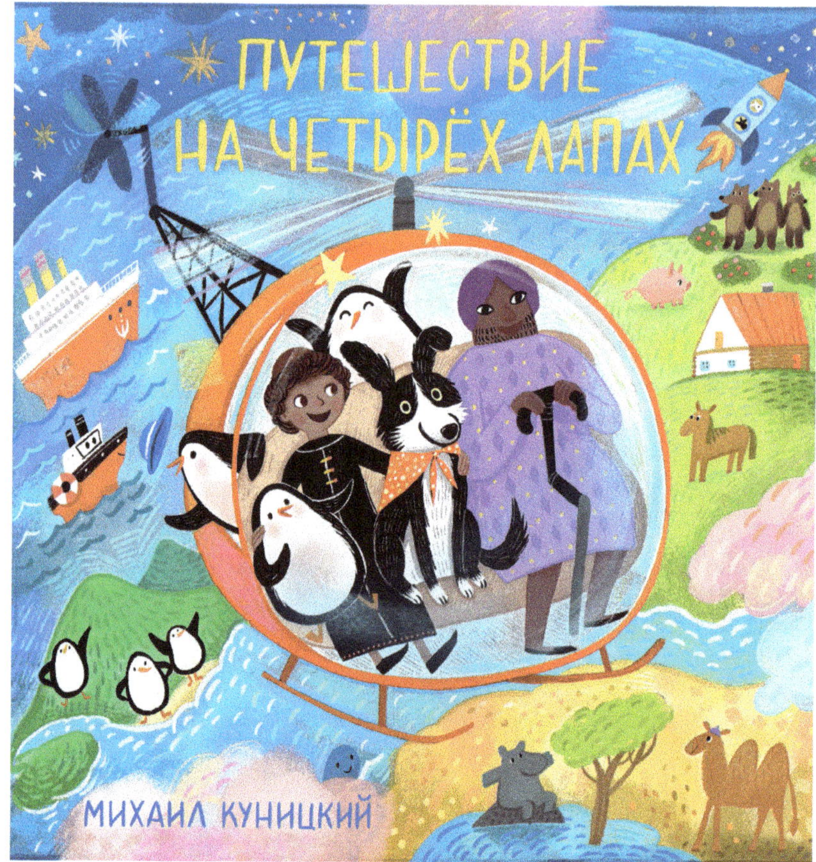

23 MONDAY

24 TUESDAY

25 WEDNESDAY

26 THURSDAY

27 FRIDAY

28 SATURDAY

29 SUNDAY

NATALIA LOSKUTOVA (KORSHUN) (RUSSIA)

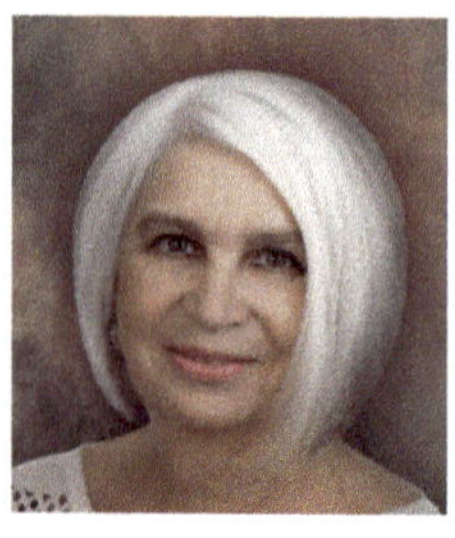

On Another Planet

It is great fun to jump over puddles of water,
The first, the second, the third. -
A spoke in our wheel
And we are on distant stars.

Everything is square-shaped,
Apples and pears
And even oranges
Are square-shaped.

I'll make a fairytale garden
Of children's blocks,
Where square-shaped citizens
Will walk.

It is great fun to jump over puddles of water,
The first, the second, the third.
A spoke in our wheel
And we are back on Earth.

03

MAY

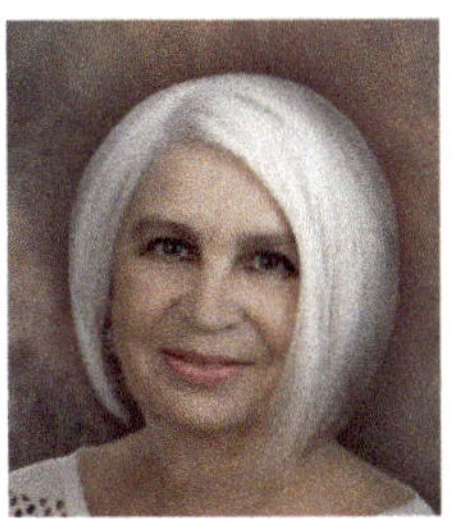

На другой планете

По лужам прыгать здорово,
Одна, вторая, третья,
Еще одно препятствие -
И на другой планете мы.

Здесь все растет квадратное,
Яблоки и груши,
И даже желтый апельсин
И тот квадратный был.

Сложу я все из кубиков,
Огромный чудо-сад,
И будут в нем квадратные
Жители гулять.

По лужам прыгать здорово,
Одна, вторая, третья,
Еще одно препятствие -
И на своей планете мы!

NIKOLAJ IVLEEV (RUSSIA)

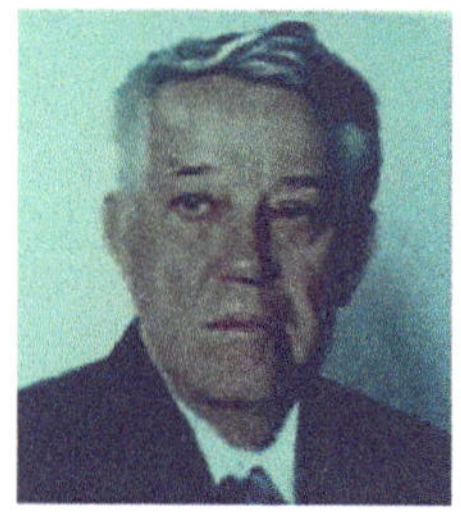

* * *

Don't sprinkle a holy tear
You are the world of cynical wickedness:
He's doomed by fate to the grave
To walk in a way that is not righteous;
He is indifferent and cruel,
like a shoestring, proud and primitive.
He is haunted by vice,
And a child's crying disgusts him!

* * *

Comrade Stalin is not our enemy!
He built for us the Gulag
He built a Gulag for us
To make camp dust.

* * *

Не окропляй святой слезой
Ты этот мир циничной злобы:
Он обречён судьбой до гроба
Идти не праведной стезёй;
Он безразличен и жесток,
Как обух горд и примитивен.
Его преследует порок,
И детский плач ему противен!

* * *

Товарищ Сталин нам не враг!
Перемежая сказку с былью,
Для нас он выстроил ГУЛАГ,
Чтоб делать лагерною пылью.

05

MAY

30 MONDAY

01 TUESDAY

02 WEDNESDAY

03 THURSDAY

04 FRIDAY

05 SATURDAY

06 SUNDAY

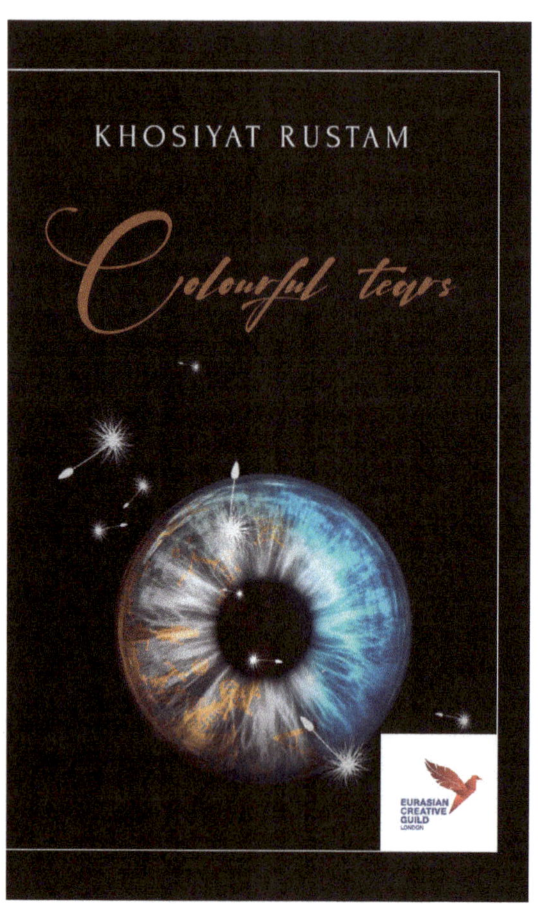

"I read every poem at least twice, my dear friend! Your heart is a planet full of secrets, concerns, compassion and love. You are a true poet, a natural poet, a pure poet as pure as you My dear poet! You're a joy to read - even your darkest poems throw light on your readers. Your talent is indisputable. As for the translators, they have done a great job. No one can tell your book is a book in translation - it looks and feels as if written in English directly. Congratulations my Dear! With all my heart I congratulate you, as my colleague, as my poet and above all as my forever friend!"

– *Albanian poet Gjekë Marinaj*

ISBN: 978-1-913356-12-5
RRP: £17.95

13

MAY

07 MONDAY

08 TUESDAY

09 WEDNESDAY

10 THURSDAY

11 FRIDAY

12 SATURDAY

13 SUNDAY

PAUL GAUGUIN (FRANCE)

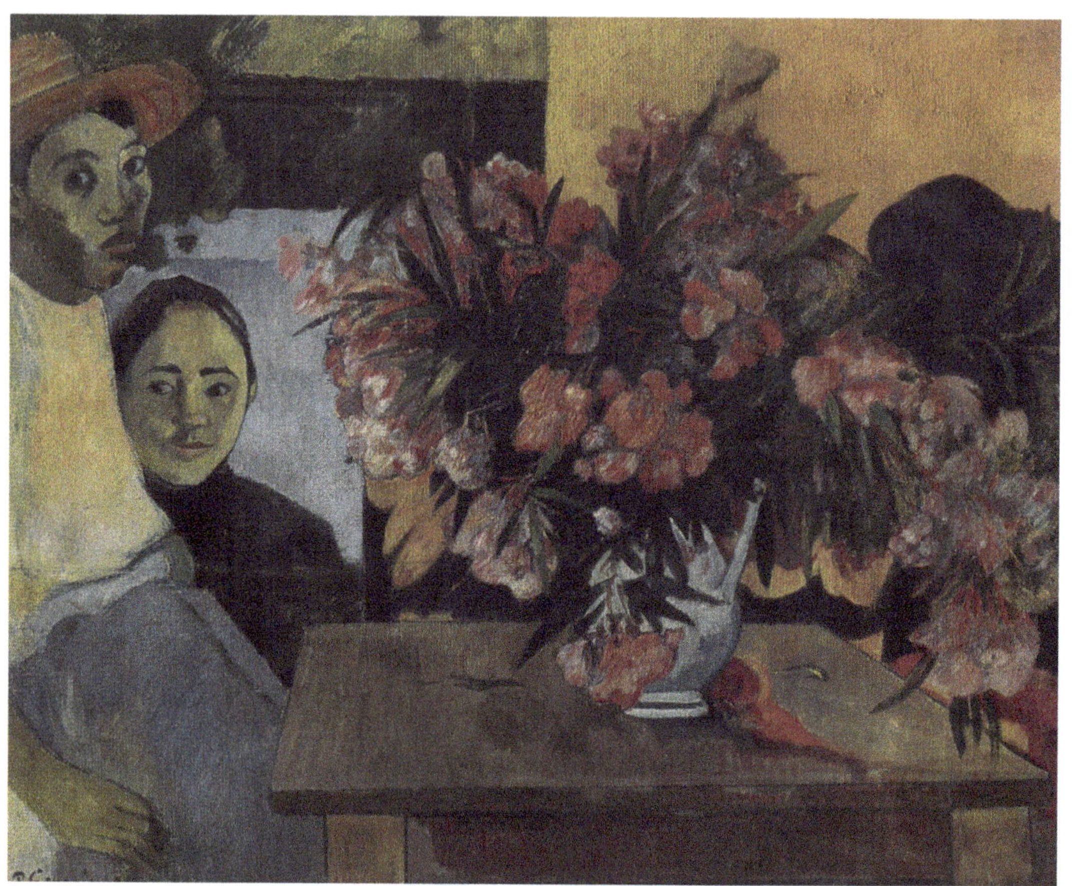

"Flowers of France", 1891

14

MAY

Mother

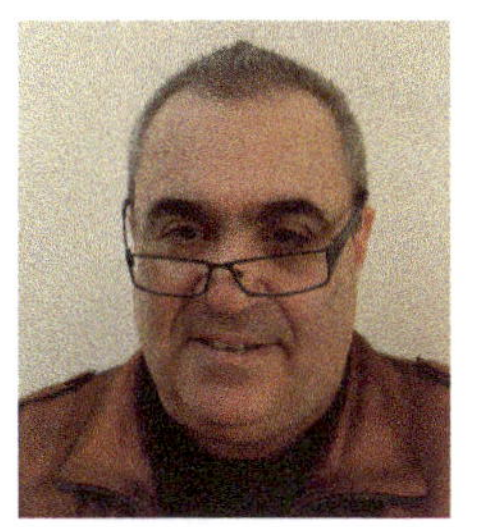

G-d has prepared a mercy for me,
And I'm thankful to G-d
All night long I dreamt of my mother,
And I touched her hand

And later on, I was hugging her shoulder
And I was clumsy and sharp,
But the world shrunk like a ball,
The rubber ball of a child.

And my soul was instantly shrunk
By a child's great love,
And the veins in the wrist swelled up,
And in my throat was a screaming sound.

And the scream was almost silent,
And I was a child again,
And there was no better moment,
But I didn't say a word

And I cried when I woke in the morning,
As if a drama had taken place,
And though the world was sullen,
I dreamt of my mother.

15

MAY

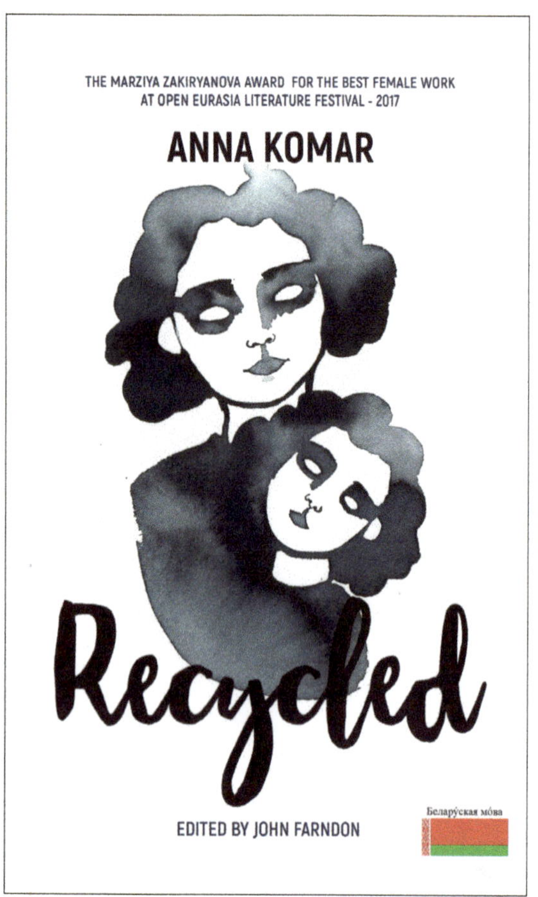

This book is a bilingual collection by a **Belarusian award-winning poet Anna Komar**. The poems in the book are strongly personal, yet they are reflections of the reality that is so familiar to many of us. Love, friendship, self-exploration, childhood memories, fears – Anna finds new ways to speak about the things we have heard so much about, and her voice is frank. The thread connecting the poems in this collection is being a woman in the strongly patriarchal society which Belarus still is. These poems are a rebellion, they touch, provoke, embarrass, get under your skin, but leave hope that the wounds will be healed, the home will be found, and love will live in it.

ISBN: 978-1-910886-81-6
RRP: £20.50

19

MAY

14 MONDAY

15 TUESDAY

16 WEDNESDAY

17 THURSDAY

18 FRIDAY

19 SATURDAY

20 SUNDAY

MARIYA PRIZNYAKOVA (RUSSIA)

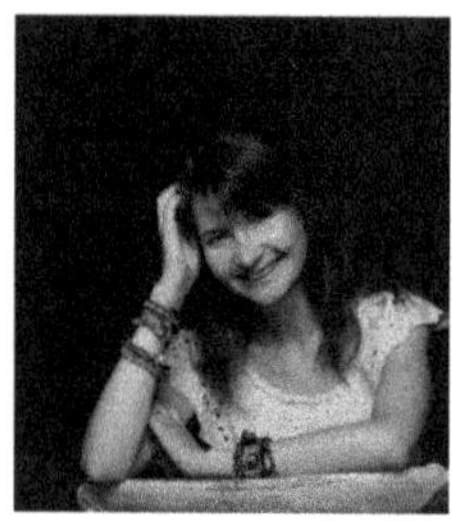

Three words

"I love you" – only three words,
but in them is a revelation from God,
summer house revitalization,
dissolution to the end;
like a bright candle – insight,
bathing in a quiet stream,
through sharp pain – enlightenment,
penetration by melting.

Where once there was a stone, there are flowers,
where the ash remained, there are sprouts;
for what was predicted in dreams, there is an awakening,
between the two banks, there are bridges.

"I love you" – only three words,
but behind them is a great river,
carrying away from the father's house,
separation into islands;
like a long spring – extension,
cutting binding ties,
through spring waters – a flowing,
creating your own muses.

Beyond all words – comprehension,
as the soul dictates we take flight;
like radiant dew, scintillation,
as great happiness starts.

20

MAY

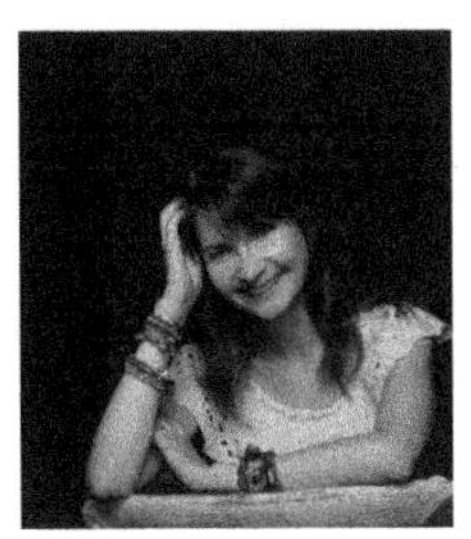

Три слова

«Я люблю тебя » – только три слова,
а в них – откровение Творца,
оживление летнего дома,
растворение до конца;
словно яркой свечой – озарение,
омовение тихим ручьем,
через колкую боль – просветление,
проницание тающим льдом.

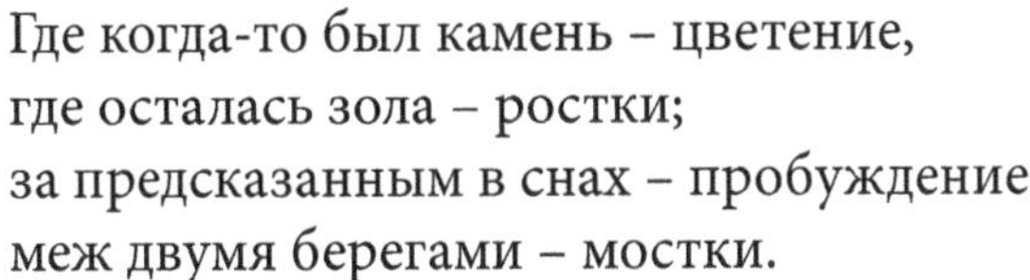

Где когда-то был камень – цветение,
где осталась зола – ростки;
за предсказанным в снах – пробуждение,
меж двумя берегами – мостки.

«Я люблю тебя» – только три слова,
но за ними – величие реки,
унесение от отчего дома,
разделение на островки;
словно долгой весны – продление,
перекромка связующих уз,
через вешние воды – течение,
созидание собственных муз.

За пределами слов – понимание,
за веленьем души – полёт;
как лучистой росы – сверкание,
как великого счастья – взлёт.

21

MAY

CHARLES BAUDELAIRE (FRANCE)

Beauty

I am fair, O mortals! like a dream carved in stone,
And my breast where each one in turn has bruised himself
Is made to inspire in the poet a love
As eternal and silent as matter.

On a throne in the sky, a mysterious sphinx,
I join a heart of snow to the whiteness of swans;
I hate movement for it displaces lines,
And never do I weep and never do I laugh.

Poets, before my grandiose poses,
Which I seem to assume from the proudest statues,
Will consume their lives in austere study;

For I have, to enchant those submissive lovers,
Pure mirrors that make all things more beautiful:
My eyes, my large, wide eyes of eternal brightness!

(translated by William Aggeler, 1954)

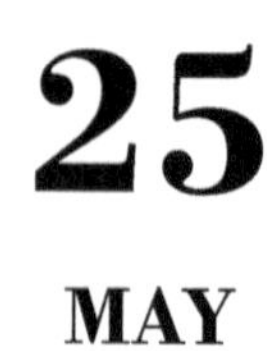

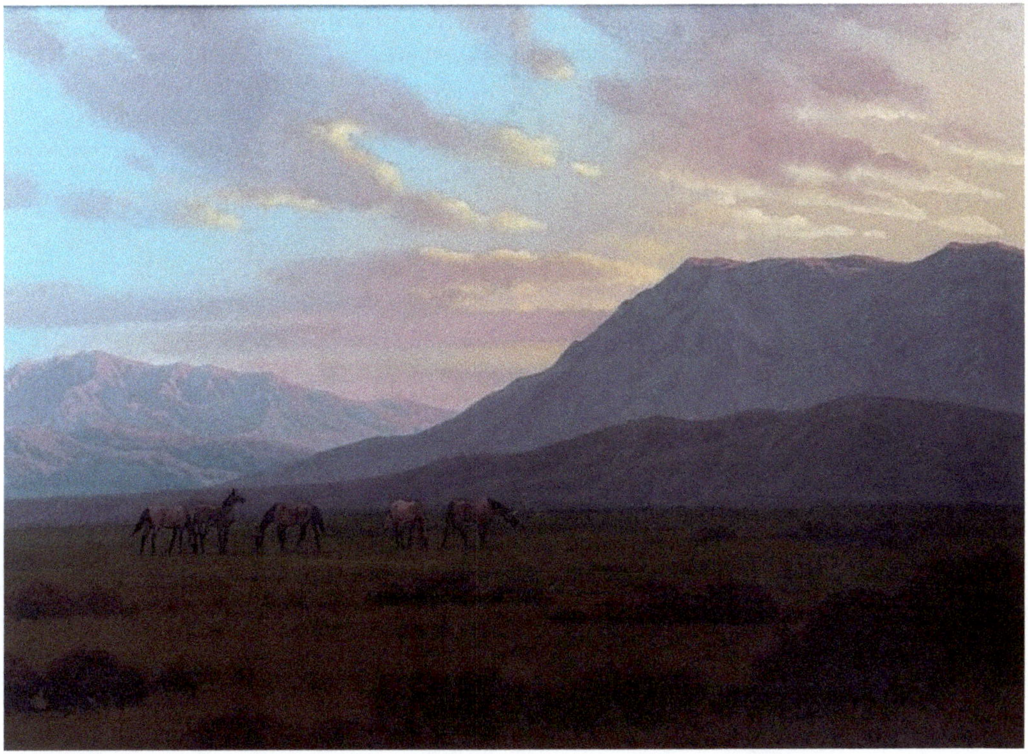

MARLAN NYSSANBAEV (KAZAKHSTAN)

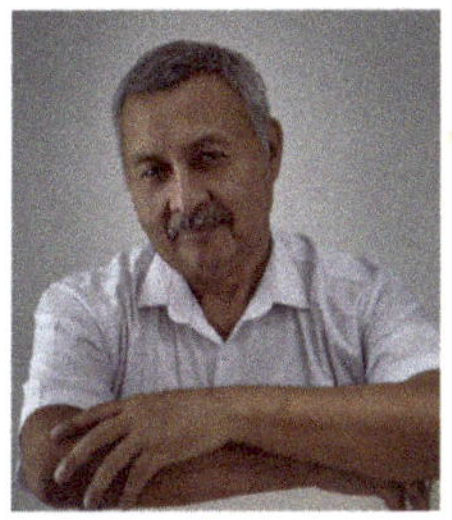

"Shybartal"
canvas, oil
70cm×90cm,
2022.

This painting was created after a meeting of members of the Eurasian Creative Guild (London) in the town of Narynkol, Almaty region.

I was inspired to paint by this heavenly place, where the majestic Khan-Tengri is, with beautiful panoramas, mountains, canyons and other beautiful landscapes. We decided next year to make an exhibition dedicated to this trip.

26

MAY

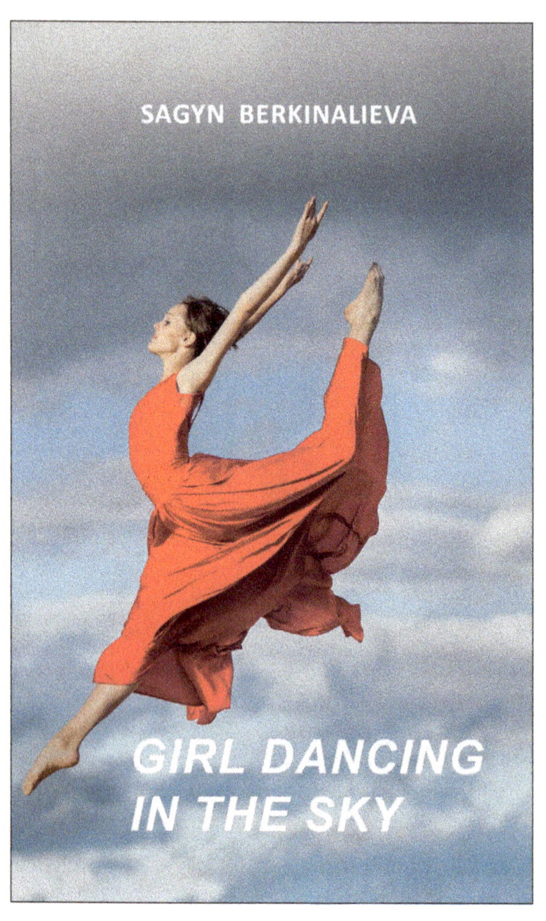

In this jewellike collection of poems from Kyrgyz poet Sagyn Berkinalieva, the poet explores her own personal destiny and her memorable insights into love, plumbing the raw feelings that cut through her heart in the course of one memorable encounter. Berkinalieva's own unique and genuine voice shines through poignantly on every page.

ISBN: 978-1913356217
RRP: £12.95

27

MAY

21 MONDAY

22 TUESDAY

23 WEDNESDAY

24 THURSDAY

25 FRIDAY

26 SATURDAY

27 SUNDAY

MARINA ALYASSOVA (KAZAKHSTAN)

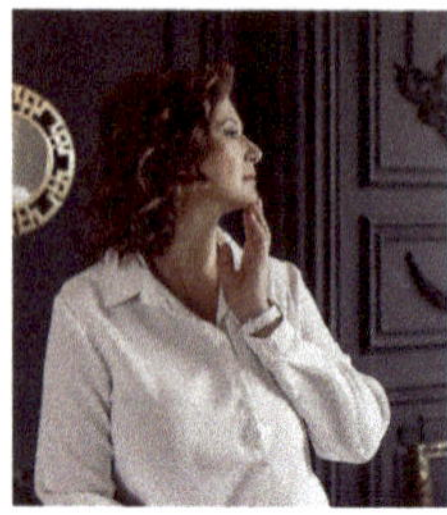

Metamorphoses

A dream lays on the city in the evening,
Streets are enlightened already at night.
The grass is silver, and thus it is freezing,
Mother Nature is now so tired.

Having left her chamber to wander,
The moon started her habitual way.
The Agent of Darkness disturbs our lumber
Sending us her unwavering gaze.

The city's noise has stopped all its motion,
The roads stay in an expectable peace.
Plunging calmly in its reflection
Of the puddles fog banks cannot cease.

Something new which is still unknown,
Destroyed fortresses and their wall,
It was born by the wondered God's moan,
And tore off their chains at all.

Unexpressive, it did really appear
In this empty mysterious space.
Time of existence flew to nowhere,
Tightening every and nothing for future days.

In this abyss of past days and future,
In this point of light, night and dark veil,
The importance became tine and usual,
Breath of spring became fragile and frail.

01

JUNE

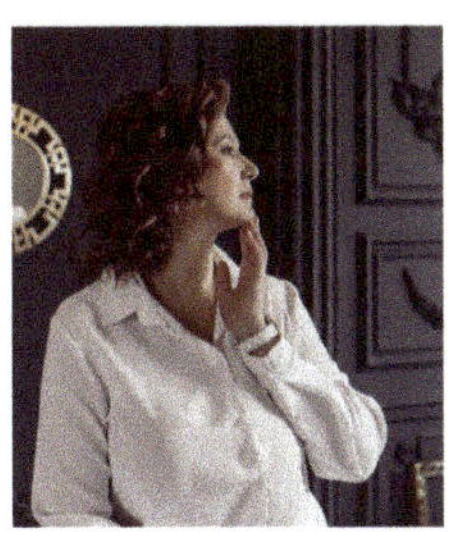

Метаморфозы

Сон опустился на вечерний город.
Зажглись на улочках ночные фонари.
И на траве засеребрился холод
За день уставшей Матушки-Земли.

И, свой чертог покинув, будто странник,
Луна по небу начала свой путь.
Заглядывая в окна, - тьмы посланник -
Мешая позабыться и уснуть.

Шум городской решил прервать движенье,
Окутала дороги тишина.
И, погружаясь тихо в отраженье
Зеркальных луж, сгустилась пелена.

И что-то новое, неведомое ныне,
Взрывая стены старых крепостей,
Рождалось в сердце раненого Бога,
Срывая прочь останки их цепей.

В пространства пустоте оно являлось,
Несказанное... Время вникуда
Рекою Бытия текло и растворялось,
Все и ничто скрепляя навсегда.

И в этой бездне будущего с прошлым,
В единой точке света, мглы и тьмы
Все важное повеяло ничтожным,
Все бренное - дыханием весны.

02
JUNE

JUAN GRIS (SPAIN)

"The Guitar", 1918

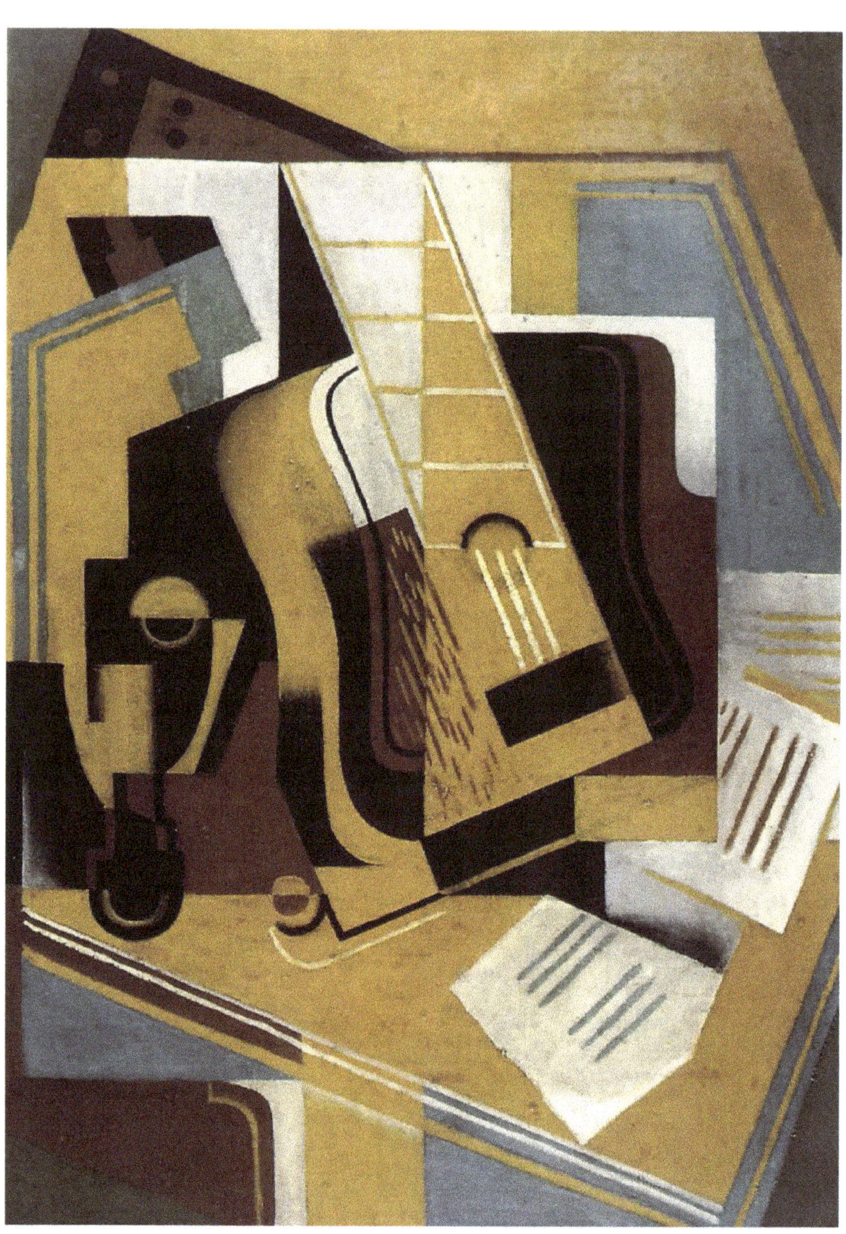

03

JUNE

28 MONDAY

29 TUESDAY

30 WEDNESDAY

31 THURSDAY

01 FRIDAY

02 SATURDAY

03 SUNDAY

IGOR KHENTOV (ISRAEL)

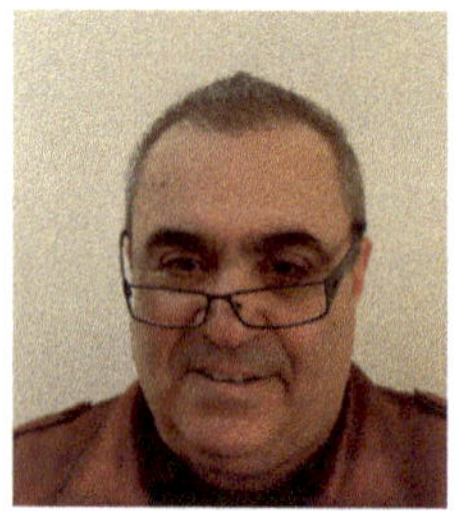

Ode to Pushkin

Curly-haired graduate of a princely school,
Lover of young muses, lover of Hymen,
Singer of native plains, connoisseur of far-off lands!
With the elastic stride of a solemn iambus
Let me adorn your crowning pose.
Not with the molasses of empty praise,
But let me lay my whole soul at your feet:
And the song of weary birds for abandoned sheaves,
And the honey of the grasses, the flight of a brave thought.
And the free wave that flies on the reef,
The rumble of starships in the shuddering black heavens,
And the feeling of the tender birth of words and rhymes.

06

JUNE

Cancer!

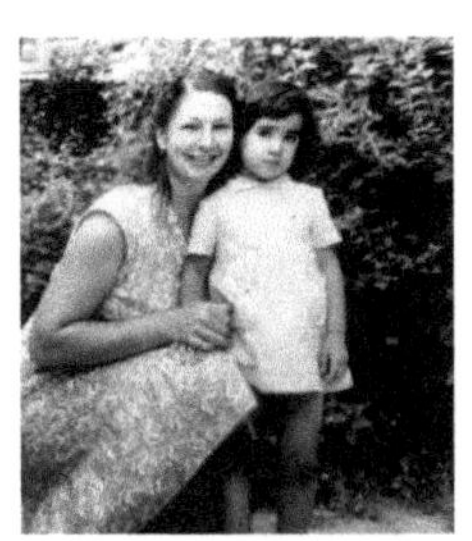

"It's all for the best" - nonsense! God takes the good ones"- no!
"He deserves it" - You say that again, enemy, and you'll get your cancer too...
Earth's fate decides who lives, the sea newt tells them where to swim,
And I'll tell them without fear: "F*ck you, I'll decide what to do with my life!"

Why does he take who he loves without arguing?
"He doesn't care who's old or young. He doesn't care who's grieving!"
Where are you, Great Men, Great Minds –
how can we save you from your "home prison"?
What sacrifice must we make to you to save our loved ones?

To get the problem seen to THERE… or do we have to give you money again?
- Who's the last one in the queue? Can I ask you...
Excuse me, everyone's in a hurry to live.
I'm walking down the corridor with her, from the doctor…
I want to say something, but she told me not to say anything.
I'm afraid to imagine what my mother thought when she found out it was her time to die.

When she fell for the first time… when that surgeon's light went out,
When, feeling no strength at all, death's tide swept her away...

Six years have passed, like yesterday. This pain tears at my soul and never relents.
I know not what my part in life is, but know about my anger, you foul cancer!

I want you to be staked to death, like a witch burned,
I want the sick man to breathe a happy breath
when he knows you're completely dead!

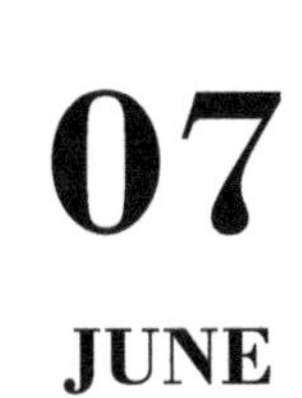

07

JUNE

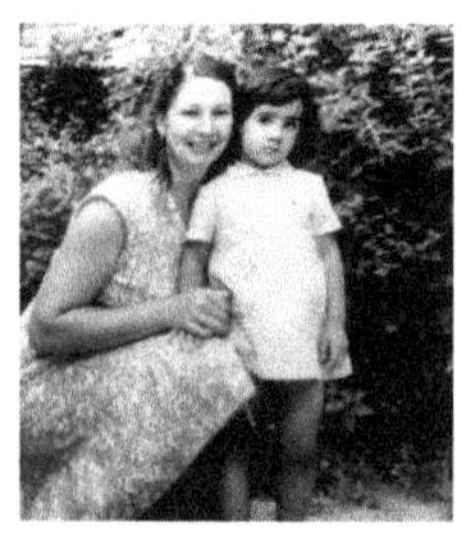

Рак!

«Всё что не делается к лучшему»-Бред! Бог забирает хороших»-Нет!
«Он заслужил» - повтори, Враг! Ещё раз скажешь-получишь свой Рак…
Судьба земная решает кому жить, тритон морской говорит куда плыть,
А я скажу им без страха «Ф*к ю», сама решу куда деть жизнь свою!

Ну почему он не ПОД а НАД и забирает кого любим не споря,
И ни по чём ему стар или млад, и всё равно ему наше горе!
Где Вы, Могучие Люди, Умы, как вас спасти из «домашней тюрьмы»?
Что в жертву вам мы должны принести, чтобы своих любимых спасти?

Чтобы проблему увидели ТАМ…или опять нужно денег дать вам,
- Кто крайний в кассу? Можно вас попросить…
- Простите, все тут торопятся Жить.
Я с ней иду по коридору от врача, хочу сказать, но мне велела молчать.
Боюсь представить, что думала Мать, когда узнала, ей пора умирать.

Когда упала на глазах в первый раз, когда тот свет у хирурга погас,
Когда совсем не чувствуя сил, её смертельный поток уносил…

Прошло шесть лет, как вчера эта боль всю душу рвёт и не гаснет никак.
Не знаю, что в моей жизни за роль, но знай презренье моё, Мерзкий Рак!

Хочу, чтоб люди тебя извели, убили колом, как ведьму сожгли,
И чтоб больной сделал радостный вдох, когда узнал, что ты полностью сдох!

08

JUNE

04 MONDAY

05 TUESDAY

06 WEDNESDAY

07 THURSDAY

08 FRIDAY

09 SATURDAY

10 SUNDAY

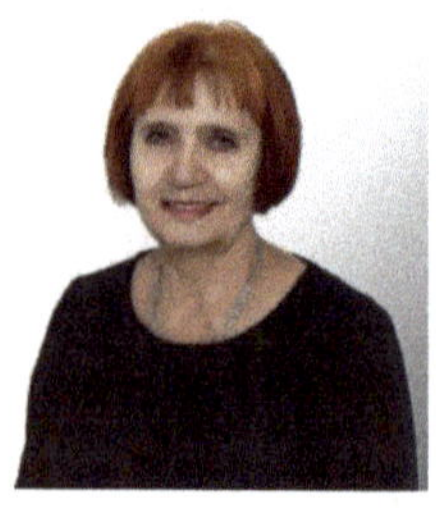

Life's Breaks

Oh let your wings soar
Wrap yourself up in the warm breeze
Dissolve the clouds in the sky
Drown happy in my feelings
Let me breathe the air
Let me spread my wings wider
To lift the mud from the bottom of my soul,
Give it to the winds with a dowry.
To float free as a bird above the Earth,
To awaken the land with a spiritual song.
To envelop it in tranquility,
To hide the Black God's abyss.

13

JUNE

Жыцця парывы

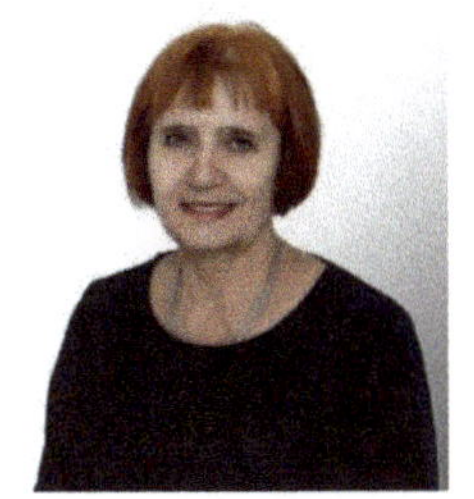

О дайце крылы ўзняцца ўвысь
Ды ў цёплы ветрык апрануцца.
У небе хмаркі растварыць,
Тануць шчаслівай у пачуццях.
Паветра дайце мне глынуць,
Шырэй расправіць ў небе крылы.
Са дна душы падняўшы муць,
Аддаць з прыданым для вятрылы.
Плыць вольным птахам над зямлёй,
Край абудзіць духоўнай песняй.
Каб агарнуў яго спакой,
Схавала Чарнабога бездань.

14

JUNE

NADEGDA BOGOVICH (RUSSIA)

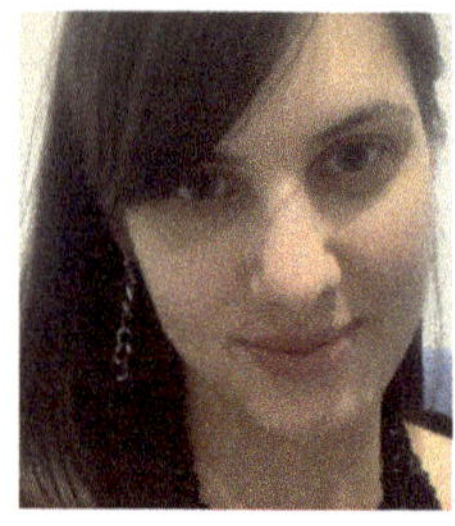

Mama Is Well!

Mama is well!
I cry out again and again!
Mama is well!
Mama is well!

The spirit is renewed in the faithfulness of God!
God is our strength and our support!
Strength within, that's the foundation!

Mama is well!
Mama is well!
I say it again and again!
Darling mother, you'll be on your feet again!

God help us!
His power is the Word!
Mama is well!
Mama is well!

Strength in love, that's the foundation!
God is our protection, there is no other!
Mama is well!
Mama is well!

Jesus, we're calling to you again!
You heard us, you're our only support!
With us in our grief, but only to
To show mercy from all bitterness!

Long days, Thou wilt saturate us again!
Thou shalt bring salvation, Thou didst give the Word!
Mama is well!
Mama is well!

15
JUNE

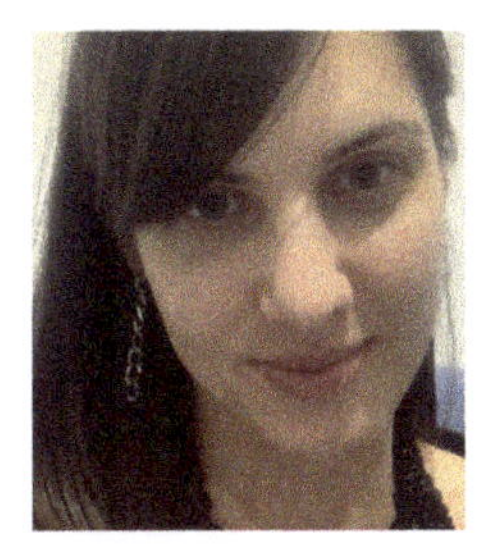

Мама здорова!

Мама здорова!
Я возглашаю снова и снова!
Мама здорова!
Мама здорова!

Дух обновляется в верности Бога!
Бог наша сила и наша опора!
Сила внутри - вот это основа!

Мама здорова!
Мама здорова!
Я повторяю снова и снова!
Милая мама, ты встанешь в строй снова!

Бог нам поможет!
Его сила - Слово!
Мама здорова!
Мама здорова!

Сила в любви - вот это основа!
Бог ты защита и нету другого!
Мама здорова!
Мама здорова!

Мы воззываем Иисус к тебе снова!
Ты нас услышал в тебе лишь опора!
С нами в скорби, но только лишь чтобы
Славу явить от всякой озлобы!

Долгими днями насытишь Ты снова!
Явишь спасение - Господь Ты дал Слово!
Мама здорова!
Мама здорова!

16
JUNE

HOCA ALI RIZA (TURKEY)

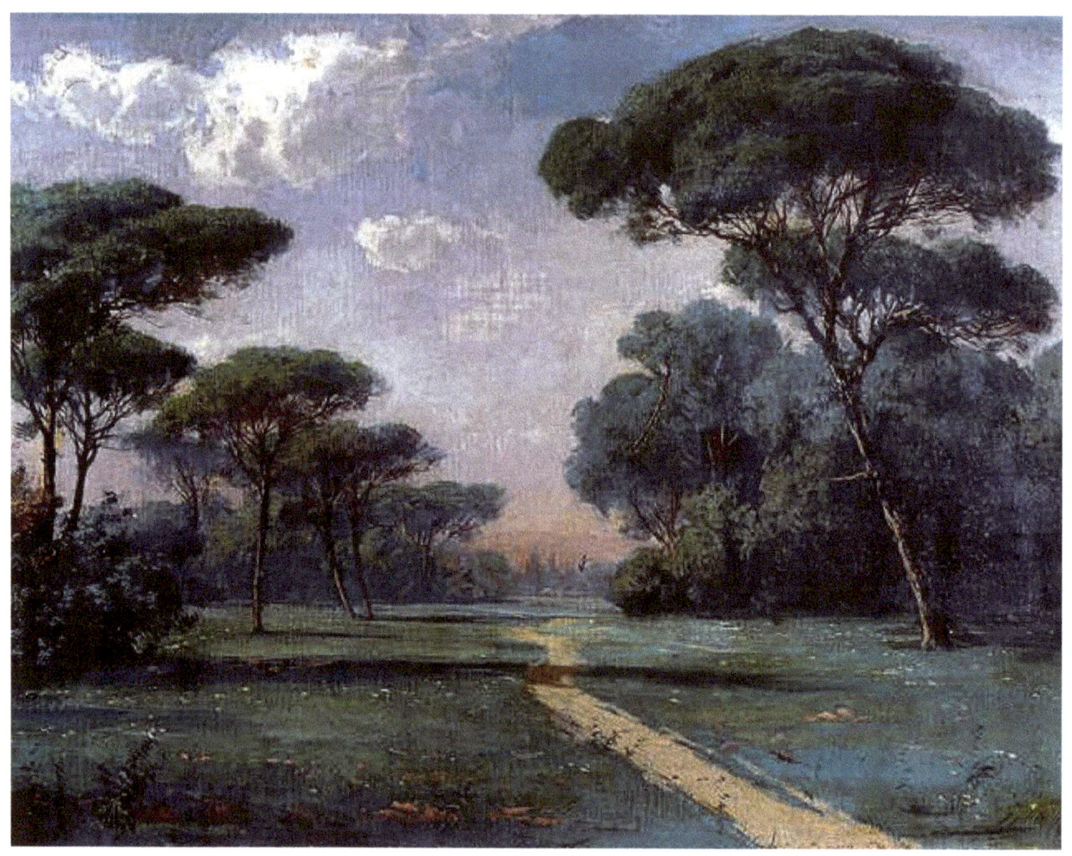

"Manzara", 1898

17

JUNE

11 MONDAY

12 TUESDAY

13 WEDNESDAY

14 THURSDAY

15 FRIDAY

16 SATURDAY

17 SUNDAY

NURGULYA OSMONKULOVA (KYRGYZSTAN)

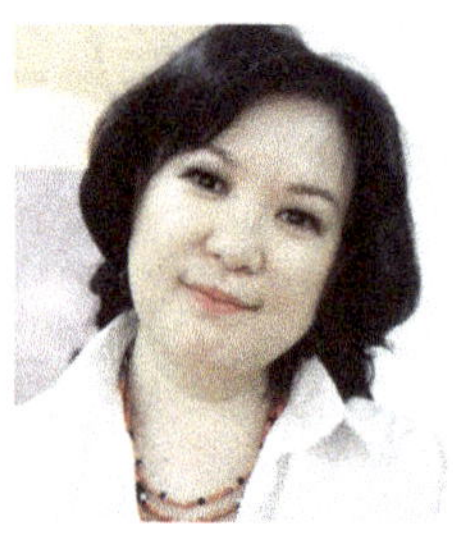

***

Big crossroads, like crosses
They have broken up our daily lives with grey concrete.
All our dreams are flying away somewhere,
The dreams that we had so nurtured in our hearts.

And the hands of the clocks are really ruthless,
They move as if they will never come back,
As if I am stuck in my not-yet-written poems,
Trying to write down the lines many times.

It is such a pity that the crossroads, like crosses in our way,
Are covered with greyish concrete.
And have separated the city into blocks.
We should plant lovely flowers there instead,
In places where people forget all their dreams.

Translation by Saltanat Mambaeva

21

JUNE

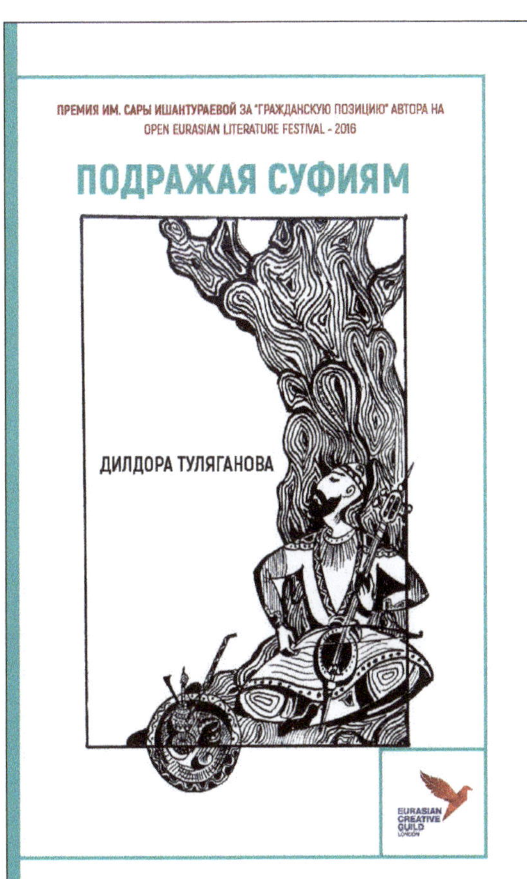

Дилдора Туляганова родом из Ташкента (Узбекистан). Ее мировосприятие формировалось под влиянием творчества Алишера Навои, Бабура, Омар Хайяма, Пушкина, Есенина и других. Позже буквально заболела творчеством великих просветителей джадидского движения Центральной Азии, таких как Бехбудий, Фитрат, Мунаввар Кори Абдурашидханова. В дальнейшем это вылилось в передачу «Ёнмаган ёзувлар» (Рукописи не горят) на Узбекском Государственном ТВ. В 1999 году, пригласили работать в «Интерньюс», затем на радио «Свобода». В 2010 году, по заказу ТРТ (Турецкой телерадиовещательной корпорации) сняла 7 документальных фильмов о диаспорах живущих в Узбекистане (уйгуры, казахи, дунгане, азербайджанцы, башкиры, поляки, русские). Участник международных научных конференций. Профессиональный журналист-исследователь, сценарист, фотограф. Поэт.

ISBN: 978-1-910886-83-0
RRP: £9.50

22

JUNE

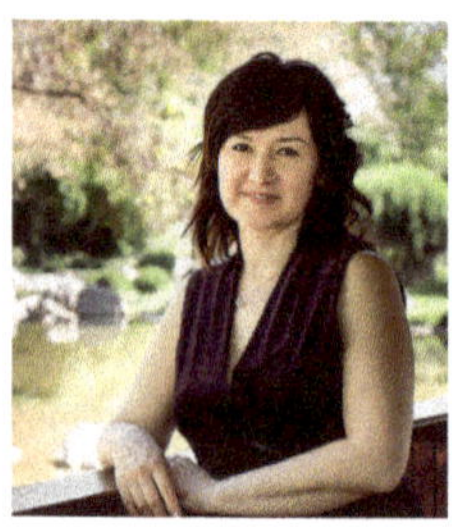

The Brooklyn Bridge

The Brooklyn Bridge
There is so much
Love, sadness,
People and events.

I'm thankful to you
For your huge size,
Warm hugs from the wind
And for sunshine.

You're always open
All your life
You're a friend
Inspiring the best times.

24

JUNE

18 MONDAY

19 TUESDAY

20 WEDNESDAY

21 THURSDAY

22 FRIDAY

23 SATURDAY

24 SUNDAY

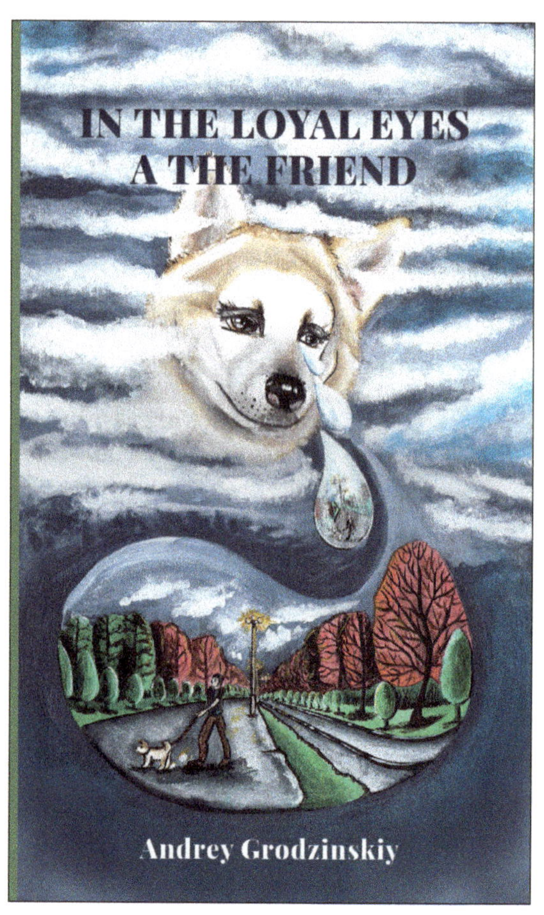

cover by by Yulia Ward

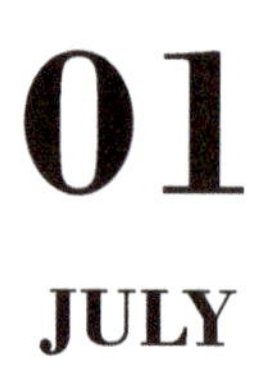

Set in Tashkent, Andrey Grodzinskiy's In The Loyal Eyes Of A Friend is a rumination on the nature of love and friendship, both with other people and with animals. It is a story about the nature of memories which is tinged with a bright but palpable sense of melancholy. Through Grodzinskiy's vividly drawn characters the reader will come to discover that it's the things you love the most which can cause you the most pain, but it's these same things that can mend your heart when you feel broken.

ISBN: 978-1913356507
RRP: £14.95

25 MONDAY

26 TUESDAY

27 WEDNESDAY

28 THURSDAY

29 FRIDAY

30 SATURDAY

01 SUNDAY

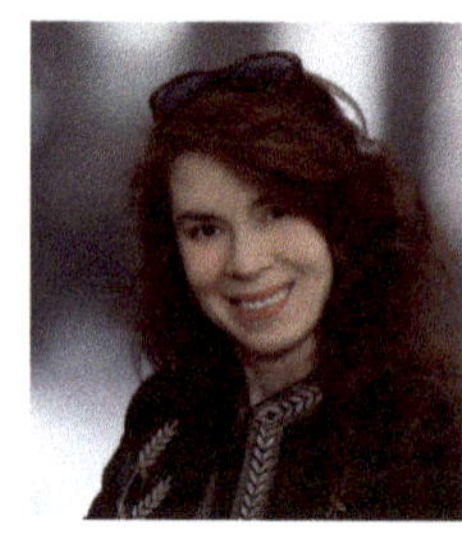

Do You Remember Christmas in Tyrol?

A collection of poems
2017-2022

Do You Remember Christmas in Tyrol?
Do you remember Christmas in Tyrol – those days of blissful obscurity?
How gloriously the powdery snowflakes fell – time-worn constellations?
The green fir tree's sultry scent, the one that lingered infinitely long,
The Milky Way? The snow on the fir trees' branches, the snow left on its branches, that we thought were poplars...?

Do you remember the house with many rooms that was crowded with guests?
Maybe that house will also remember things that we have not yet said...
The day that used to be, the day that has passed, that has taken its steps with care,
And of the untimely departed, the mournful cross by the roadside...

The day is a barrier, the snow is a barrier, there are barriers on the wooden roofs...
Once among the uninvited guests, we did not intend to flee.
We are lost in the captivity of the Alps, in Prägraten, on another planet...
The Alps rise – an obelisk, a silent starry obelisk,
The one that knows not of death, the high Eternity...!

The Blizzard Is Playing Hide And Seek Again...

Neither cold nor hot – under that long gaze...
...the candle of memory flickers behind the long snowfall...

*

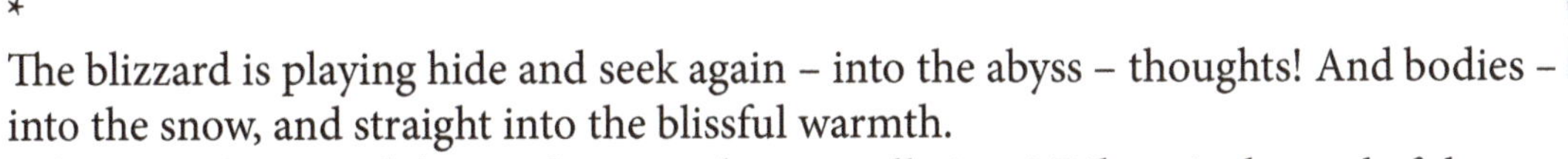

The blizzard is playing hide and seek again – into the abyss – thoughts! And bodies –
into the snow, and straight into the blissful warmth.
Where are the snowflakes? Where are the constellations? Where is the oval of the moon? Faces?
In this beauty of obscurity, we vanish without end.

We disappear, we disappear, we disappear, we disappear,
Like snow, we melt, we rain...
A ski trail, and – tea, and – hide-and-seek
Of dark rooms. Blizzard – away!
Here your friend, the night, will fall.

Head over heels in the night, unclothed and unadorned,
You're a laughing man, tired of walking and mischief...
...Fever. A fireplace. And – the deaf night, where, tumbling down from the heights,
We melt on a carpet of fur, like snowflakes,
Like snowflakes, melting, melting,
Defenceless and pure.

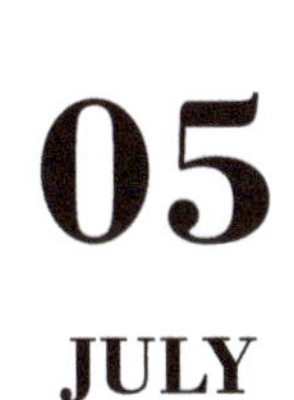

05

JULY

YULIA OLSHEVSKAYA-HATZENBÖLLER (GERMANY)

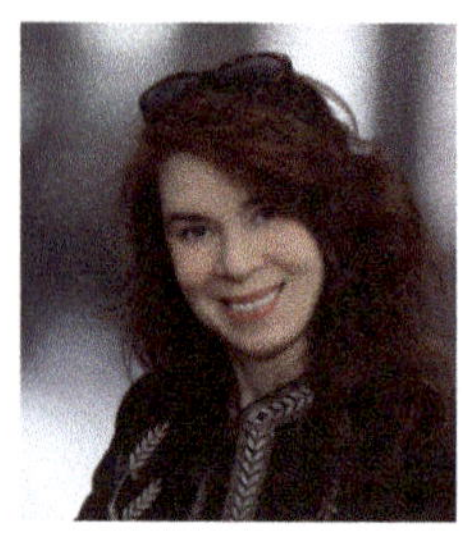

Дорога пилигримов
(Осенних листьев — охра и шафран...)

Осенних листьев — охра и шафран,
И льдистой дымкой тронутое, злое,
Початком кукурузным налитое,
Ночное небо.
Ladenburg. Туман.
Лебяжий всплеск над лунною водою...

Мне видится огромный зимний сад,
Рождественской дороги пилигримов
Огни далекие,
что страждущих манят...
Фахверки одинокие стоят,
И осень, как чума, проходит мимо.

Глубокой полночи разлитое тепло,
Где облаков, что крыльев лебединых,
Прозрачны перья...
Вставший на крыло
На этот час — или на миг единый,
Взлетает Голос,

И за ним — душа,
В небесный плен,
Без права возвращенья...
Стою в садах полночных, не дыша,
И все вокруг — свечение, круженье,
Смех серебра...

Ladenburg, Weinheim, 15 сентября 2014

06

JULY

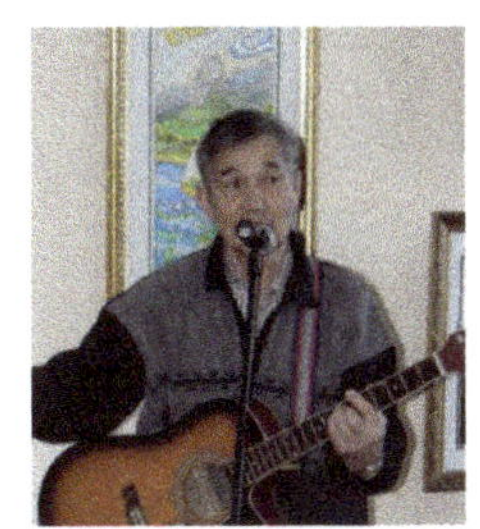

Forgive Me This Weakness

Forgive me this weakness, but I want so much to
groan and throw myself into your arms
I want to be warm in my soul
Let it come to us in September

The years and days and months fly away
The windmill's sails call to destiny
Only faith's strings sing to us.
But the memory is the soul that mourns.

Forgive me this weakness, but I celebrate
That I've walked a different road in life.
And stood at the source of the stream.
And the river carried me to the sea.

And the souls will come together.
It doesn't matter if there's only pennies in it.
But a hand on our shoulders,
When our vanity befalls us.

Forgive me this weakness and the old ones,
The years have gone by.
But with cheek to shoulder,
I'll honour their memory.

I will! I was not ignorant out of spite,
I'll mend my soul's tender skin.
And with hope I'll shout again:
"I love this life! I love it!".

07

JULY

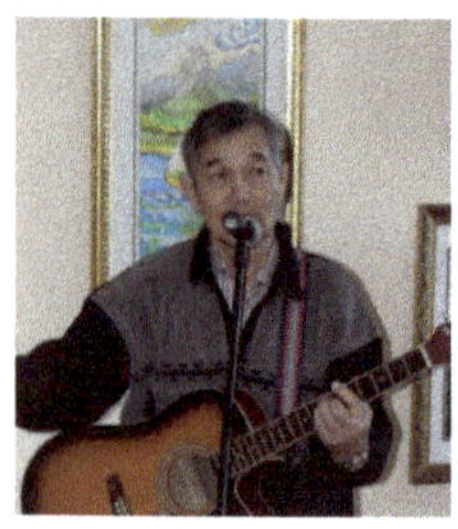

Прости эту слабость

Ты прости эту слабость, но хочется
Застонать и в объятия броситься.
И душой раствориться в тепле.
Пусть оно к нам пришло в сентябре.

И слетают года, дни и месяцы.
Правят парус судьбы крылья мельницы.
Только веры нам пела струна.
Ну, а память оплачет душа.

Ты прости эту слабость, я праздную,
Что по жизни дорогой шёл разною.
И стоял у истока ручья.
И рекой уносило в моря.

И зови не зови, души сходятся.
Не беда, что гроши только водятся.
Но ложится на плечи рука,
Если нас достаёт суета.

Ты прости эту слабость и прежние,
Было дело - ушли годы вешние.
Но, прижавшись щекою к плечу,
Память светлую им отмолчу.

Отмолю! Не со зла был невеждою,
Залечу я души кожу нежную.
И с надеждою вновь закричу:
“Я люблю эту жизнь! Я люблю!”

08

JULY

02 MONDAY

03 TUESDAY

04 WEDNESDAY

05 THURSDAY

06 FRIDAY

07 SATURDAY

08 SUNDAY

GENNADY GOROVOY (ISRAEL)

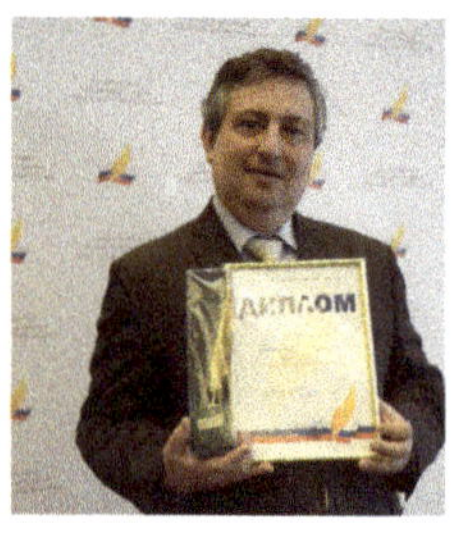

Appeal to God

How beautifully the flowers are blooming,
Yellow leaves are falling,
I'm in awe of the beauty,
It's good to be born into this world.

The sun shines and warms us,
The sunrises amaze us...
I want to soar like Pegasus
And see it all from above.

I want to fly over the land, over the grass
Over mountains and forests,
To see that other world
Not as we see it, you and me

Where children always play
Where no one ever gets sick,
Where we live in peace and friendship forever:
Muslims, Christians, Jews...

Where there are no wars and no dictators,
Where people's quarrels melt away;
People love, everybody loves
Old and young

13

JULY

I wish you well
I beg, love one another,
Let each one of you have everything:
Status, money, a wife, a friend...

And then the wars will disappear,
There'll be no reason to fight, no reason to quarrel;
I wish you all well,
I wish you all the good that you can do

I wish you all the good things in the world,
The world will be a better place, a brighter place,
I beseech thee, God, I beseech thee,
Help me to do it sooner.

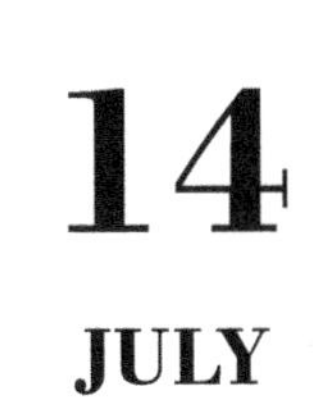

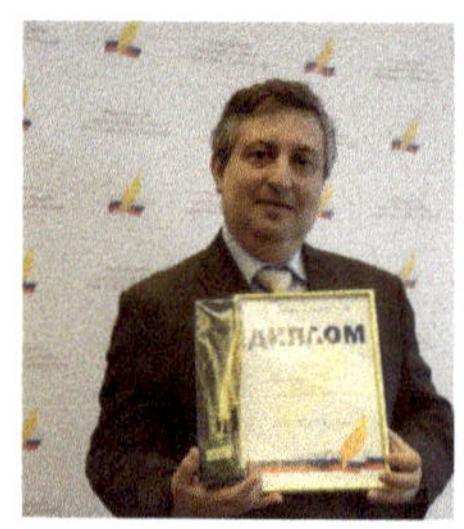

Обращение к Богу

Как красиво цветут цветы,
Опадают желтые листья,
Я в восторге от красоты,
Хорошо в этот мир родиться.

Солнце светит и греет нас,
Восхищают собой рассветы...
Я хочу взлететь, как Пегас,
И увидеть все сверху это.

Пролететь над землей, травой,
Над горами и над лесами,
Чтоб увидеть тот мир- другой-
Не такой, как мы видим с вами.

Где гуляют дети всегда,
Где никто никогда не болеет,
Где живут в мире-дружбе всегда:
Мусульмане, христиане, евреи...

Где нет войн, и диктаторов нет,
И растаяли ссоры людские;
Люди любят, любимы все-
Пожилые и молодые.

15

JULY

Я хочу добра пожелать,
Умоляю: "Любите друг друга,
Пусть у каждого будет все:
Статус, деньги, жена, подруга..."

И исчезнут войны тогда,
Ведь нет поводов драться-ругаться;
Я желаю вам всем добра,
Позитивными оставаться.

За добро отплатят добром,
Мир улучшится, станет светлее,
Умоляю я, Бог, тебя,
Помоги сделать это скорее.

16

JULY

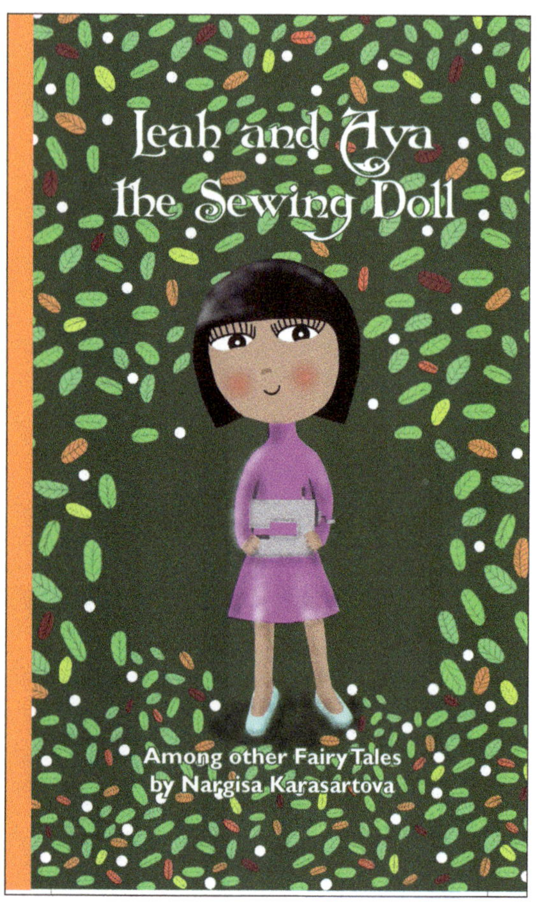

The book *"Leah and Aya the Sewing Doll"* by the author Nargisa Karasartova, is intended for children of preschool and primary school age. This book contains fairy tales that can be beloved by any child, tales that are distinguished not only by their fascinating plots, but also because they teach kindness, friendship, and justice. Many heroes of these fairy tales are usually mistaken or misunderstood, but eventually learn to love and accept themselves as they are. The stories teach valuable lessons, they show that our world is responsive and that any misunderstanding can be corrected, the heroes know how to ask for forgiveness and how to forgive. These fairy tales show that a happy ending depends on each of us, that we ourselves must have a good heart, inner strength and are open to the world around us.

ISBN: 978-1913356453
RRP: £17.50

09 MONDAY

10 TUESDAY

11 WEDNESDAY

12 THURSDAY

13 FRIDAY

14 SATURDAY

15 SUNDAY

ALEKSANDRA VLASOVA (UK)

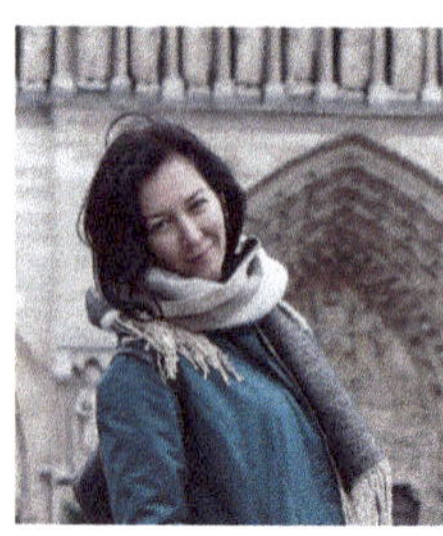

***

Black water, gold of lights
Old slug, along your river Neva
Past the Hermitage, the palace bridge, the cathedral
Hans carries me into the distance under the rustle of the waves

Black water, gold of lights
An old slug walks along the Neva
Past, Hermitage, Palace Bridge, Cathedral
Where is proud old Hans taking me?

***

Черная вода, золото огней
Старый тихоход, по Неве твоей
Мимо Эрмитаж, дворцовый мост, собор..
Ганс несёт меня вдаль под шелест волн

Черная вода, золото огней
Старый тихоход по Неве идёт
Мимо, Эрмитаж, Дворцовый мост, Собор
Гордый старый Ганс куда меня несёт?

22

JULY

16 MONDAY

17 TUESDAY

18 WEDNESDAY

19 THURSDAY

20 FRIDAY

21 SATURDAY

22 SUNDAY

VICTORIA LEVIN (ISRAEL)

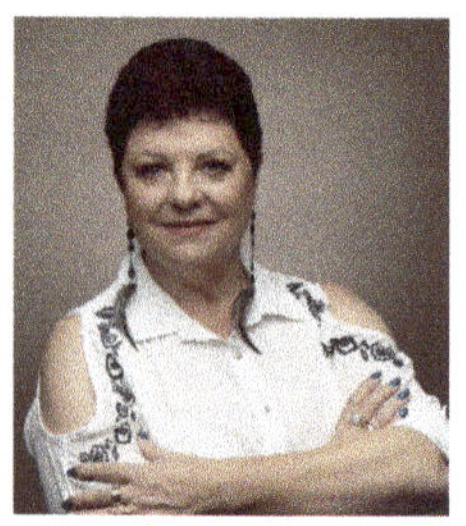

By the brook of Harod

It is said that this is where the biblical David defeated Goliath,
it is said that here Saul was slain in the valley of Israel.
At the foot of Gilboa, the brook* flows quietly into the Jordan,
and then by a waterfall in a canyon it still flows.

And the basalt rocks here have suffused, and the songs of the Tanakh,
the blast of green power and the drunken March of Israel,
spins its jets and rings in the springtime nakhal,
oozing out of the rain clouds - and straight into history!

Here the Mamelukes drank with the Mongols, and the future collapse
of their horde, the proud nakhal tinkled and rolled its waters.
He who came to battle will remain in cursed ashes,
and his people will in time come to be ashamed.

I stand on the bridge. My heart will beat with fear
from high canyons in the depths of Tanachian truths.
The surroundings still smelled of fresh greenery...
of milky and slightly sticky leaves.

July 23

23

JULY

**The Harod nakhal (brook), located at the foot of Mount Gilboa, runs through the valley of Israel and flows into the Jordan.*

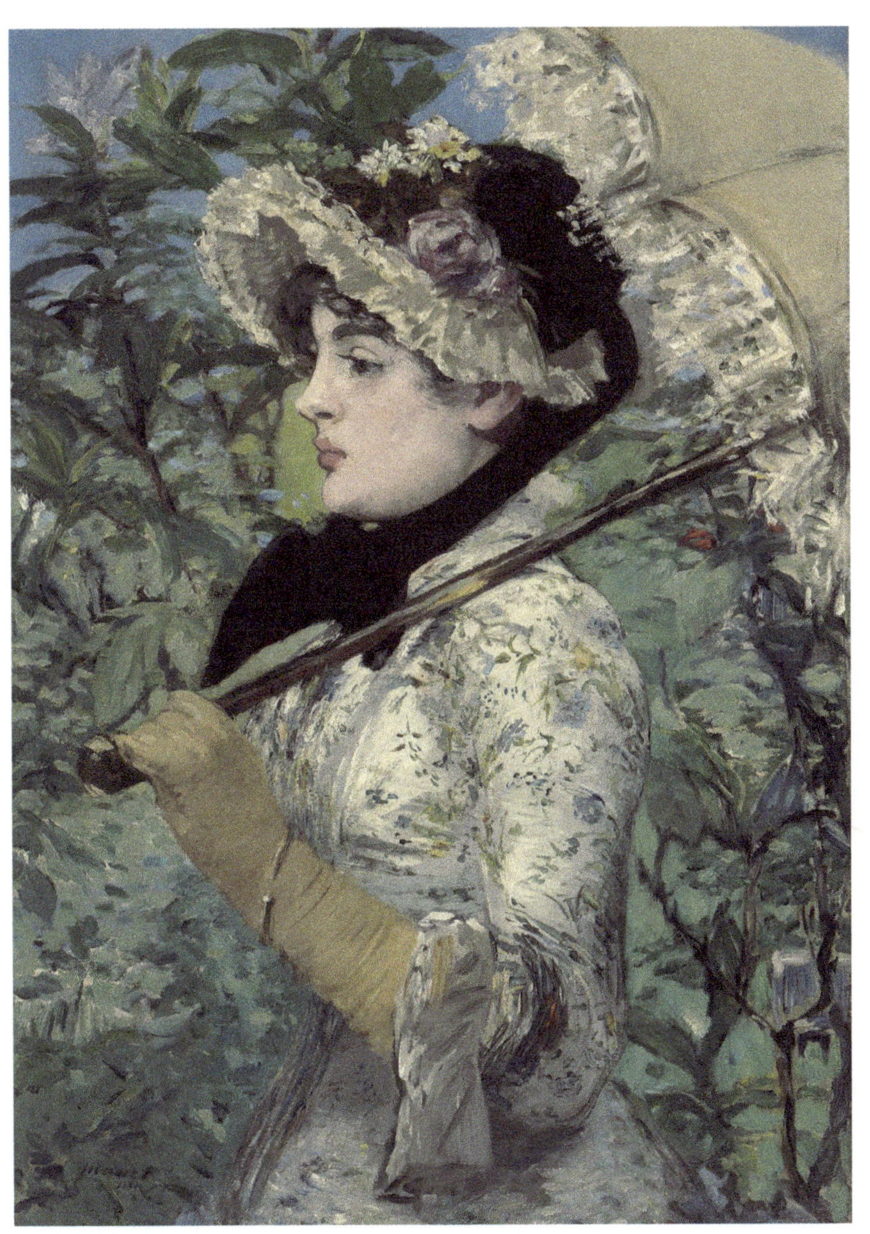

"Spring", 1881

24

JULY

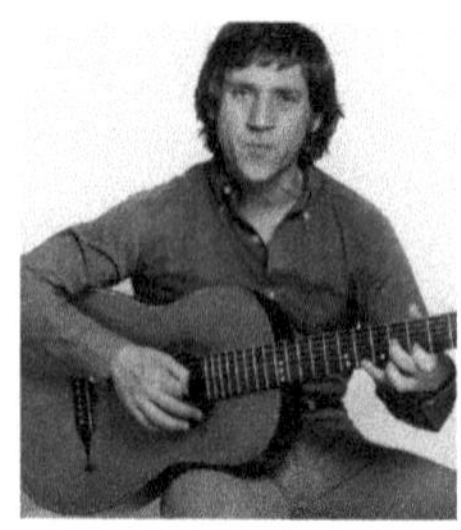

The Ornery Horses

On a cliff over a chasm, in my sled and nearly slipping,
I am lashing at my horses. I am rushing, I am whipping.
Drinking fog and gulping gale… Am I running out of air?
It's the end! I see it clearly with a jubilant despair.
Slow down for me, horses! Slow down for me!
Don't you let my whip drive you on!
But I wound up with these horses so ornery…
Didn't finish my life, will not finish my song.
I'll let my horses drink. One more verse I will sing.
Just a little bit longer I'll cling to the brink.
I will perish like a feather blown away by the tornado,
And the sled across the snow will drag me, leaving deep striations…
Bring it down to a walk, my horses! – We can make it there later! –
Won't you stave off my arrival at the final destination!
Slow down for me, horses! Slow down for me!
Ease your gallop and just trot along!
But I wound up with these horses so ornery…
Didn't finish my life, cannot finish my song.
I'll let my horses drink. One more verse I will sing.
For a split second longer I'll cling to the brink.
We have made it. Can't be late when you're invited to God's table.
But why do I hear angels chanting, and their voices sound so evil?
Or is that a crazy sleigh bell crying, choking in its rattle,
As I'm yelling at my horses to slow down just a little?
Slow down for me, horses! Please, slow down for me!
I am begging you: hold back your run!
But I wound up with these horses so ornery…
Didn't finish my life, let me finish my song!
I'll let my horses drink. One last verse I will sing.
For a split second longer I'll cling to the brink.

Written by
Vladimir Vysotsky

Translated by
Vadim Astrakhan

Sponsored by
Vysotsky in English
(vvinenglish.com)

25
JULY

Summer

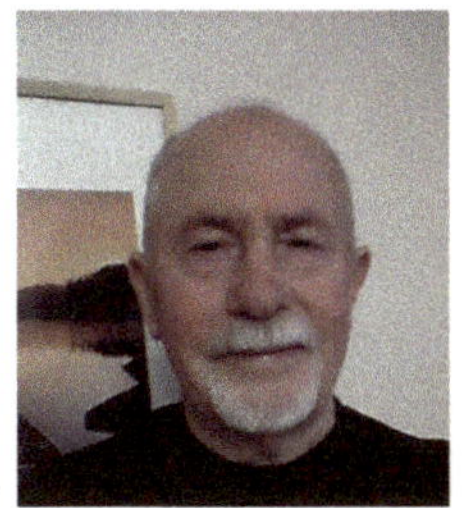

Dusted on the roadside
An orange-brown flower.
Above it a cautious creeper flutters,
Sticking its thin proboscis.
The fidget-body flutters silently
Like a fish, like a hummingbird, up and down.
On the leaves the sun has gilded the dust
The sun has gilded the leaves with the ancient pattern of golden woven vestments.
The pine needles warmed by the scorching sun
The pine needles are scented with the fragrance of incense.
The soul, in harmony with the heavenly world,
Like a reveller, fluttering vertically.
And all the world around is a vast Temple of God.

26

JULY

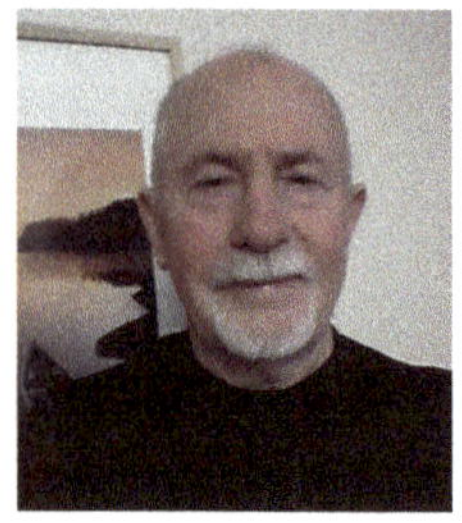

Лето

Припорошённый пылью придорожной
Оранжево – коричневый цветок.
Над ним трепещет бражник осторожный,
Вонзая остро тонкий хоботок.
Парит бесшумно тело-веретёнце
Как рыбка, как колибри - вверх и вниз.
На листьях пыль позолотило солнце
Узором древним златотканых риз.
Палящим солнцем разогретая хвоя
Дохнула ладана благоуханьем.
Душа, в гармонии с небесным мирозданьем,
Чуть-чуть пьянея от земного бытия,
Стремится ввысь, в заоблачные дали,
К духовным, невещественным мирам,
Как бражник , трепеща, по вертикали.
А мир вокруг - огромный Божий Храм.

27

JULY

Black butterfly

when the black butterfly of the night
spreads anger, weakness
fluttered
he cloaked the colours, the eyes
he breathed silence
took away the breath

don't be afraid, she said

aflame
the colours came alive

I knew everything from the first
look
give me your hand
open your mouth

a colourful butterfly flew up
I always believed

that day for the first time, she was able to fall
asleep
to wake up
she knew

she tasted a strawberry pie
so she's a few crumbs closer now

the distance is only a few drops of water
after how many does it cease to be an ocean?

how to travel the distance
over the ultramarine seas
lapis lazuli blueness
it is not darkness

I always believed even then

28

JULY

ADAM SIEMIEŃCZYK (UK)

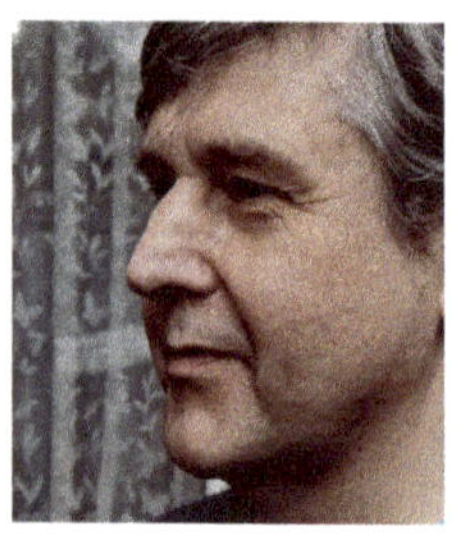

Czarny motyl

gdy czarny motyl nocy
rozpostarł gniew słabość
załopotał
przysłonił barwy oczy
tchnął milczenie
pozbawił oddechu

nie bój się powiedziała

płomiennie
ożyły kolory

wszystko wiedziałam już od początku
spójrz
daj mi rękę
otwórz usta

wzleciał barwny motyl

zawsze wierzyłam

tego dnia po raz pierwszy mogła
zasnąć
obudzić się
wiedziała

skosztowała ciastka truskawkowego
więc jest o kilka okruchów bliżej

odległość to tylko kilka kropel wody
od ilu przestaje być ona oceanem?

jak przebyć dystans
ponad morzami ultramarine
lapis lazuli niebieskość
nie jest ciemnością

zawsze wierzyłam nawet wtedy

29

AUGUST

23 MONDAY

24 TUESDAY

25 WEDNESDAY

26 THURSDAY

27 FRIDAY

28 SATURDAY

29 SUNDAY

VITALIY SHEVCHENKO (HANAMITY) (RUSSIA)

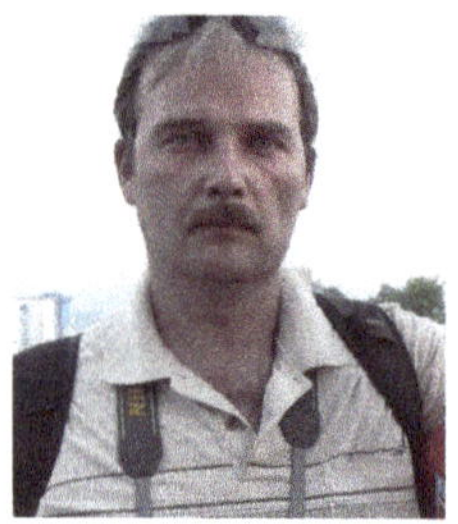

The portrait of my beloved wife Natalie, my muse and inspiration.

30

JULY

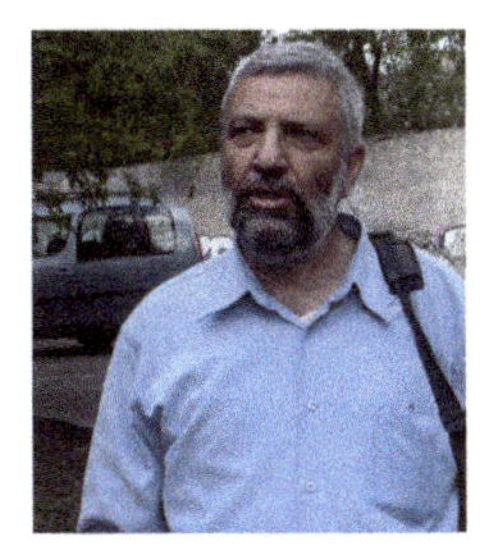

Cache

Germans, Germans on all sides,
The Germans, the Germans are overhead!
The Germans are looking for our secret hiding place
The sound of motorbikes, sirens howling.
There's a hundred of us, and a stone cloak
The cache spreads over us all...
If only the executioner would not come!
Sleep, my little Noemie!

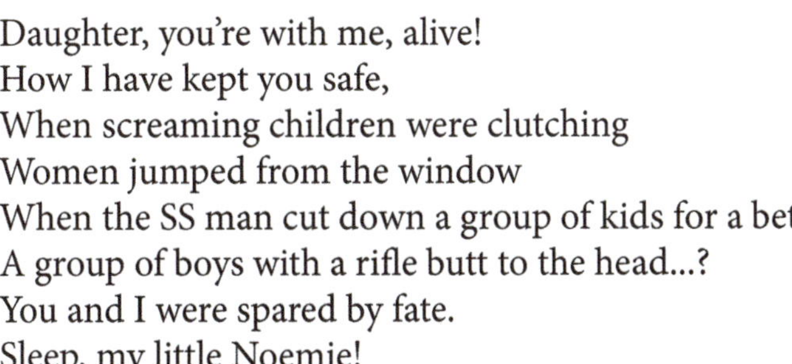

Daughter, you're with me, alive!
How I have kept you safe,
When screaming children were clutching
Women jumped from the window
When the SS man cut down a group of kids for a bet
A group of boys with a rifle butt to the head...?
You and I were spared by fate.
Sleep, my little Noemie!

Your father's arms will not save you.
My poor Izzya, in a ring of smoke
He came to God's judgment on high
Straight from the hot chimneys of Auschwitz.
It's just the two of us to drag
The eternal burden of Jewish happiness...
Shh! No shouting! They'll find us! Silence!
Sleep, my little Noemie!

01

AUGUST

ALEXANDER KAZARNOVSKY (ISRAEL)

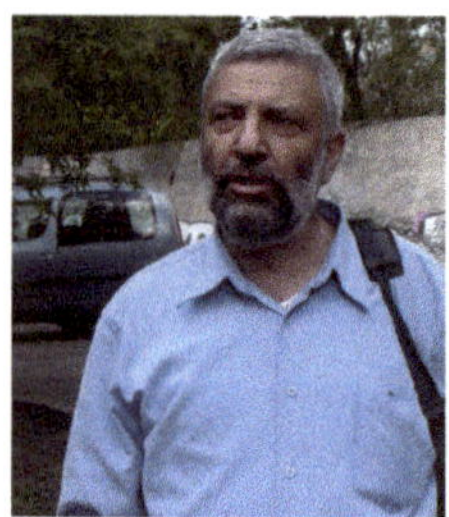

Why are you crying, daughter, what is it?
You mustn't cry, be quiet now…
It's frightening to think, there's a hundred of us here...
Hear the shooting upstairs more and more.
Well, for God's sake, don't cry! Don't cry!
Darling, this is no time to cry.
The boogeyman will come... Not the boogeyman, the hangman.
Sleep, my little Noemie.

Oh, all the screaming and screaming. And you...
What are you looking at? What are you waiting for?
We're all stalks of the same grass!
We're all in the same bloody spiral.
Oh, my God! Silence her cry!
O Lord! That we all may not die!
That we may continue to breathe and live
Sleep, my little Noemie...

O God! You demand sacrifice, but You yourself
Thou wilt weep and cast thy children to ruin.
"Abraham led his son to the knife,
Yiftach's daughter fell on the altar!
Daughter! My life! The light of my eyes!
My pain! The seed of my fathers!
I beg you one last time –
Sleep, my little Noemie...

02

AUGUST

That's it. It's silent. How heavy.
The night has erased the last echo.
When the hand is heavy, it slips
From your frozen throat
I do not want to scream or sob:
My daughter, my hands, my hands!
You, who have fallen asleep forever,
Sleep my little Noemie.

We are all stalks from one grass.
You're my undead weed!
Soon we'll go out into the world
I'll carry you to my chest.
The sky will sing its psalms to us.
The stars will read their poems to us.
The hills will whisper in silence:
"Sleep, my little Noemie!"

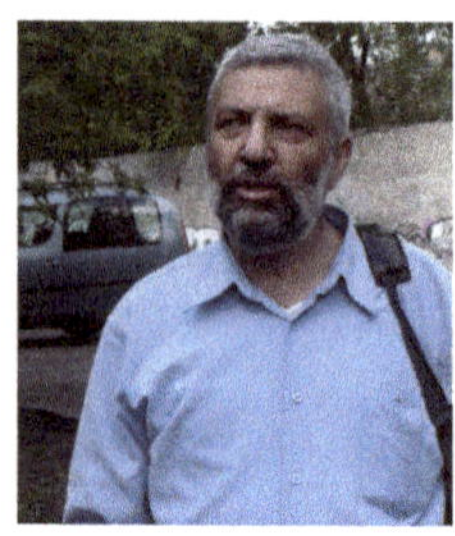

Схрон

(в схронах обитатели гетто прятались от облав. Тех, кого находили, отправляли на уничтожение)

Немцы, немцы со всех сторон,
Немцы, немцы над головой!
Немцы ищут наш тайный схрон –
Треск мотоциклов, сирены вой.
Нас здесь сто, и каменный плащ
Схрон расстелил над нами над всеми...
Только бы не пришел палач!
Спи, моя маленькая Ноэми!

Доченька, ты со мной, живая!
Как я тебя уберечь смогла,
Когда кричащих детей сжимая,
Прыгали женщины из окна,
Когда эсэсман на пари срубал
Стайку ребят прикладом в темя?...
Нас пощадила с тобой судьба.
Спи, моя маленькая Ноэми!

Руки отца тебя не спасут.
Бедный мой Изя колечком дыма
К Богу явился на горний суд
Прямо из жарких труб Освенцима.
Нам лишь вдвоем с тобой волочить
Счастья еврейского вечное бремя...
Тссс! Не кричать! Нас найдут! Молчи!
Спи, моя маленькая Ноэми!

04

AUGUST

Что ты расплакалась, дочка, что?
Плакать нельзя, замолчи сейчас же
Страшно подумать – ведь нас здесь сто...
Слышишь – стрельба наверху все чаще.
Ну, ради Бога, не плачь! Не плачь!
Милая, плакать сейчас не время...
Бука придет... Не бука – палач.
Спи, моя маленькая Ноэми.

Ох, все кричит и кричит. А вы –
Что вы глядите? Чего вы ждете?
Все мы стебли одной травы!
Все мы в одном крововороте.
Господи! Крик ее заглуши!
Господи! Чтоб не погибли все мы!
Чтобы и дальше дышать и жить –
Спи, моя маленькая Ноэми...

Боже! Ты требуешь жертв, а Сам
Плачешь, детей Своих бросив на плаху.
Сына под нож повел Авраам,
Пала на жертвенник дочь Йифтаха!
Доченька! Жизнь моя! Свет моих глаз!
Боль моя! Отцов моих семя!
Я умоляю в последний раз –
Спи, моя маленькая Ноэми...

ALEXANDER KAZARNOVSKY (ISRAEL)

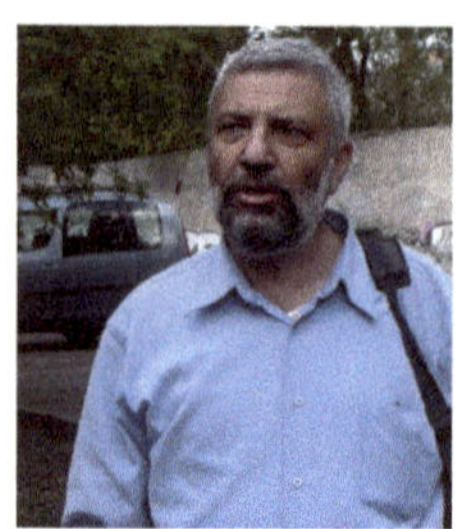

Все. Затихла. Как тяжела.
Ночь последнее эхо стерла.
Отяжелевши, рука сползла
С твоего застывшего горла
Только б не вскрикнуть, не зарыдать:
Дочь - мою – руками – моими!
Ты, заснувшая навсегда,
Спи моя маленькая Ноэми.

Все мы – одна трава на стеблях.
Травинка ты моя неживая!
Скоро мы выйдем в мир, и тебя
Я понесу, к груди прижимая.
Небо споет нам свои псалмы.
Звезды прочтут нам свои поэмы.
И в тишине прошепчут холмы:
"Спи, моя маленькая Ноэми!"

06

AUGUST

30 MONDAY

31 TUESDAY

01 WEDNESDAY

02 THURSDAY

03 FRIDAY

04 SATURDAY

05 SUNDAY

GĀO FÈNGHÀN (CHINA)

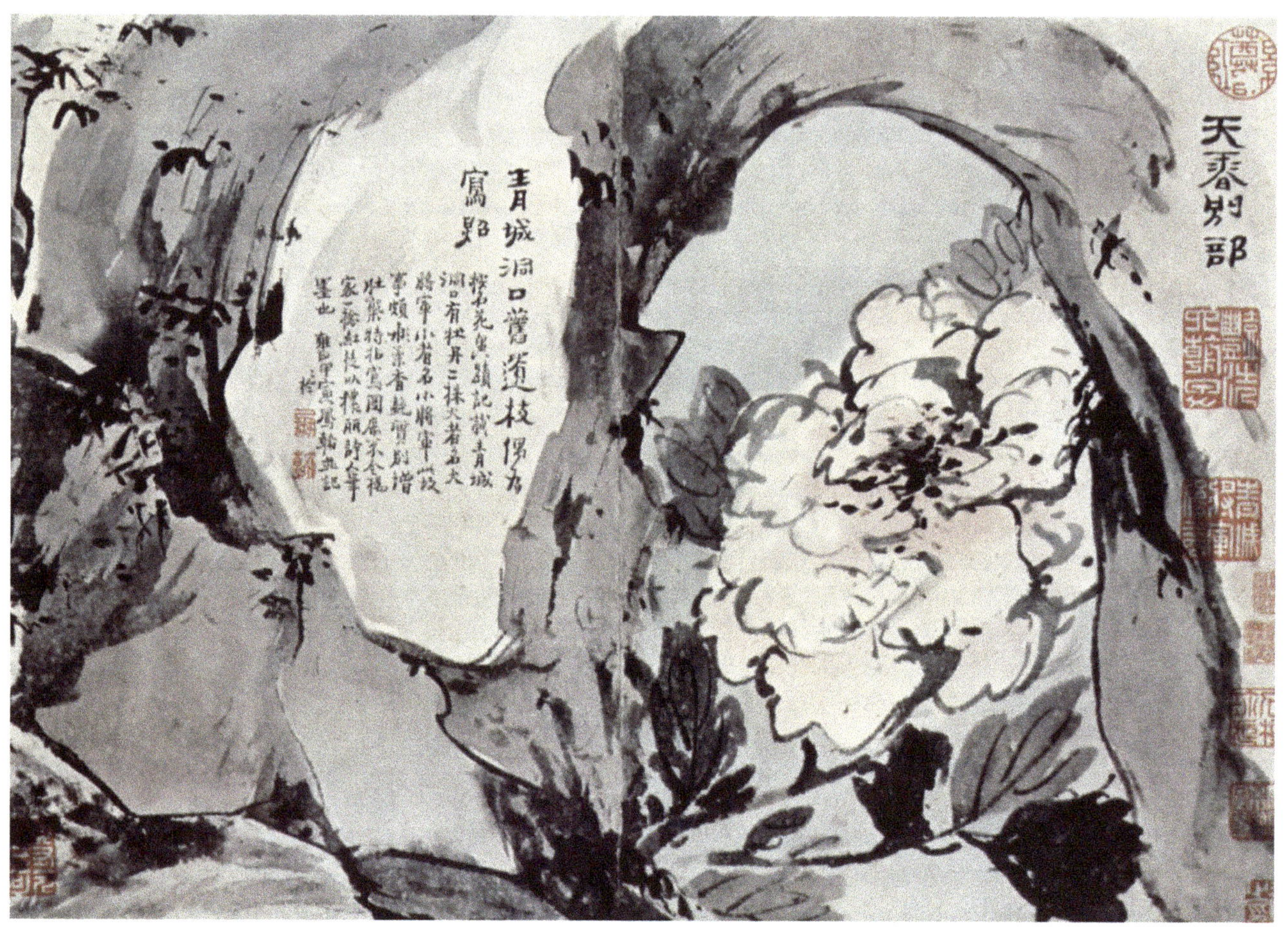

"Peonies and rocks", 1734

07

AUGUST

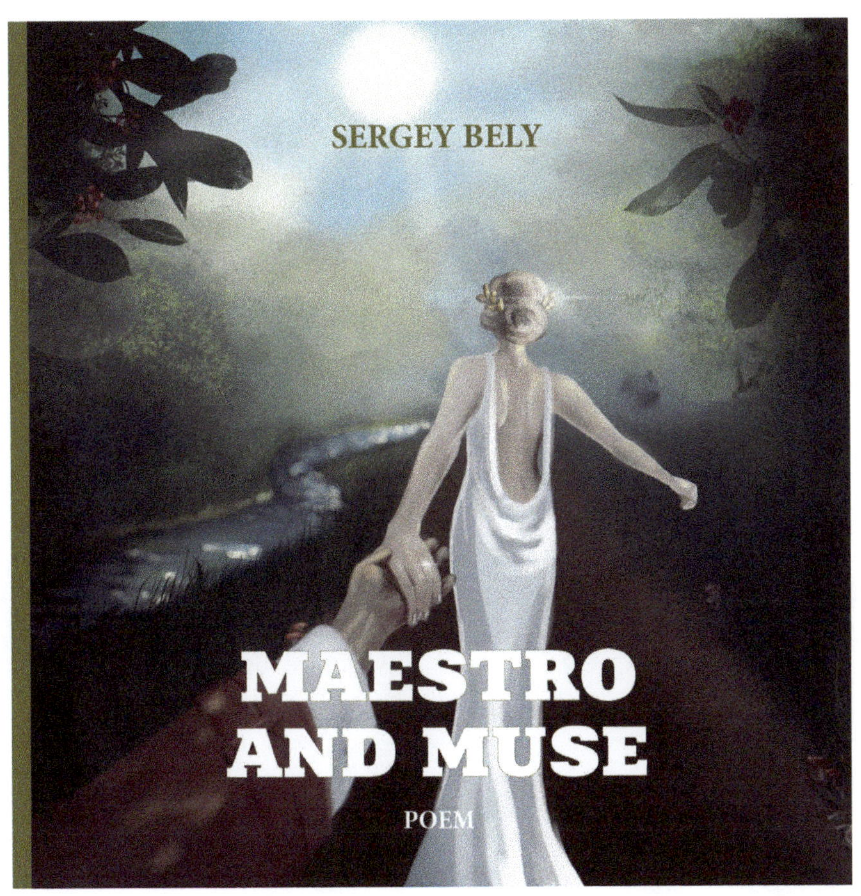

The Maestro is the main character, and he is married to his Muse. They have a romantic life full of adventure, travel and kindness. It is full of positive experiences while negative events are taking place in the world, and Satan and his servants are playing their wicked game on Earth.

ISBN: 978-1913356392
RRP: £17.50

Acquaintance With the Muse

The long-awaited moment has come:
The Maestro saw her without lowering his eyes -
Like a ray of the sun, sweetly appearing to shine and arise.
She was his reason, his hymn,
A reason for them to create together,
He wanted her to become his Muse and only for him.
'What else do I need for happiness
Apart from you, will you be my Muse?'
'As you say, Maestro; I will only have you.'

They went, having met on Khreshchatyk:
The Maestro phoned his Muse and invited her to Khreshchatyk.
They went to the Globus Shopping Centre, already in an embrace;
They were destined to create: she was to become his Muse soon.

The next day he made an offer to his bright, beautiful Muse.

They went on a date
And he, taking a bouquet of scarlet roses, said:
'Be my muse and my wife forever;
Shine like the sun in my life!'
Taking his Muse's hand and kissing it, he gave her the bouquet.
'Are you ready to become my lawful wife and my bright sunny Muse?
Are you ready to share with me both pain and joy?
Are you ready to forgive?
Are you ready to inspire me?
Support and warm me like the sun?
I fell in love with you in Khreshchatyk already.

What do you say, my love and sun, are you mine already?'
'I agree to be your wife;
To support and inspire and never let you go.
To be together through storm, sun, hail and heavy rain;
To share with you poverty, and the joy of life and love.'

The Maestro put a ring on her finger;
The engagement took place: there was simply no other choice;
And eight days later, the Maestro signed in the registry office with his sunny girl.

They lived together in a little room in his old apartment.
A larger apartment came later, way up high;
And Maestro - he created, he wrote.

A dark man came to visit them: it was the dark creature, Satan, who stood with two servants beside him.
They rang the doorbell,
Those two servants: a dog and a pig.
At that very moment, the servants and Satan took the guise of people.
And Satan, wearing a classic suit and tie,
And he with a cane of old age,

Suddenly turned ten years younger.
The dog stood with him, and the pig was the youngest.
The Maestro opened the doors for them
And Satan immediately said:
'Ah, kind fellow, I learnt you married your Muse - and a beauty at that - she must be the light of your life;
I want to sincerely congratulate you.'

(from a poem "Maestro and Muse")

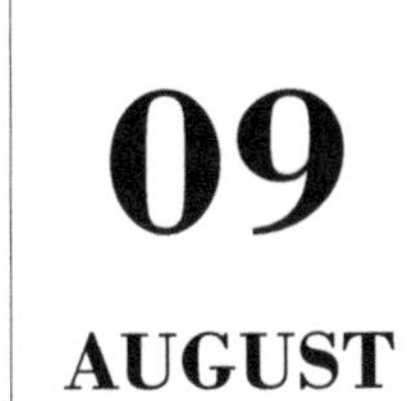

Maestro - glavnyy geroy, zaklyuchil brak s Muzoy, u nikh romantichnaya zhizn', polnaya priklyucheniy, puteshestviy i dobroty. Ona nasyshchena mnogimi pozitivnymi momentami, v to vremya, kak v mire proiskhodyat negativnyye sobytiya. Satana i yego slugi vedut svoyu zluyu igru na Zemle...

The maestro is the main character, he married the Muse, they have a romantic life full of adventure, travel and kindness. It is full of many positive moments, while negative events are taking place in the world. Satan and his servants are playing their wicked game on Earth ...

ISBN: 978-1913356286
RRP: £17.50

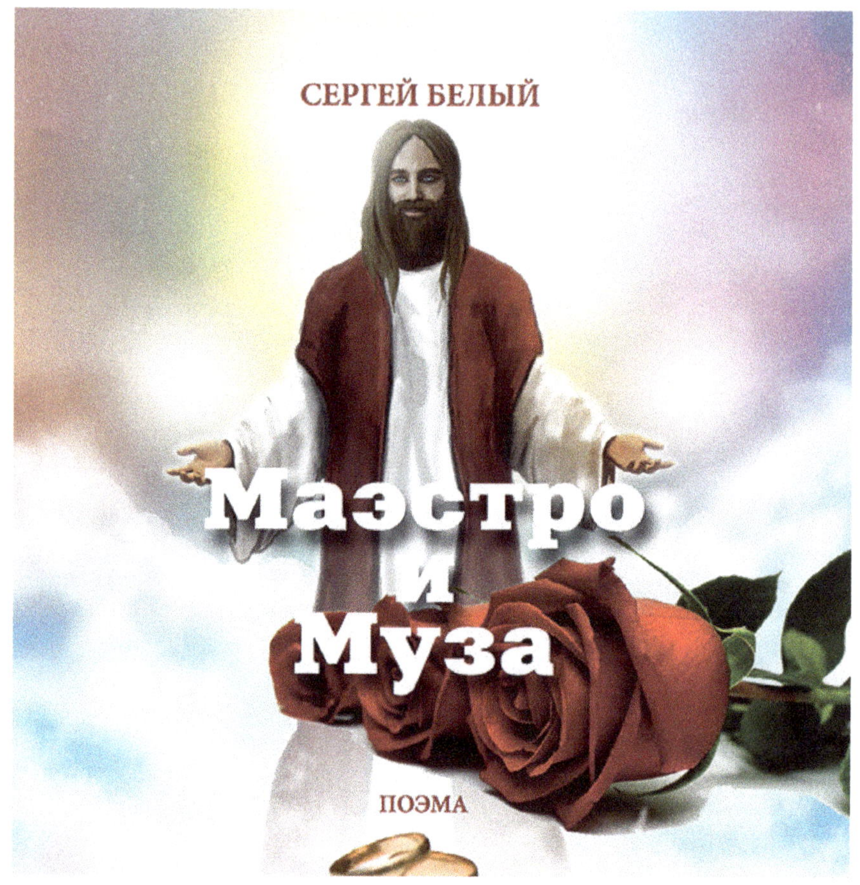

13 MONDAY

14 TUESDAY

15 WEDNESDAY

16 THURSDAY

17 FRIDAY

18 SATURDAY

19 SUNDAY

ALEKSANDRA VLASOVA (UK)

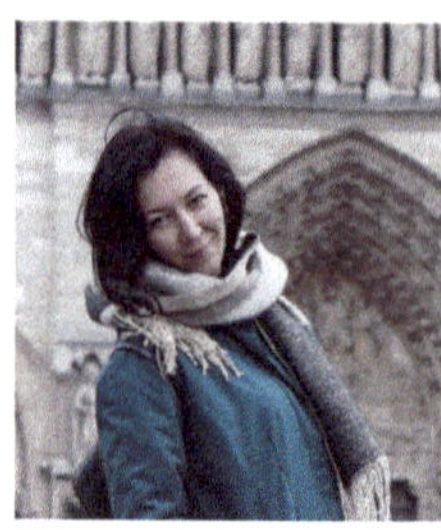

***

Fields, fields, latitudes
Under blue skies
Here you forget who you are
You stand all alone

Grasshopper rustles in the grass
The moth flutters
And the horizon is far away
Sunset light

All is well, dear
Land, fields, meadows
But I changed it all
To foreign shores..

***

Поля, поля, широты
Под небом голубым
Здесь забываешь кто ты
Стоишь совсем один

В траве шумит кузнечик
Порхает мотылёк
И горизонт далече
Закатный огонёк

Все хорошо, родное
Земля, поля, луга
Но променял все это
На чужие берега..

26

AUGUST

20 MONDAY

21 TUESDAY

22 WEDNESDAY

23 THURSDAY

24 FRIDAY

25 SATURDAY

26 SUNDAY

"Shaki han palace interier"

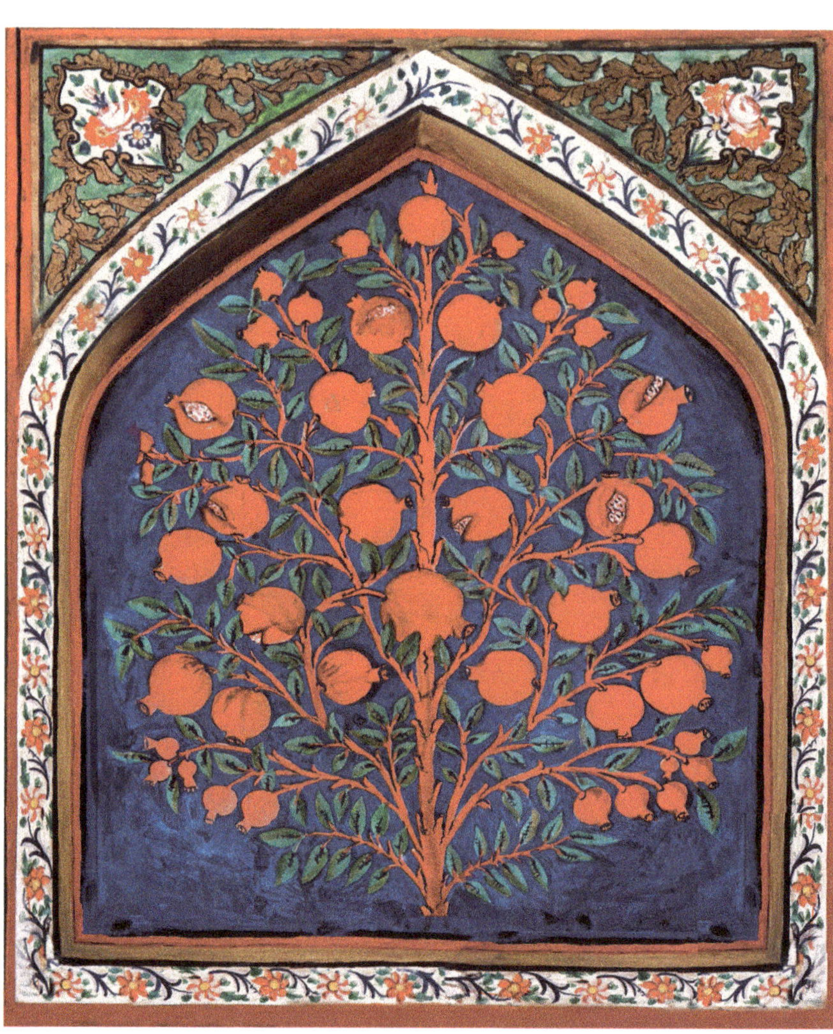

28

AUGUST

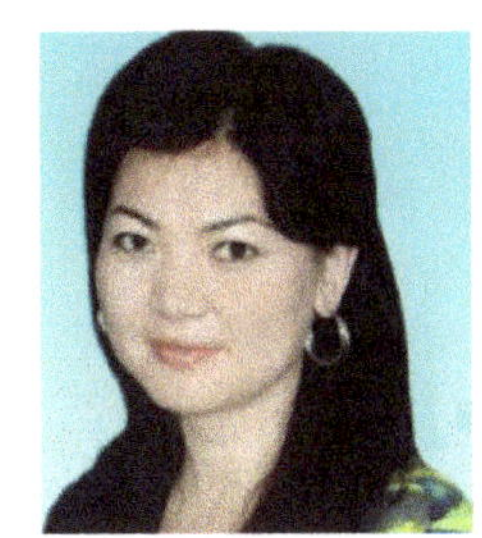

Your Heart

Your heart is so big,
It is my cradle,
Lull me into a golden sleep
tuk-tuk, the sound is music to my ears.

I'll cover myself with a blanket of stars,
I'll unravel my plaits before I go to sleep.
It's nice here, comfy, new,
my scarlet, warm home.

I'll dwell in your heart and never come out,
and I'll be here whether it is night or day
and like the tune of a maplewood flute,
My heart will play my love to you.

ELENA ANANYEVA (GERMANY)

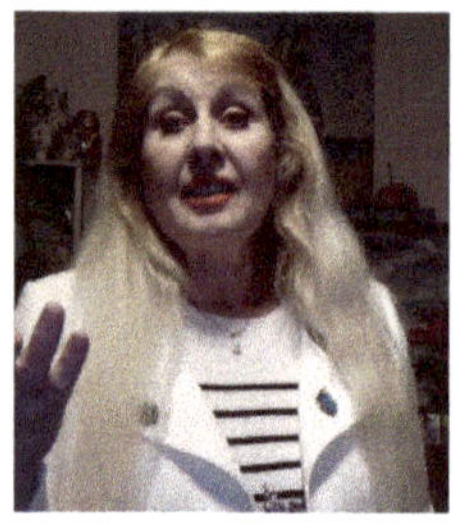

Leda, Zeus and battle

Early in the morning
Leda in a merry splash.
The royal retinue of sunny Sparta
guarding her, admiring her.

Across the sea, the seas are different,
by the Black Sea - Ukraine is there.
Only Leda didn't know about it -
It's only the childhood of the World.

There was no America
and 11th of September,
the Earth hadn't exploded,
was not falling from the sky.

It's time to go back
to the childhood of the World.
Not by means of war.

(Fragment of the poem)

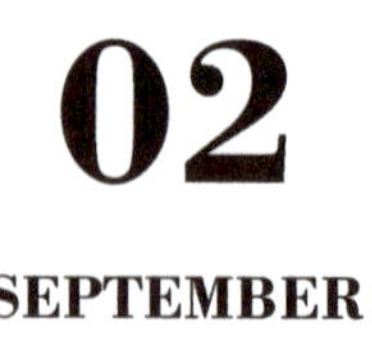

27 MONDAY

28 TUESDAY

29 WEDNESDAY

30 THURSDAY

31 FRIDAY

01 SATURDAY

02 SUNDAY

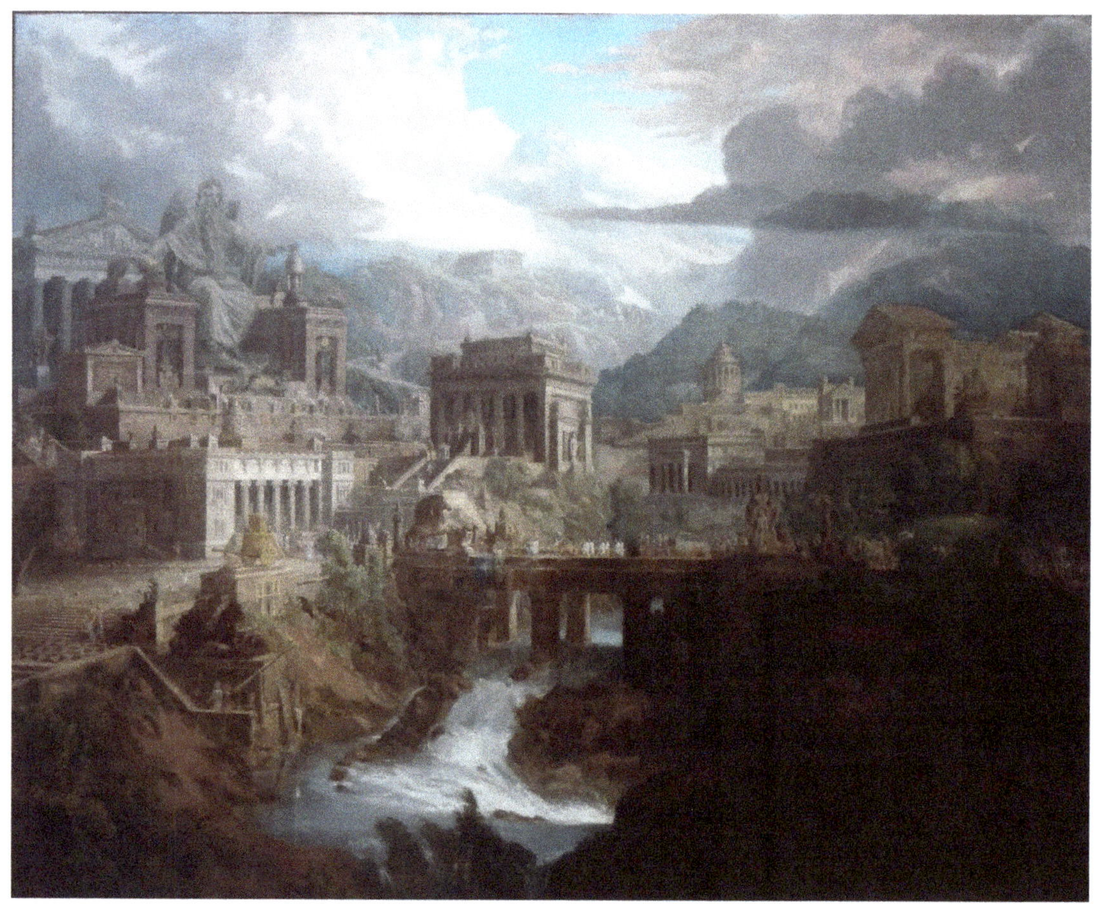

"Colossal statue of Zeus in the ancient Greek city of Lebadeia", 1819

05

SEPTEMBER

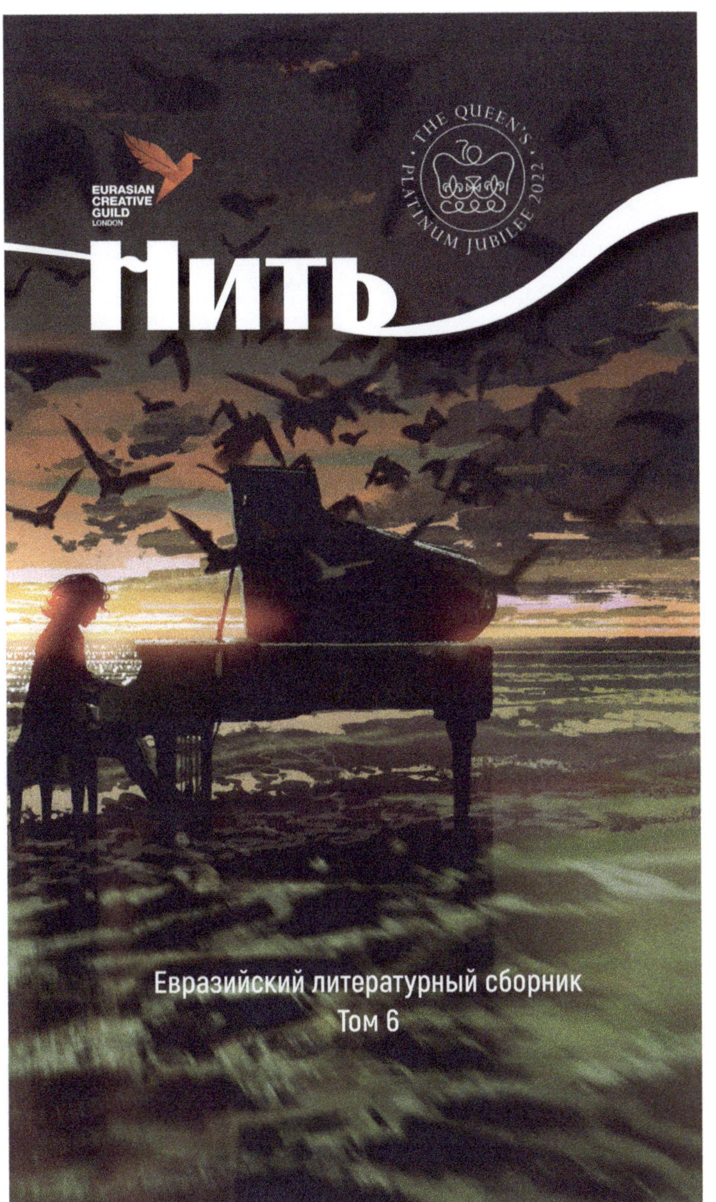

Our sixth collection comes out in 2022. This year in the UK was a year of joy and grief at the same time. This year was marked with the platinum anniversary of the reign of Queen Elizabeth II – an event more than outstanding! Elizabeth II was the first reigning British monarch to celebrate 70 years of sitting on the throne. Can you imagine how many generations have changed before her eyes? How many cultural trends have passed through her life? And in the same year, Her Majesty the Queen passed away…

In honor of this, ECG (London) and Hertfordshire Press (UK) decided to devote the sixth issue of the already legendary almanac Thread-6 to the memory of Her Majesty the Queen Elizabeth II. This almanac reflects both the diversity of cultures and the connection of generations, and this year it contains works not only in Russian, but also in English. We hope that this unique edition will find the warmest response from you, dear readers.

ISBN: 978-1913356552
RRP: £17.50

06

SEPTEMBER

Знакомство с музой

Настало долгожданное мгновение:
Маэстро увидал ее, не опуская глаз -
Как солнца лучик, мило появилась, чтоб засиять еще не раз.
И повод появился у него
Чтоб вместе им творить.
Хотел он, чтобы она Музой стала только для него.
- Что нужно нам для Счастья?
Ты будешь Музой для меня?
- Как скажешь! Маэстро, у меня есть только ты!!!

Пошли они, встретившись на Крещатике:
Маэстро Музе позвонил и на Крещатик пригласил.
Спустились в ТЦ «Глобус» в обнимочку уже.
Творить им было суждено: ей Музой стать так скоро суждено.

На следующий день он сделал предложение Музе солнечной своей.

Пришел он на свидание,
Прихватив с собой букет из алых роз:
Будь музой и женой навсегда моей!!!
Сияй, как солнце в жизни ты моей!!!
Взяв руку Музы и поцеловав, букет он ей отдал.
- Готова стать законною женой и Музой солнечной моей?
Готова ты делить со мной и боль и радость?
Готова ты прощать?
Готова ты меня так вдохновлять?
Поддерживать и солнцем согревать?
Тебя я полюбил на том Крещатике уже!!!
Что скажешь ты, любовь моя и Солнце ты мое уже?

09

SEPTEMBER

- Согласна быть твоей женой!!!
Поддерживать тебя и вдохновлять, и никогда не отпускать!!!
Быть вместе в бурю, солнце, град и дождик сильный, проливной!!!
Разделить с тобой и бедность, и радость жизни, и любовь!!!

Маэстро на руку надел кольцо.
Помолвка состоялась: другого просто было не дано.
А через восемь дней Маэстро расписался в ЗАГСе с солнечной своей!

И жили они вместе в комнатушке, в хрущевке старой у него.
Квартира побольше позже появилась, высоко.
Маэстро - он творил, писал;
Пришел к ним в гости Черный человек,
он же Черный Сатана и двое слуг с ним рядом,
Стояли и звонили в дверь!
Те двое слуг: собака и свинья!!!
В этот раз стояли слуги с Сатаной: все трое в обличии людей.
На Сатане - костюм классический и галстук.
И с тростью он, преклонных лет,
Помолодел вдруг лет на десять.
Стояла собака с ним, а свинья была там самой молодой.
Маэстро открыл им двери
И Сатана тут сразу произнес:
Добрейший человек! Узнал я, что женился ты на Музе и красавице,
она - свет Очей!
Хочу поздравить искренне тебя.

(отрывок из повести "Маэстро и Муза")

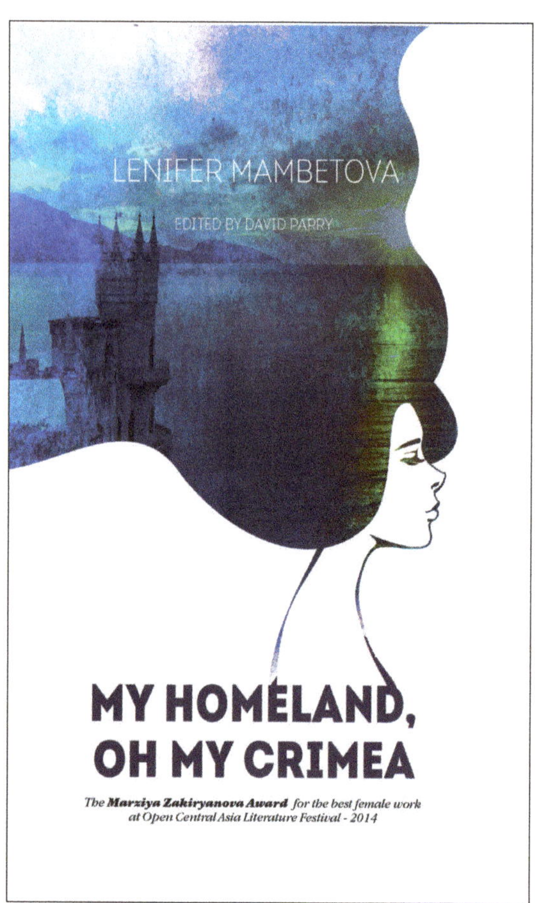

The hands of our ancestors are ever active. Weaving, as they do, their signs and marks into everything manifest. Hardly a surprise, on reflection, since the departed have always heavily outnumbered those presently surrounding us. Yet, realizing the unending power of our forebears may shock unwary observers, while openly unsettling the faint of heart. After all, ancestral influences can take challengingly repellent, unrepentantly grotesque, or even divinely aesthetic expression. All meaning, on the level of the Global Text, poets usually fall into a necessary burlesque when such spectres appear in verse. In which case, introducing *My Homeland, Oh My Crimea* in its first English edition is not simply an honour, but also a reminder of our common humanity. Moreover, as the first Crimean-Tartar poetry collection ever published in the English-speaking world, it is an extremely rare privilege. Certainly, Lennifer's terse and highly evocative style will delight her new readerships. Reminding them through politicized image and lamenting symbol that writer's "learn" prose, although they "express" poetry. The latter being an act of healing, along with the possibility of genuine transcendence.

ISBN: 978-1-910886-04-5
RRP: £17.50

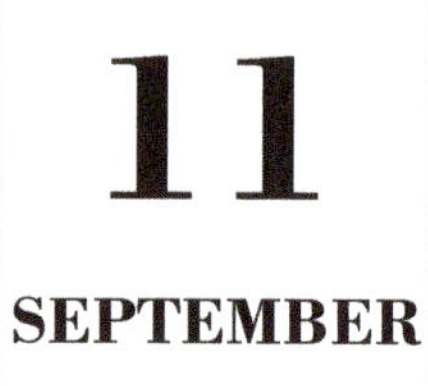

03 MONDAY

04 TUESDAY

05 WEDNESDAY

06 THURSDAY

07 FRIDAY

08 SATURDAY

09 SUNDAY

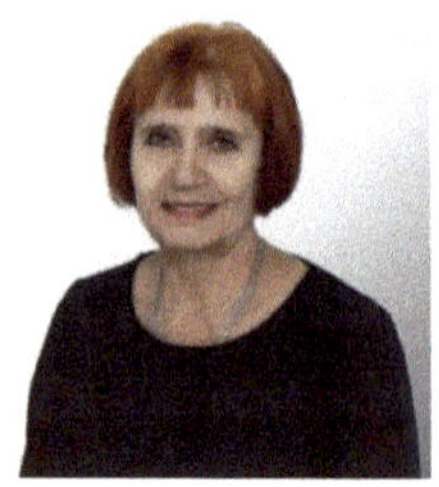

Waiting for the Dawn

Sunshine, come out from the clouds,
Mop up my tears with your rays
The dawn is waiting for us
Lost on the road
Give us an ear to hear
The notes of falsity in the chorus.
The stooges of our mother
Not to be welcomed in the vastness.
Give us the sight of an eagle
To see the soot in flight.
Give us strength on the edge of the virgin soil,
That it shall not wither in the swamp.
Give us the gift of reason,
Understanding and conscience,
That we may not bend in the wind,
Nor hide our rays in shadow.

15

SEPTEMBER

Зачакаўся нас світанак

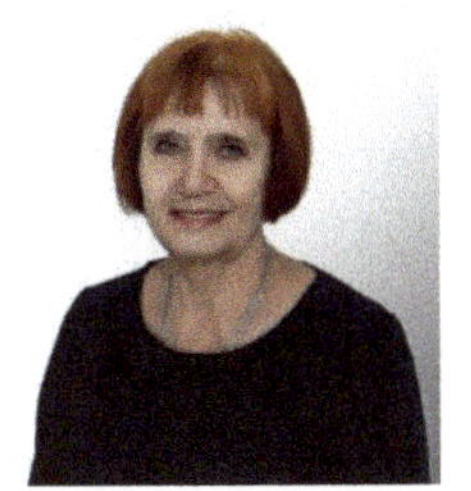

Выйдзі сонейка з-за хмарак,
Сабяры праменьчык слёзы.
Зачакаўся нас світанак
Заблукаўшых у дарозе.
Падары нам слых, каб чулі
Ноты фальшы ў пераборах.
Стогны роднае матулі
Не віталі на прасторах.
Падары нам зрок арліны
Сажу бачыць у палёце.

Моцы дай на край цалінны,
Каб не чах ён у балоце.
Падары нам розум светлы,
Разуменне і сумленне,
Каб не гнуліся ад ветру,
Не схавалі промні ценем…

16

SEPTEMBER

The Yarn is a bouncy little ball of curiosity who enjoys rolling around his owner's floor. However, something was bothering the little Yarn, everyone around him has a 'name', his cat friend 'Purr', his owner 'Tosha', all of them have names, identities.

The Yarn felt that if he stayed in the cramped drawer of the equally cramped room he resided in, he would never be able to explore the outside world and discover who he really is, who knows, maybe he's no different from the 'Sun' outside his window, bright, happy and brave enough to help his friends in need.

ISBN: 978-1913356606
RRP: £24.95

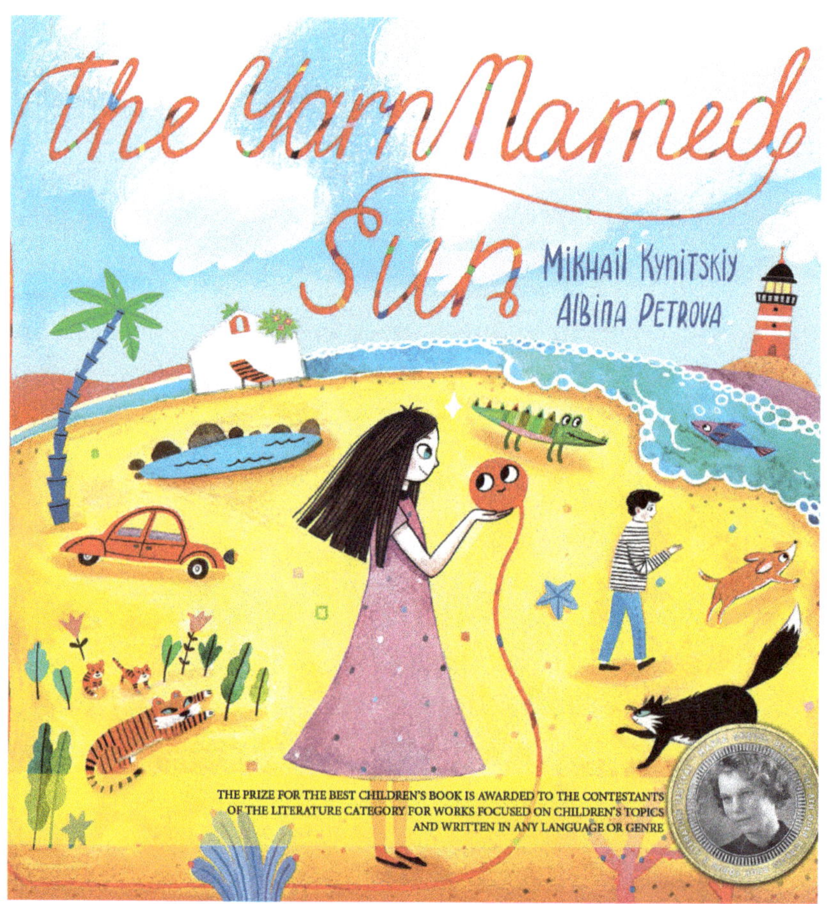

fully illustrated book for kids, illustrator Albina Petrova

10 MONDAY

11 TUESDAY

12 WEDNESDAY

13 THURSDAY

14 FRIDAY

15 SATURDAY

16 SUNDAY

TATYANA MENDYBAEVA (KAZAKHSTAN)

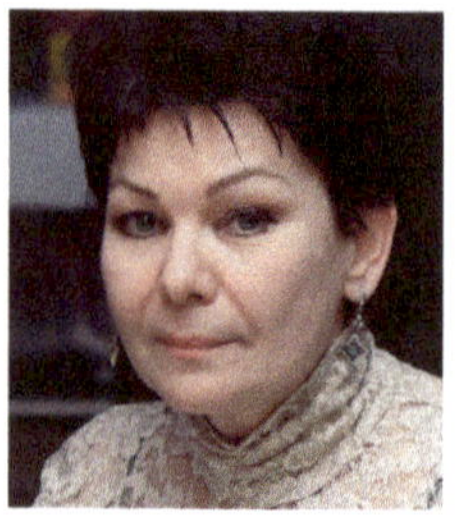

"Zebra"
Paper, mixed technique.
*29*21 cm, 2020*

Illustration for the verse "Zebra" from the book "The ABCs". Verse and pictures of animals from A to Z.

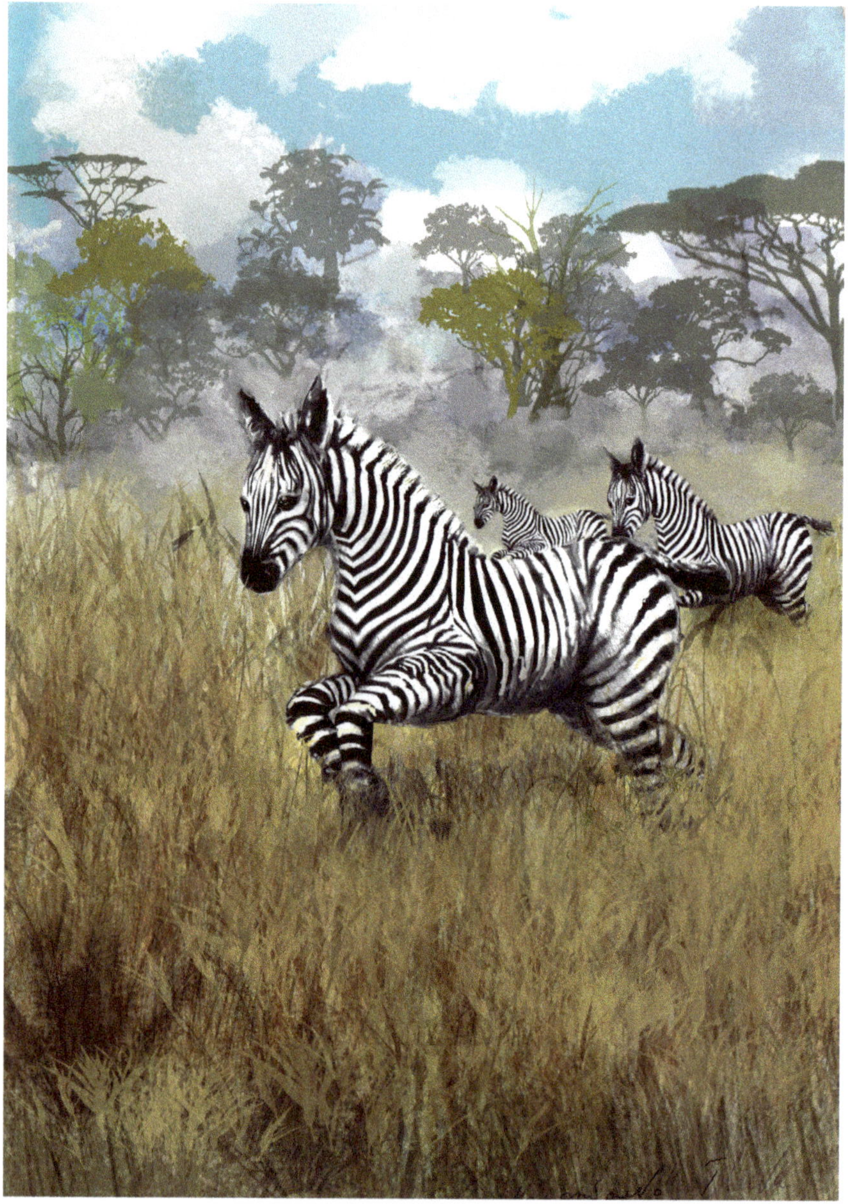

***

Here's a striped zebra galloping somewhere.
People wonder what those stripes mean.
Maybe it's the horse's disguise:
Black for night and white for day?

19

SEPTEMBER

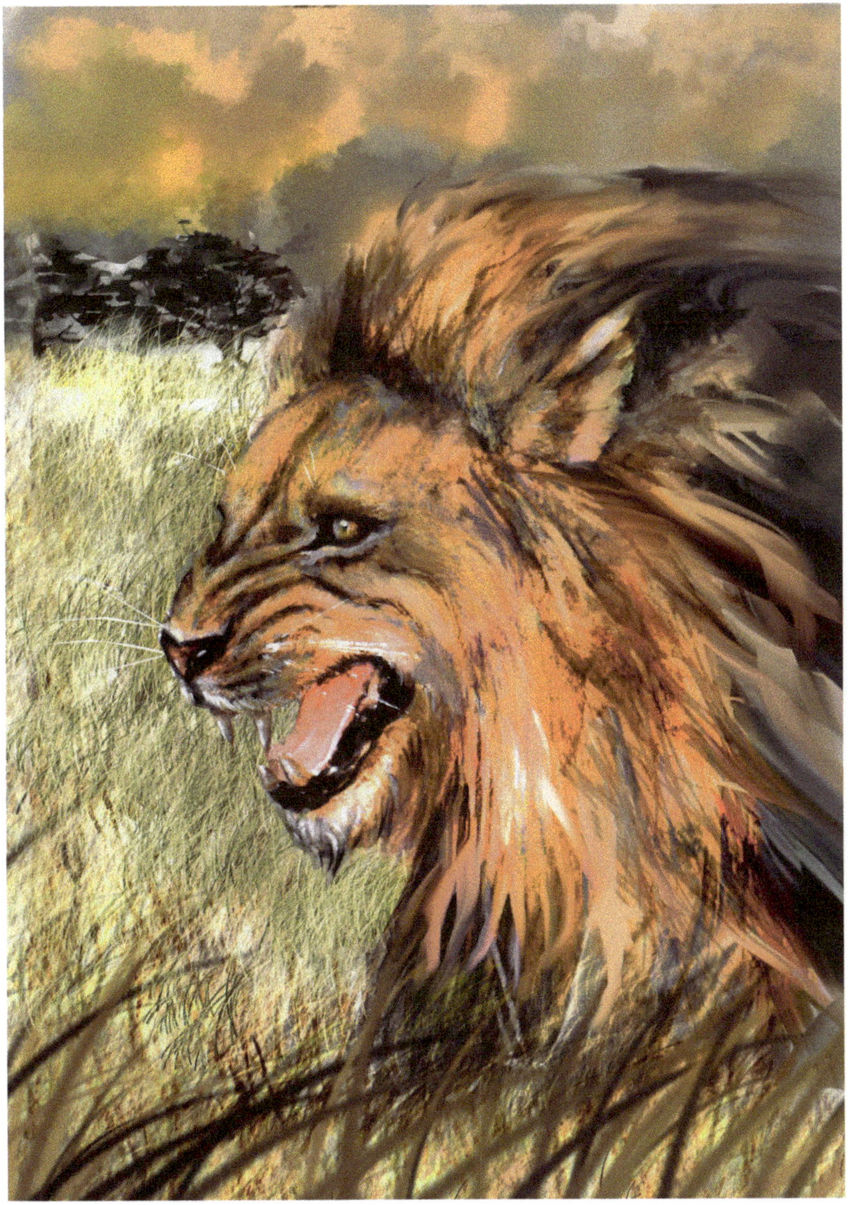

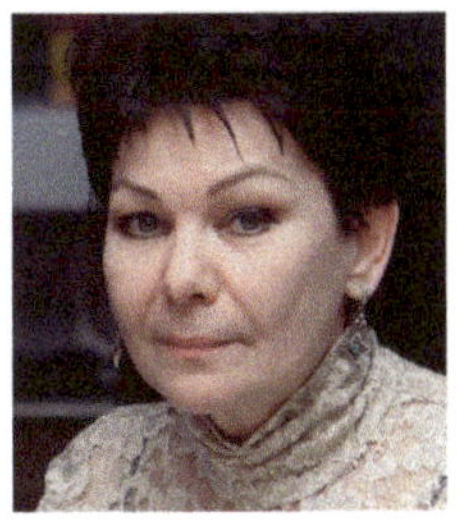

"Lion"
Paper, mixed technique
*29*21 cm, 2019.*
Illustration for the verse "Lion" from the book "The ABCs". Verse and pictures of animals from A to Z.

***

There's a roar across the savan-nah, across the savannah,
And out of the lion's mouth a yellow fang appeared...
The lion's pride is out, out to hunt...

20

SEPTEMBER

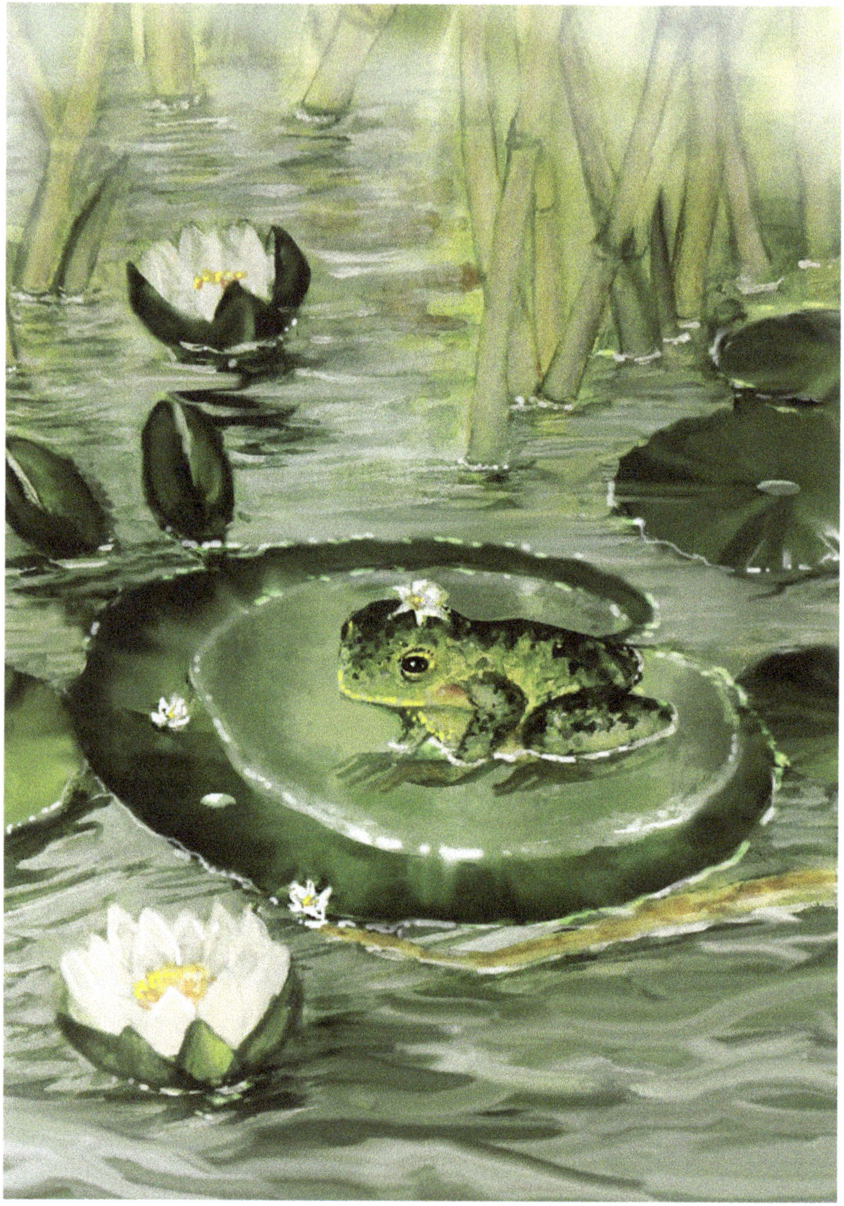

TATYANA MENDYBAEVA (KAZAKHSTAN)

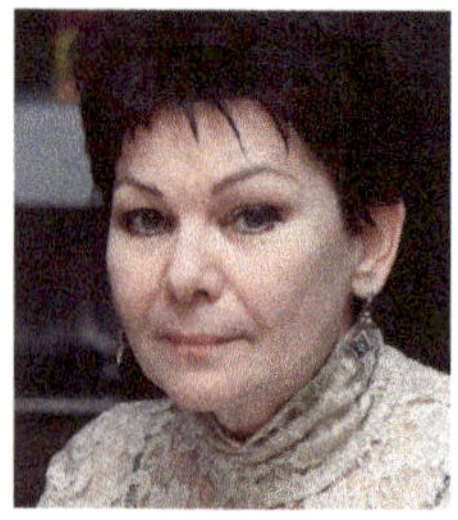

"Frog"
Paper, mixed technique
*29*21 cm, 2019.*
Illustration for the verse "Frog" from the book "The ABCs". Verse and pictures of animals from A to Z.

***

The frog wants very much
To be a beautiful princess.
I'm going to disappoint you, froggy,
But your dreams won't come true.
That's only in fairy-tales
No princess lives in a pond...

21

SEPTEMBER

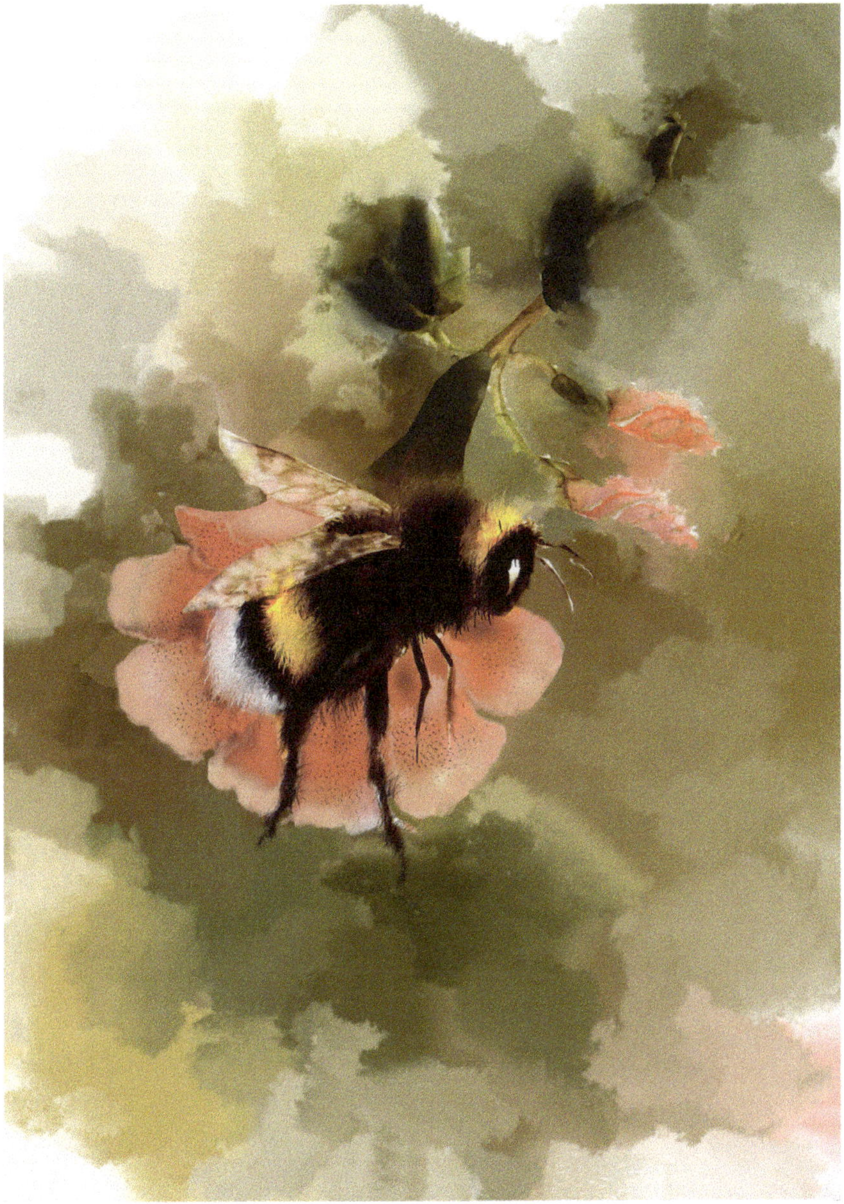

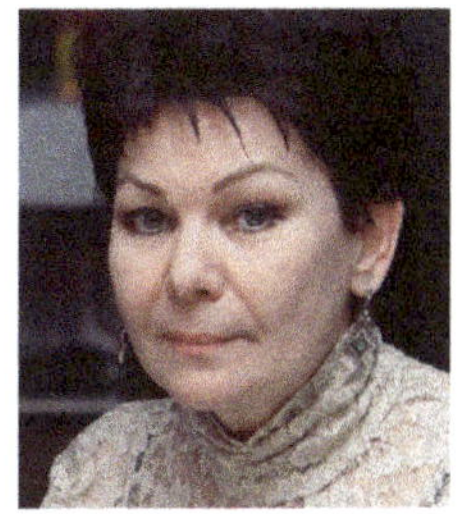

"Bumblebee"
Paper, mixed technique
*29*21 cm, 2019.*
Illustration for the verse "Bumblebee" from the book "The ABCs". Verse and pictures of animals from A to Z.

***

Black and white and gold,
Softly velvet and fluffy
The bumblebee came down to the flower
To collect pollen and sap.

22

SEPTEMBER

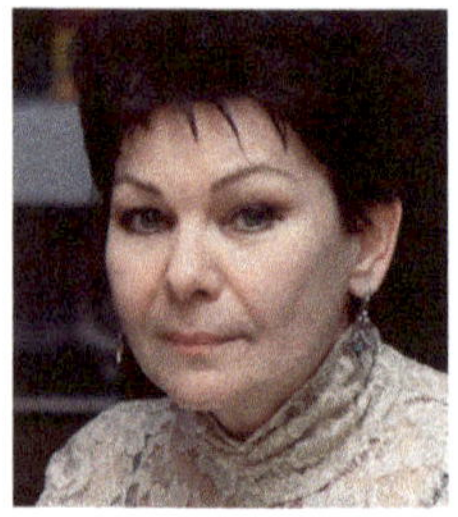

"Elephant"
Paper, mixed technique
*29*21 cm, 2019.*
Illustration for the verse "Elephant" from the book "The ABCs". Verse and pictures of animals from A to Z.

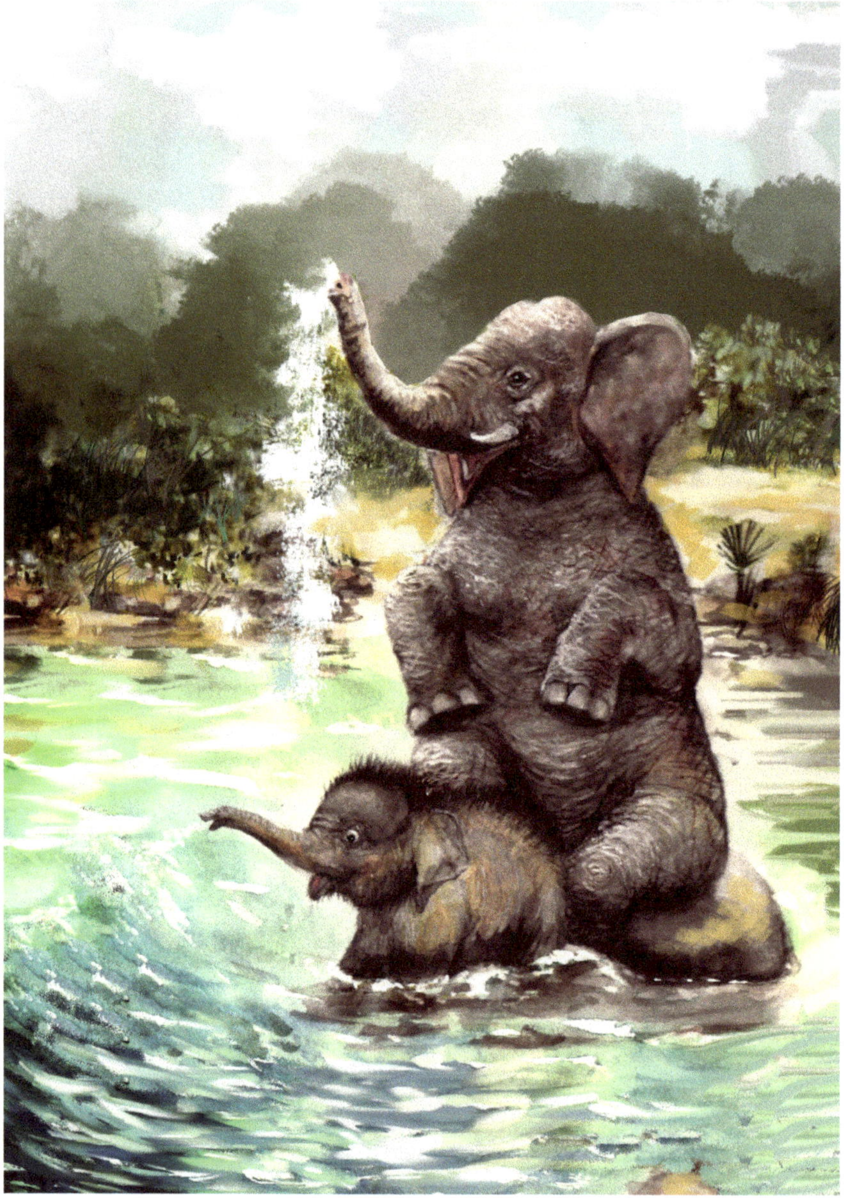

***

Mama elephant is bathing her baby
She's been looking for a bath for her baby.
Any bath is too small for an elephant!
In the river she bathes her baby elephant.

23

SEPTEMBER

17 MONDAY

18 TUESDAY

19 WEDNESDAY

20 THURSDAY

21 FRIDAY

22 SATURDAY

23 SUNDAY

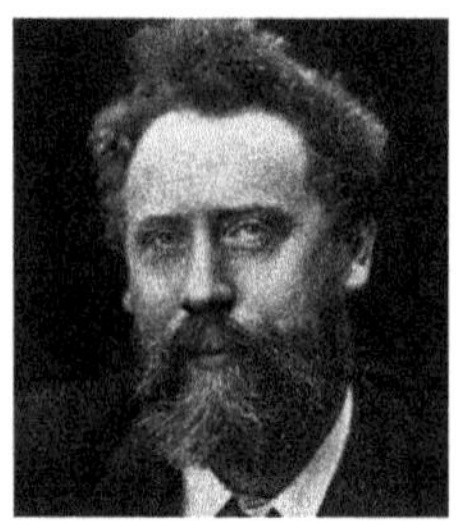

To My Mother

Chiming a dream by the way
With ocean's rapture and roar,
I met a maiden to-day
Walking alone on the shore:
Walking in maiden wise,
Modest and kind and fair,
The freshness of spring in her eyes
And the fullness of spring in her hair.

Cloud-shadow and scudding sun-burst
Where swift on the floor of the sea,
And a mad wind was romping its worst,
But what was their magic to me?
Or the charm of the midsummer skies?
I only saw she was there,
A dream of the sea in her eyes
And the kiss of the sea in her hair.

I watch her vanish in space;
She came where I walked no more;
But something was passed from her grace
To the spell of the wave and the shore;
And now as the glad stars rise,
She comes to me, rosy and rare,
The delight of the wind in her eyes
And the hand of the wind in her hair.

25

SEPTEMBER

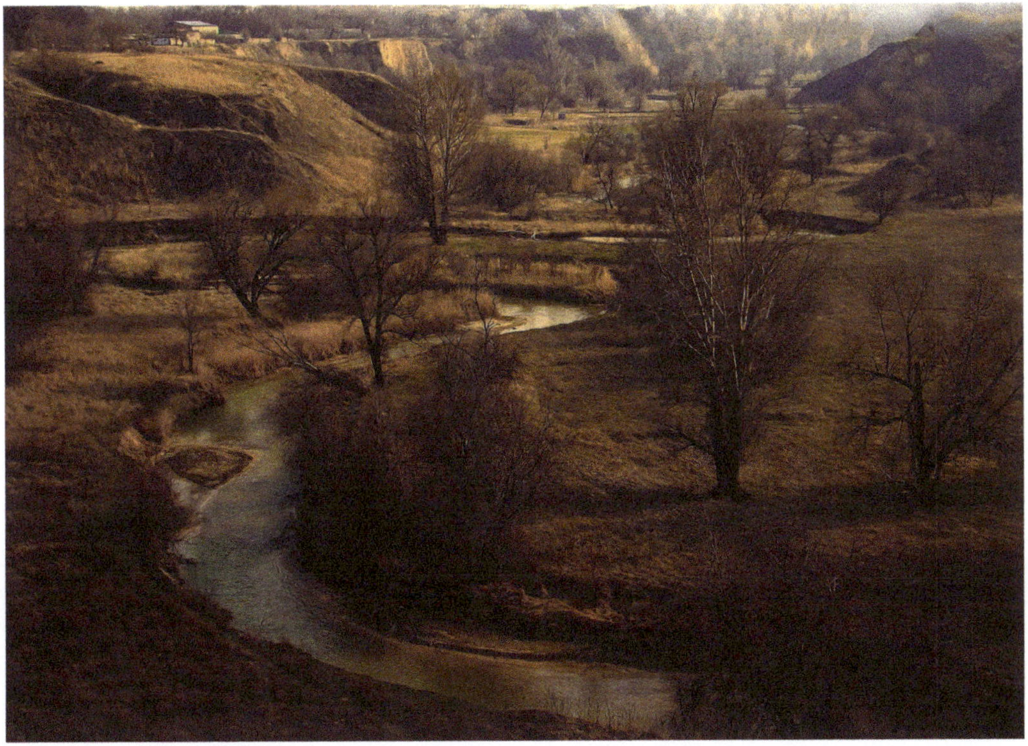

EDUARD KAMENSKIKH (KAZAKHSTAN)

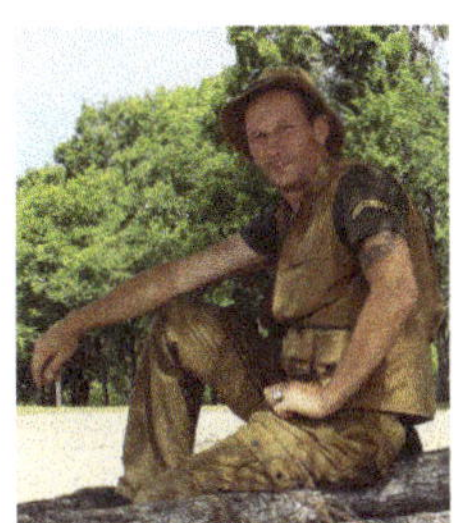

"Sadness" – an autumn landscape in the Almaty region of Kazakhstan

26

SEPTEMBER

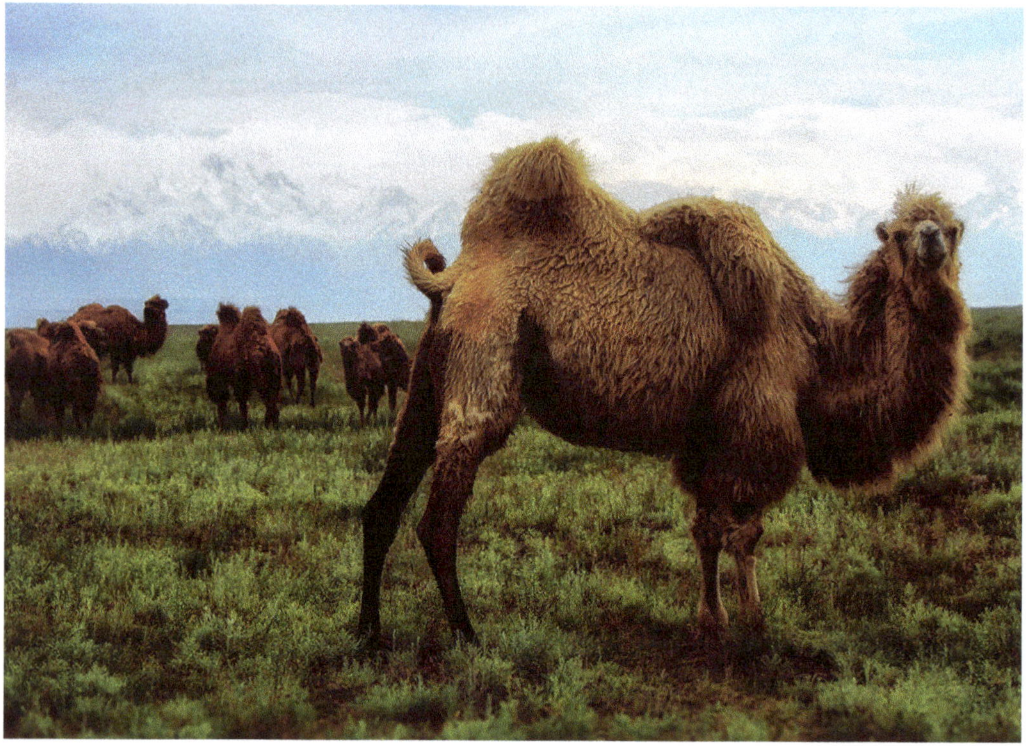

EDUARD KAMENSKIKH (KAZAKHSTAN)

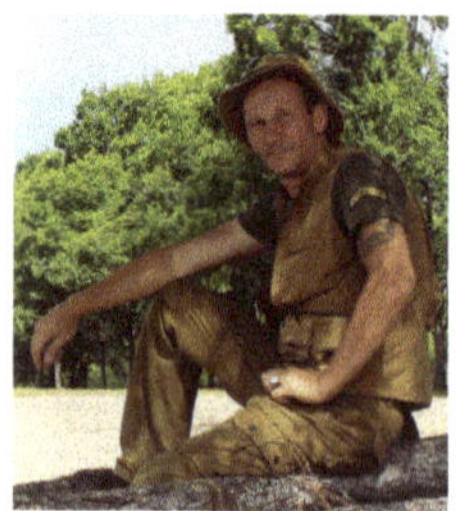

"A ship of the desert" – Camels in the foothills of Zailiyskiy Alatau (the subject has given permission for its image being used. Just kidding)

27

SEPTEMBER

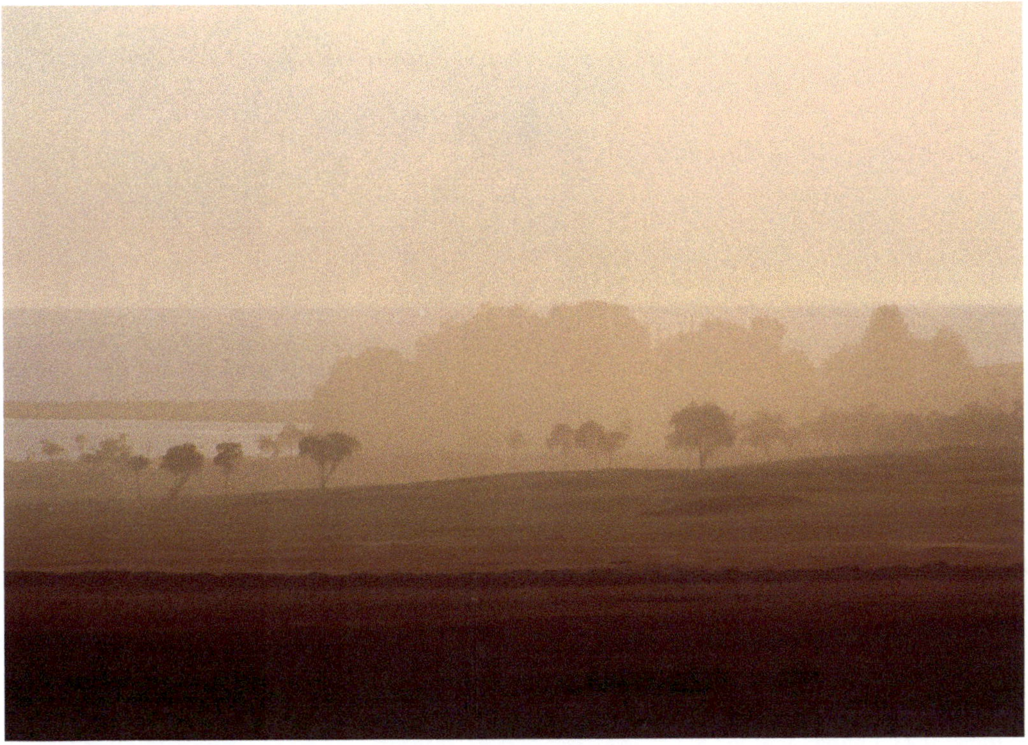

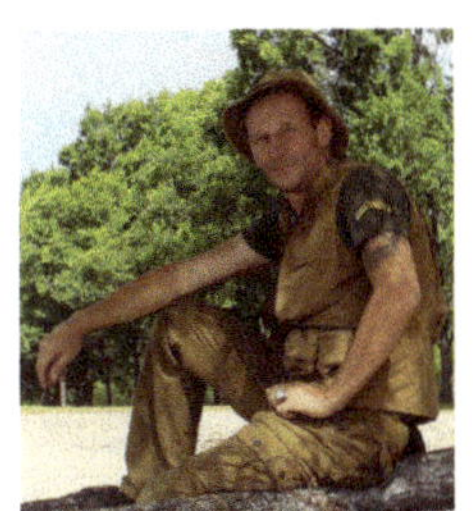

"Fog" – a foggy morning near Lake Issyk-Kul

28

SEPTEMBER

ARUAI TASMAGANBETOVA (KAZAKHSTAN)

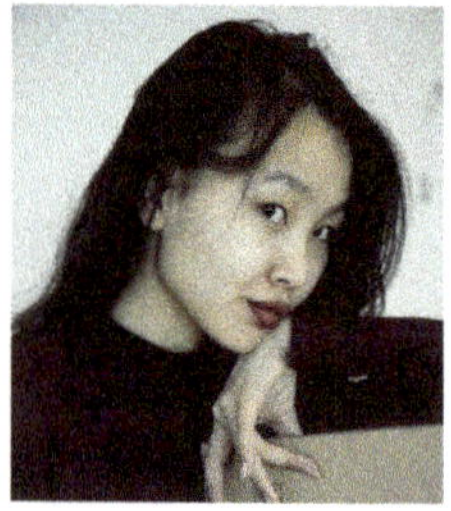

"Amazon Sak"
Size 50/60
Watercolour

I love horses, even though I have never owned one.
I belong to formerly nomadic people who are descended from the Scythians.

The Scythians were among the first to ride wild horses.
Not surprisingly, in their culture the myth of the Centaur appeared. The image of centaurs supposedly came from the imagination of civilised – but not yet horse-riding – peoples, who first came across horse riders in some northern nomadic tribes, like the Scythians. The painting "Amazon Sak", where I depict a young girl on horseback shooting from a bow, is made with watercolours.

Looking at this composition, you can understand how the myth of the Centaur appeared.

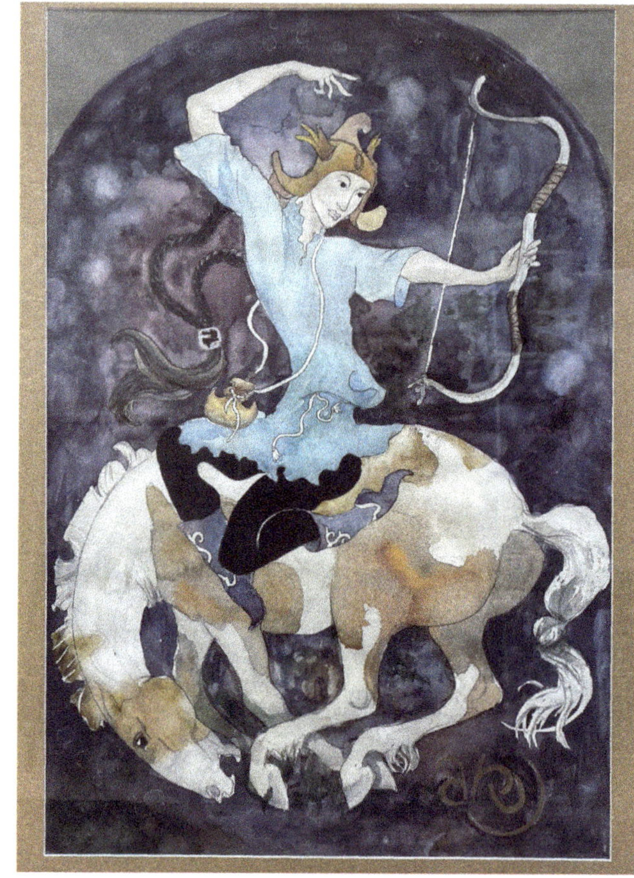

29

SEPTEMBER

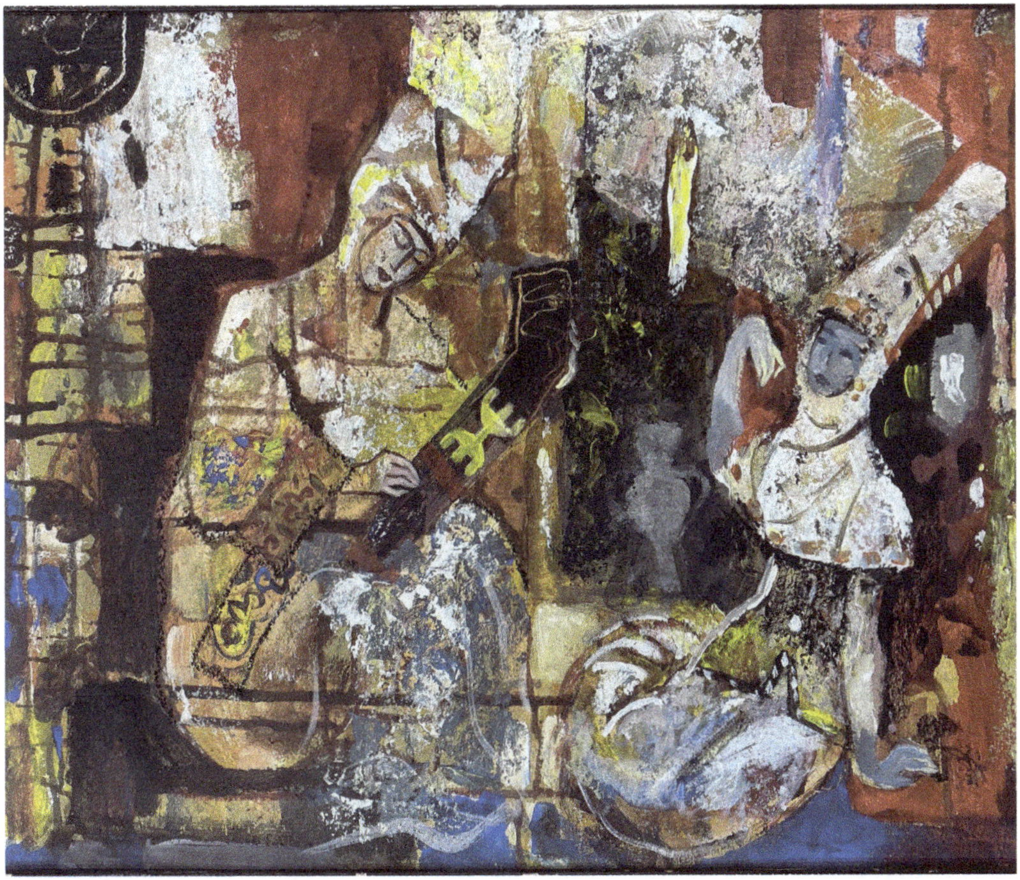

ARUAI TASMAGANBETOVA (KAZAKHSTAN)

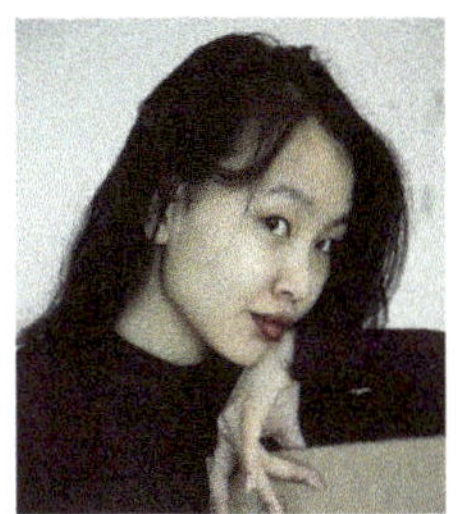

"Education"
Size 50/65
Acrylic, canvas
2019

30

SEPTEMBER

GULNARA DZHOLDOSHBEKOVA (KYRGYZSTAN)

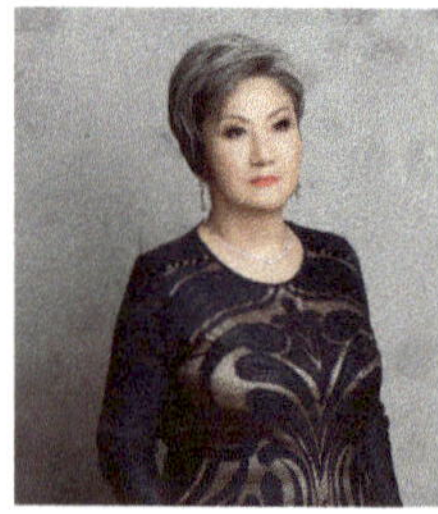

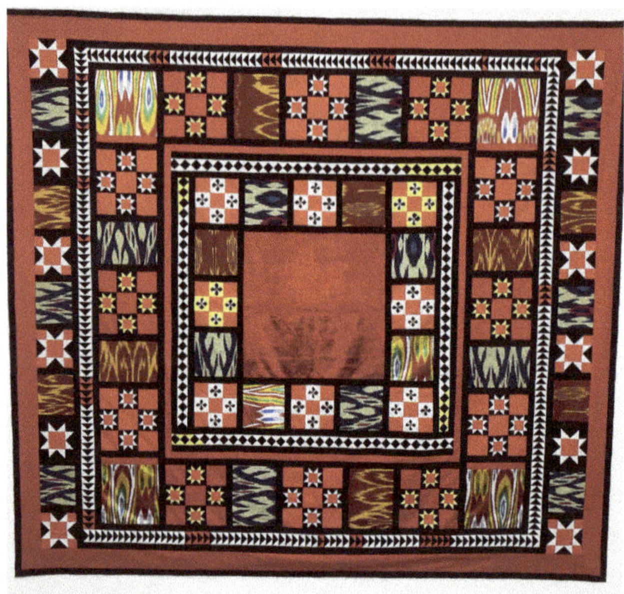

"The bridal veil"
Technique: patchwork.
Material used: cotton fabric
221*246

In the olden days, the kurak (patchwork) technique was used to give magical powers to the bride. The custom was to give a large number of items made with this technique as a bride's dowry. A few weeks before the wedding her female relatives would gather to make "Kurak koshogo", which was given as a wedding gift. It was believed to ward off evil spirits by protecting the home of the bride and groom. This is a revival of the old traditions!

This panel is called "The bridal veil". By making it, I thought of my daughter. I put into it all my heart and a mother's love, as well as my best wishes!

01

OCTOBER

24 MONDAY

25 TUESDAY

26 WEDNESDAY

27 THURSDAY

28 FRIDAY

29 SATURDAY

30 SUNDAY

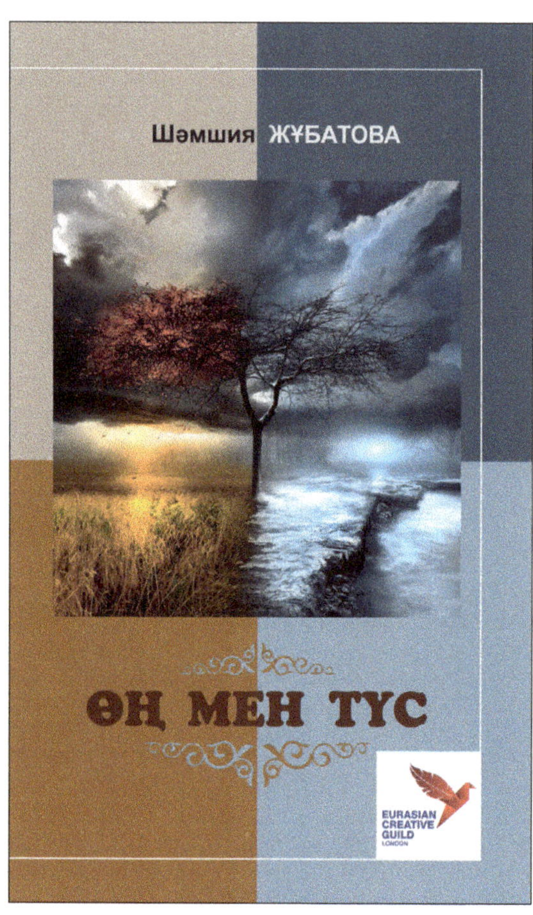

Книга «Өң мен түс» написана в жанре поэзии. Привлекает читателя особенностью стиля, многогранной содержанию слова. Автор очень рано начала свой творческий путь. В итоге достигла словесное мастерство, красочный художественный мотив, могла передать их в своем творчестве. Вышли десять сборников автора в жанре поэзии и прозы.

«Сердце матери» - так называется очередная поэма поэтессы. Это - первое поэтическое произведение написанное на небе. Излитая цепочка на 1500 строк, которая родилась в течении 2-3 часа на авиалайнере, произвела огромное впчатление читателей и создала аншлаг в аэропорту.

Сборник Шамшии Жубатовой своего рода - исповедь души, историей любви человечеству, родному краю, детям. Простата изложения сложного мировоззрения-достоинство словесного мастера. Книга является открытием Мира, совершенно нового Времени, прихода и рождения другого поколения.

Стихи вошедшие в сборник характеризуются смелостью, выразительным акцентом, скоростью мыслей.
Книга «Өң мен түс» -спокойный и тихий голос постоянно звучащий внутри каждого из нас. Нужно только научиться слушать их.

ISBN: 978-1-910886-69-4
RRP: £9.50

01 MONDAY

02 TUESDAY

03 WEDNESDAY

04 THURSDAY

05 FRIDAY

06 SATURDAY

07 SUNDAY

MARIYA PRIZNYAKOVA (RUSSIA)

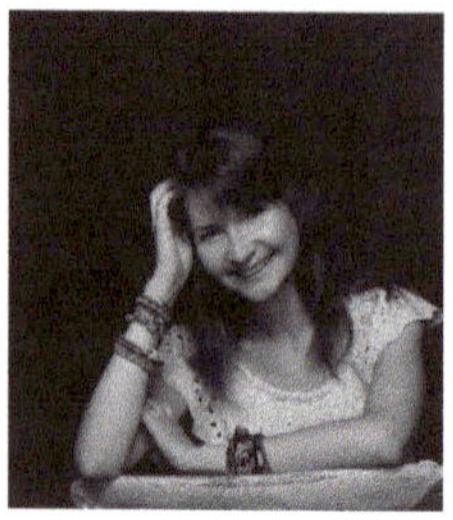

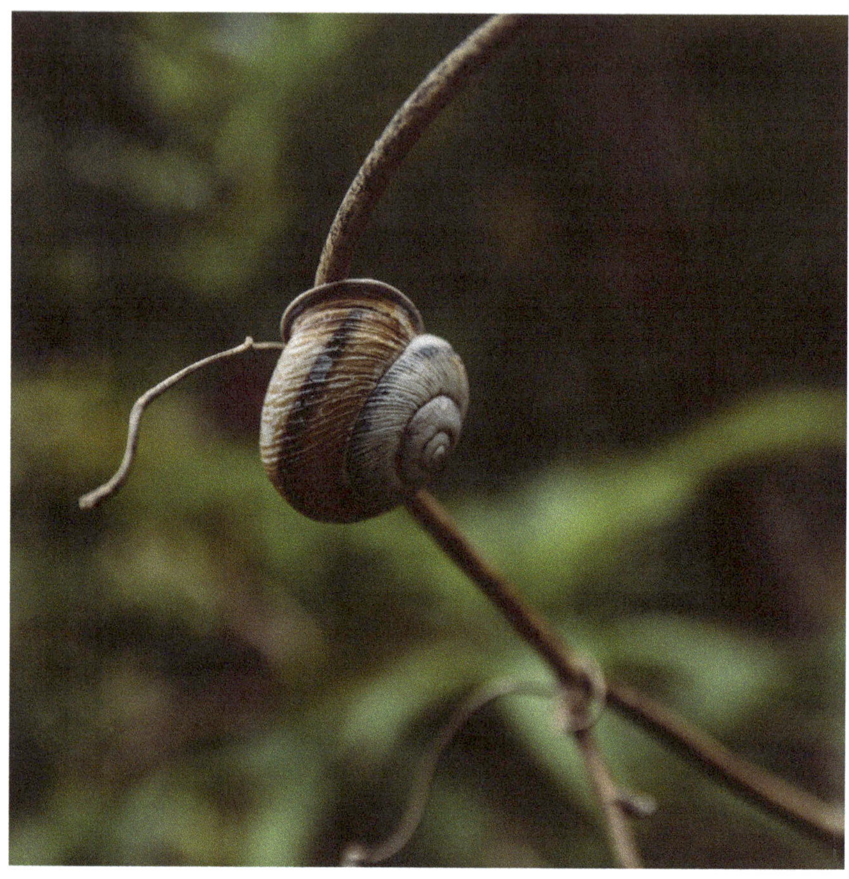

"Snail"
Date: September 2021.
Digital art photography.
Size: 8.64 Mb; 3712x3712.

I took this photo while walking along the semi-wild slopes of the small town of Novy Afon in Abkhazia. The snail on its stalk hung almost over the very path along which I passed. She shone so enticingly with her round sides that I couldn't resist taking a picture of her.

11

OCTOBER

09 MONDAY

09 TUESDAY

10 WEDNESDAY

11 THURSDAY

12 FRIDAY

13 SATURDAY

14 SUNDAY

ATTILA JOZSEF (HUNGARY)

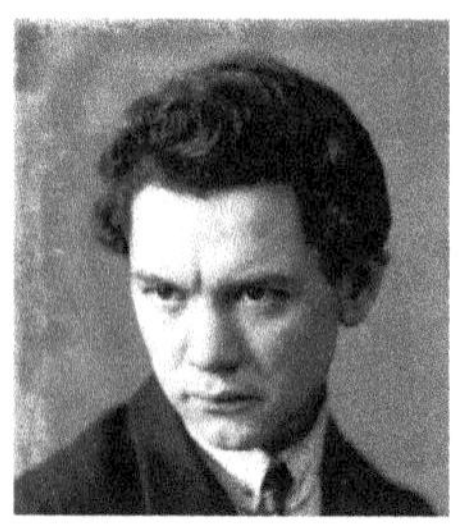

Lullaby

The sky is letting its blue eyes close;
The house its many eyes closes, too.
The quilted meadow lies in a doze:
Go to sleep softly, little one, do.

The wasp and beetle are both asleep;
Their heads are down on their feet, and through
Darkness, a drone in the dark they keep:
Go to sleep softly, little one, do.

The tram has fallen asleep as well,
And while its rattling slumbers, too.
It tings in its sleep a little bell:
Go to sleep softly, little one, do.

The coat is sleeping across the chair,
The tear is sleeping where it's worn through;
No more to-day will it stretch the tear:
Go to sleep softly, little one, do.

The ball and whistle are both at rest.
So is the wood where the picnic grew.
Even your sweets by sleep are possessed:
Go to sleep softly, little one, do.

All will be yours in the crystal ball;
You'll be a giant, it will come true;
But just let your little eyelids fall:
Go to sleep softly, little one, do.

A fireman, soldier, herder of sheep,
You'll be all three, and each will be you.
See, your mother is falling asleep:
Go to sleep softly, little one, do.

translated by Vernon Watkins

17

OCTOBER

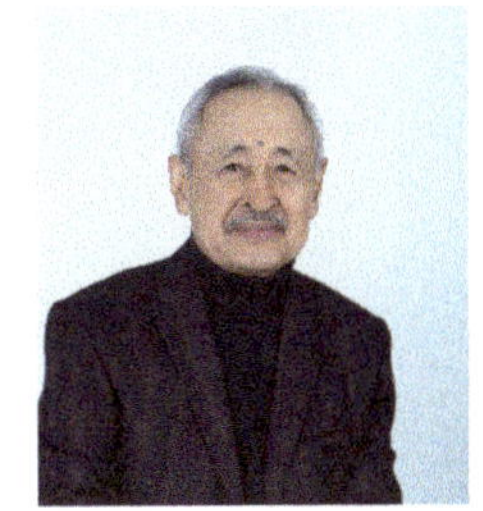

"Reflection"
Technique: oil, orgalite
23.6Ñ…31.5 inches

*A finalist in the "TOP-25 Artworks of Eurasia" contest; a member of the Eurasian Creative Guild (London).

Rajnish Osho: "The less the artist's personality is in the picture, the more talented he is!"

The philosophical basis of style methodology in the Eastern tradition is that of revealing the internal "Self", and the concept of Karl Gustav Jung about the essence of the creative process, which consists of turning to unconscious structures of the personality, the archetypal content. Jung said that each of us has someone who is millions of years old inside ourselves. That's why my purpose as an artist is to creatively actualize these archaic layers of the structure of my personality. My creative credo is not in the image, but in the expression of my inner world, which is much deeper and richer than the world perceived by imperfect sensory organs. In addition, I am a representative of the culture of my ancestors, their nomadic civilization, where artistic creativity is based on a kind of improvisational insight. The basis of such creativity is not empirical knowledge and skills, but the disclosure of the flow of emotions and feelings, which themselves are shed on the canvas. My compositions are made according to the spirit; that is, in autopilot mode. First I feel, and only then I think and conceptualize.

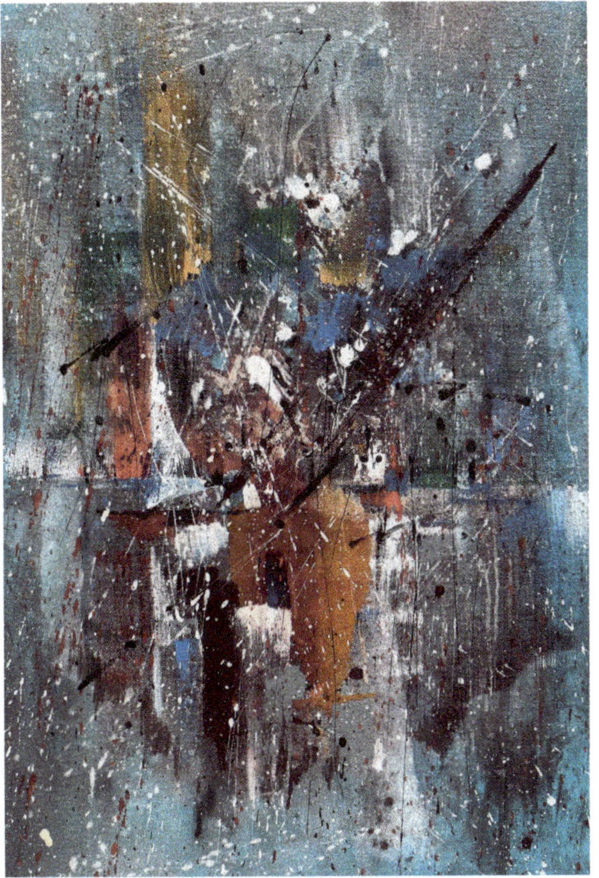

18

OCTOBER

WILLIAM SHAKESPEARE (UK)

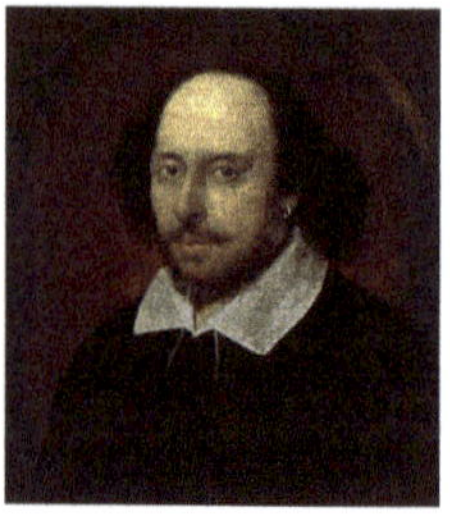

Sonnet 134

So, now I have confess'd that he is thine,
And I myself am mortgaged to thy will,
Myself I'll forfeit, so that other mine
Thou wilt restore, to be my comfort still:

But thou wilt not, nor he will not be free,
For thou art covetous and he is kind;
He learned but surety-like to write for me
Under that bond that him as fast doth bind.

The statute of thy beauty thou wilt take,
Thou usurer, that put'st forth all to use,
And sue a friend came debtor for my sake;
So him I lose through my unkind abuse.

Him have I lost; thou hast both him and me:
He pays the whole, and yet am I not free.

Сонет 134

Ты друга моего смогла пленить,
И я готов в плену твоем остаться,
Затем, чтоб вновь свободным с другом быть,
И нашей мирной жизнью наслаждаться.

Но и теперь остался он рабом:
Ты ж непреклонна, он – уступчив снова,
Я за него ручаюсь и вдвоем
Сменяем наши узы на оковы.

Ты чарами смогла нас оплести,
Как ростовщик, дерущий беспощадно:
Теперь меня и другу не спасти:
Его я потеряю безвозвратно.

Расплатиться с тобой он – все равно,
Мне пленником твоим быть суждено.

21

OCTOBER

Поэтический перевод с английского Михаила Ананова

15 MONDAY

16 TUESDAY

17 WEDNESDAY

18 THURSDAY

19 FRIDAY

20 SATURDAY

21 SUNDAY

IGOR KHENTOV (ISRAEL)

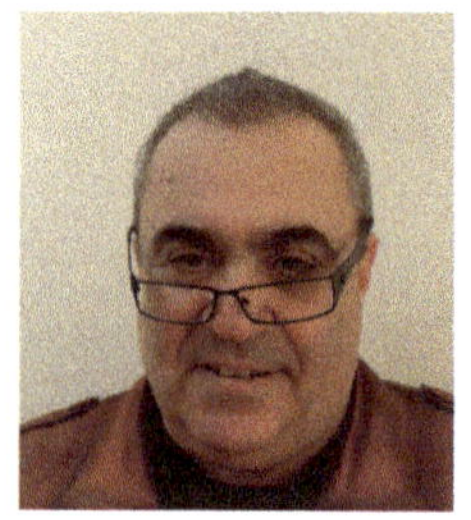

Fallen Leaves

Montmartre is subdued on an autumn night,
Like, indeed, the whole French capital,
But the chestnut leaves were swirling,
Decorating the streets they fell on.

From the silence came: "I love you, forgive me,
I'll get a divorce, I can't go on like this!" –
Under a streetlight, forgetting caution,
The director put a statistician in a taxi.

He emptied his wallet at the brothel,
On an ornate bench, hugging a tripod,
An unknown artist drank a Beaujolais
With Monet's ghost on his mind.

Thinking that Paris was the foundation of all foundations,
And honouring the universe itself,
The Seine, which carries its waters unhurriedly,
Was framed in its sleeping sails.

And in the restaurant no-one was ready for bed:
A violin and a saxophone were playing,
And a black man in a tuxedo sang in a sweet baritone
The timeless blues of Monsieur Joseph Cosmas.

22

OCTOBER

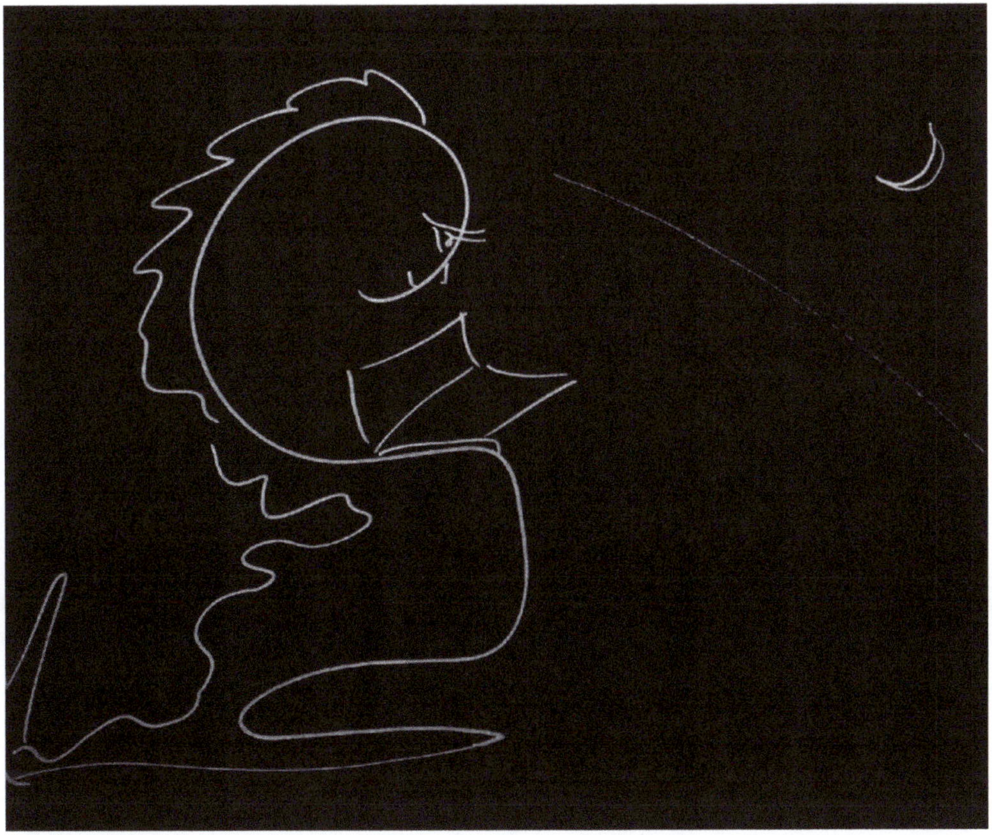

ELENA BEZRUKOVA (KAZAKHSTAN)

"The Dragon" 11.7x8.3 inches

A finalist in the "TOP-25 Artworks of Eurasia" contest, and a member of the Eurasian Creative Guild (London).

Made on grafella, "The Dragon" reflects the author's directions of creativity: projective graphics and miniatures for paintings.
Projective graphics originated in the late nineties in Kazakhstan. This graphic art reveals the emotional and spiritual perception of the world, reflected in an intuitively laid line.

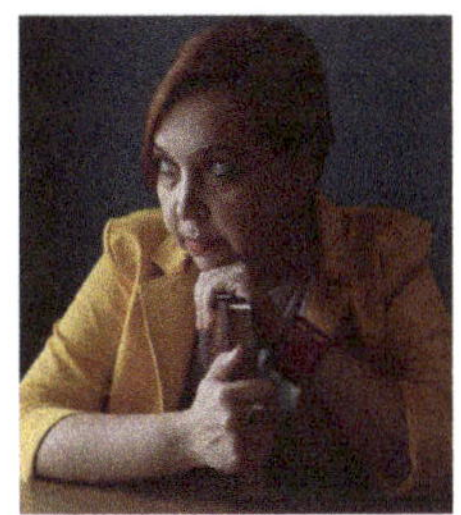

Projective graphics are a sort of echo of primitive art, shamanism and art therapy in modern psychology. They are simple, concise, look great in the interior of any style, have the property of harmonizing the emotional state of the viewer and developing his spatial-creative thinking.

Technique: projective graphics

25

OCTOBER

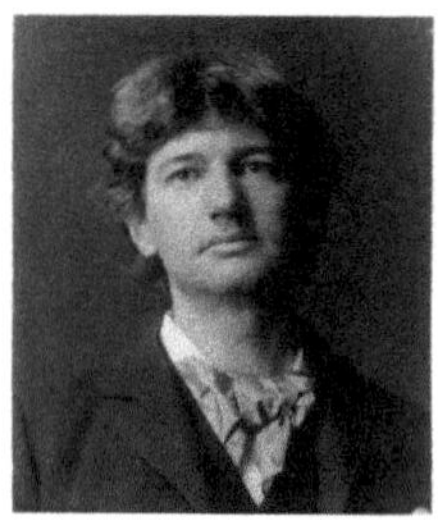

A Wood-Path

At evening and at morning
By an enchanted way
I walk the world in wonder,
And have no word to say.

It is the path we traversed
One twilight, thou and I;
Thy beauty all a rapture,
My spirit all a cry.

The red leaves fall upon it,
The moon and mist and rain,
But not the magic footfall
That made its meaning plain.

26

OCTOBER

22 MONDAY

23 TUESDAY

24 WEDNESDAY

25 THURSDAY

26 FRIDAY

27 SATURDAY

28 SUNDAY

LENA GOGOLEVA (RUSSIA)

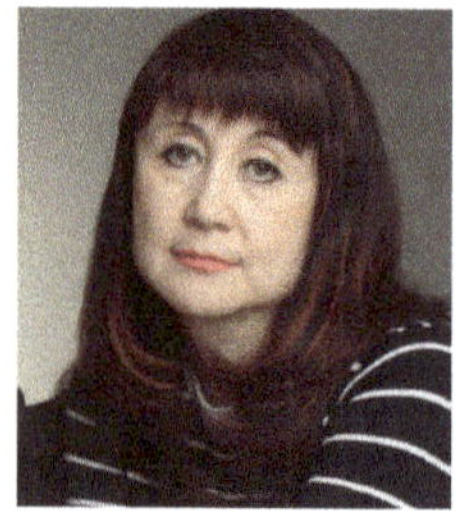

"Blessing"
Cardboard. Acrylic.
Mixed technique.
70 × 50 cm . 2015.

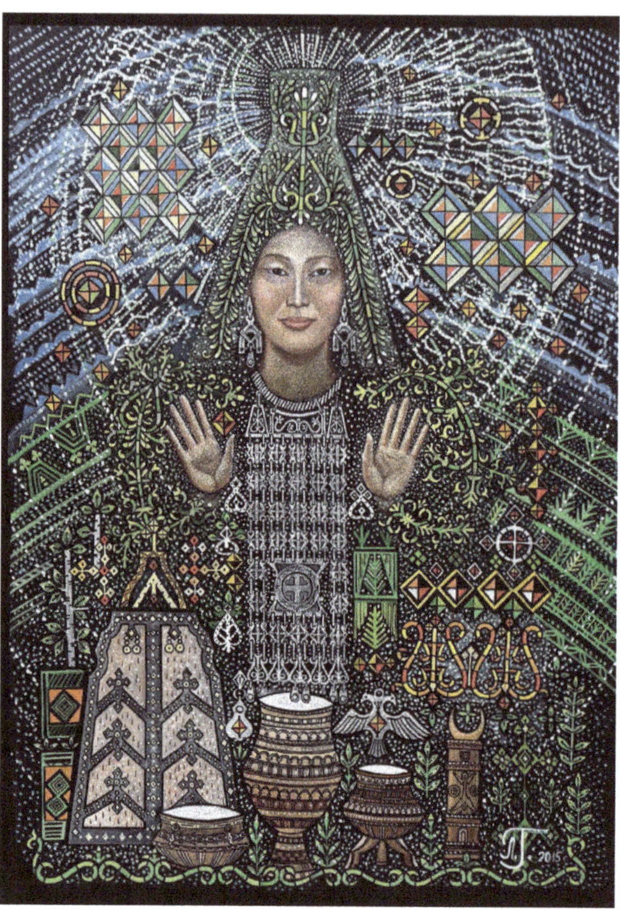

A blessing is a wish for goodness, success and happiness.
Lena Gogoleva's painting wishes well the Goddess Aysyt herself - a Yakut goddess who is the patroness and giver of children and litter of pets.

The picture is painted in the style of "conceptual ornamentalism". Each ornament is not a simple decoration but a certain sign - symbol: growing young grass, trees, water pouring down from the sky, wooden vessels filled to the brim with milk. The birch-bark door Happakchi, a symbol of the beautiful bride; the two-headed oxoku bird, a symbol of men's wisdom and sagacity.

The ornament in this concept is a kind of coded sign, a symbol.
A person who knows the symbolism of the ornament can easily "read" the message of the author: "I wish you good, peace, prosperity and well-being! ".

03

NOVEMBER

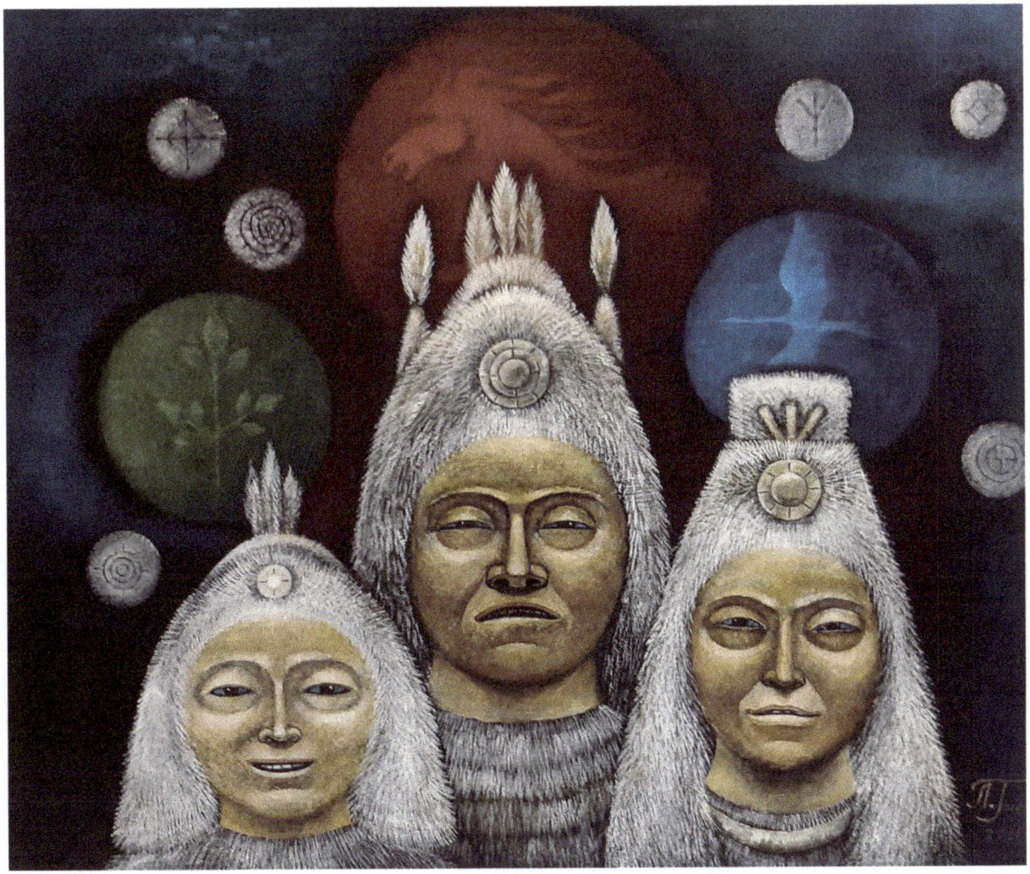

LENA GOGOLEVA (RUSSIA)

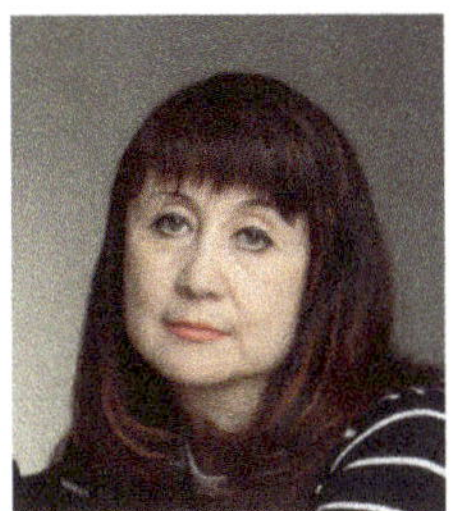

"Family"
Canvas on cardboard. Acrylic.
Mixed technique.
70 × 90 cm, 2021.

Family is the most important thing in human life. A traditional family teaches love, care, wisdom and responsibility. Family members give strength, support in difficult moments and give confidence in the future.

This is especially important for people living in the North, in extreme climatic conditions where winter is most of the year and the temperature reaches - 50 degrees below zero.
A family will not let a man die, as he is the strength of a family, nor a woman, who is its spirit. The child is a young growing tree with strong roots and a beautiful crown pointing towards the future.

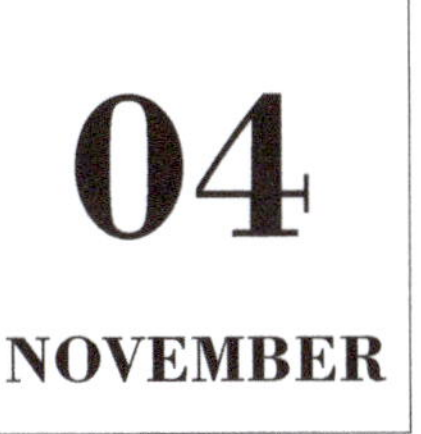

KAREL HYNEK MÁCHA (CZECH REPUBLIC)

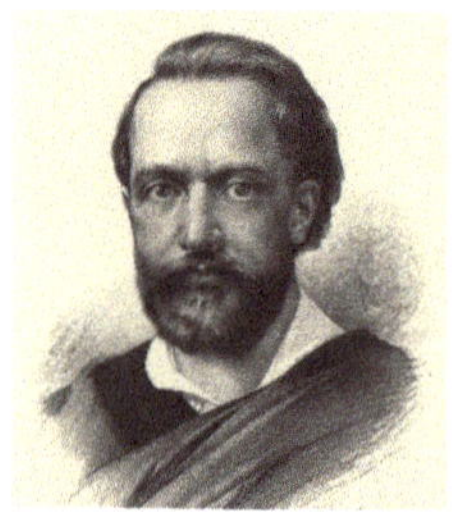

***

Late evening, on the first of May -
The twilit May - the time of love.
Meltingly called the turtle-dove,
Where rich and sweet pinewoods lay.
Whispered of love the mosses trail,
The flowering tree as sweetly lied,
The rose's fragrant sigh replied
To love-songs of the nightingale.
In shadowy woods the burnished lake
Darkly complained a secret pain,
By circling shores embraced again;
And heaven's clear sun leaned down to take
A road astray in azure deeps,
Like burning tears the lover weeps.

***

Byl pozdní večer - první máj -
večerní máj - byl lásky čas.
Hrdliččin zval ku lásce hlas,
kde borový zaváněl háj.
O lásce šeptal tichý mech;
květoucí strom lhal lásky žel,
svou lásku slavík růži pěl,
růžinu jevil vonný vzdech.
Jezero hladké v křovích stinných
zvučelo temně tajný bol,
břeh objímal je kol a kol;
a slunce jasná světů jiných
bloudila blankytnými pásky,
planoucí tam co slzy lásky.

(translated by Edith Pargeter)

05

NOVEMBER

29 MONDAY

30 TUESDAY

31 WEDNESDAY

01 THURSDAY

02 FRIDAY

03 SATURDAY

04 SUNDAY

NADEGDA BOGOVICH (RUSSIA)

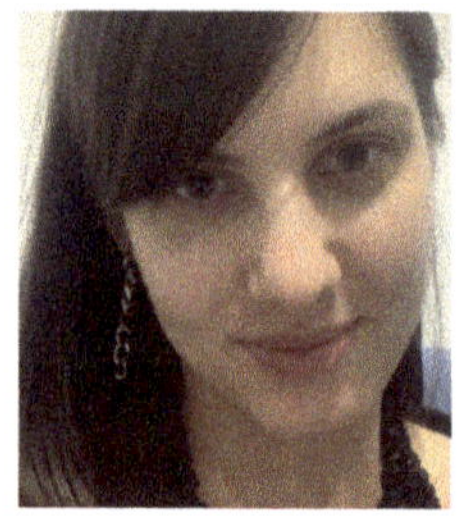

Write, Write with Anticipation...

Write, write with anticipation,
Write with a little oblivion...
Write with a special emotion,
Write about the house in the village,
Write about it and about yourself,
Your children, your family:
Write about your dreams in silence...

Write about him and of love,
Write from your heart and not in silence...
Write of your friendship,
About the tenderness of your soul.

Write, but don't hurry,
Talk to me about him,
About the fragility of his soul!

Write about you and your love!
You've already found one another.
Don't rush time,
Trust me and rest.

Fill your heart with love
So that you have the strength to go to him.
He will be faithful to the love
That you can find.

07

NOVEMBER

For therein lies the salvation of the soul,
But, Daughter, don't be in a hurry.
You need to toughen up
You've got to get stronger.

And then you'll go to him,
To him alone in the world.
And you'll write a novel,
Just the way he said it would be!

He is my beloved son,
His soul is bright.
I know what is damaged,
And so tormented to the end...
His soul is with me always!

I know he is looking for me...
I am ready to guide him on his path.
I am always changing,
I gave my word, I am faithful always.

Do not forget me...
And build your house on the rock.
Then neither wind nor storm
Can separate your clan.

Now you know the secret,
Of happy couples
Now you know love
You've got it in your hearts
And I will protect you

NADEGDA BOGOVICH (RUSSIA)

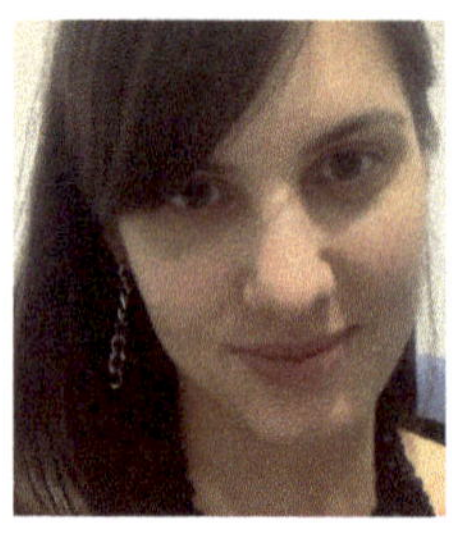

To take care of each other and help each other
And you're my dream now
But just listen to me

And I'm always ready to tell you
To show you what is best to do
I've just been waiting for you for so long,
Now everything in heaven is decided

And you just have to trust me
And don't resist your destiny...
You have touched me with your heart,
Now I am with you for all eternity.

And time will put everything in its place
You'll get my advice, and yes
Love will be yours to the fullest!

08

NOVEMBER

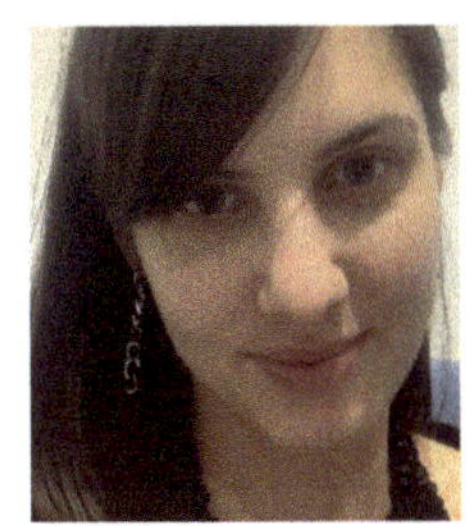

Пиши, пиши с предвосхищеньем…

Пиши, пиши с предвосхищеньем,
Пиши хоть в маленьком забвенье...
Пиши с особым умиленьем,
Пиши о доме в поселенье,
Пиши о нем и о себе,
О детях ваших, о семье:
О всех мечтаньях в тишине…

Пиши о нем и о любви,
Пиши от сердца не молчи…
О дружбе вашей напиши,
О нежности своей души.

Пиши, но только не спеши,
О нем со Мной поговори,
О хрупкости его души!

Пиши о вас и о любви!
Друг друга вы уже нашли.
И время ты не торопи,
Доверься Мне и отдохни.

Наполни сердце ты любви,
Чтоб был ресурс к нему идти.
Он верен будет той любви,
Которую смогли найти.

09

NOVEMBER

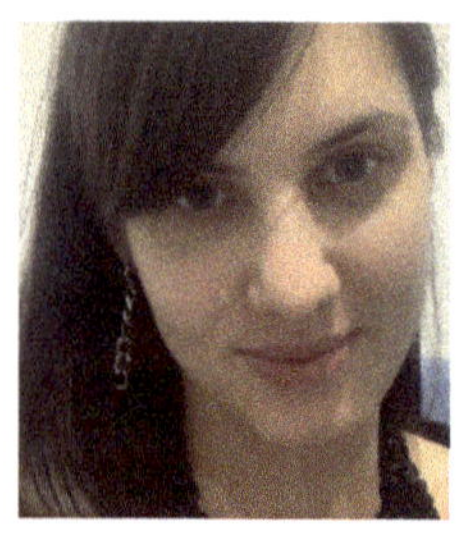

Ведь в ней спасение души,
Но только Дочка не спеши.
Окрепнуть нужно ты пойми,
Убрать осколки изнутри.

И вот тогда пойдёшь к нему,
К нему на свете одному.
И вы напишите роман,
Такой как есть, как он сказал!

Он - сын любимый для Меня,
Душа его она светла.
Я знаю, чем повреждена,
И так измучена до дна...
Его душа со Мной всегда!

Я знаю ищет он Меня…
Я направлять готов в стезя.
Я неизменен никогда,
Я слово дал, Я в нем всегда.

Не забывайте обо Мне…
И стройте дом ваш на скале.
Тогда не ветер ни буран,
Не смогут развести ваш клан.

Теперь вы знаете секрет,
Счастливых пар от всех их бед.
Теперь познали вы любовь,
У вас в сердцах она живет.
А Я вас буду защищать,

10

NOVEMBER

Беречь друг друга, помогать.
И вы Моя теперь мечта,
Но только вслушайтесь в Меня.

А Я всегда готов сказать,
Как лучше сделать, показать.
Я просто ждал вас так давно,
Что все на небе решено.

А вы лишь доверяйте Мне,
И не противитесь судьбе...
Коснулись сердцем ВЫ Меня,
Теперь Я с вами на века.

А время все расставит на места:
И будет вам совет и да,
Любовь познаете сполна!

OSMAN HAMDI BEY (TURKEY)

"The Tortoise Trainer", 1906
(Turkish: Kaplumbağa Terbiyecisi)

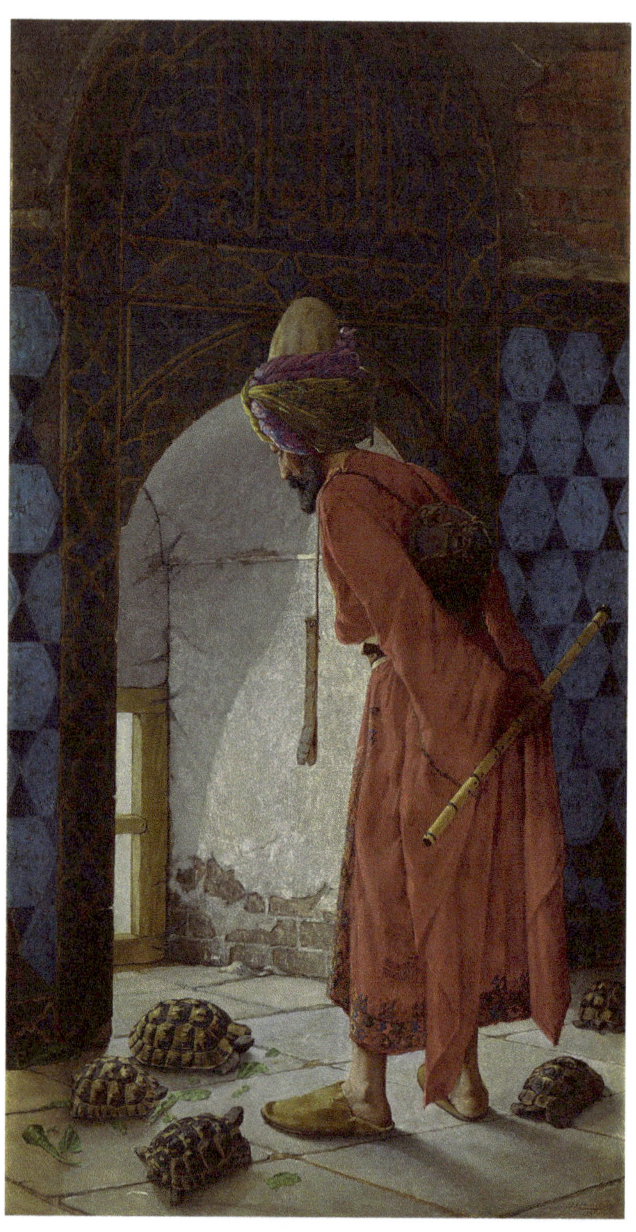

11

NOVEMBER

05 MONDAY

06 TUESDAY

07 WEDNESDAY

08 THURSDAY

09 FRIDAY

10 SATURDAY

11 SUNDAY

"Dancing dervishes", 1480-1490

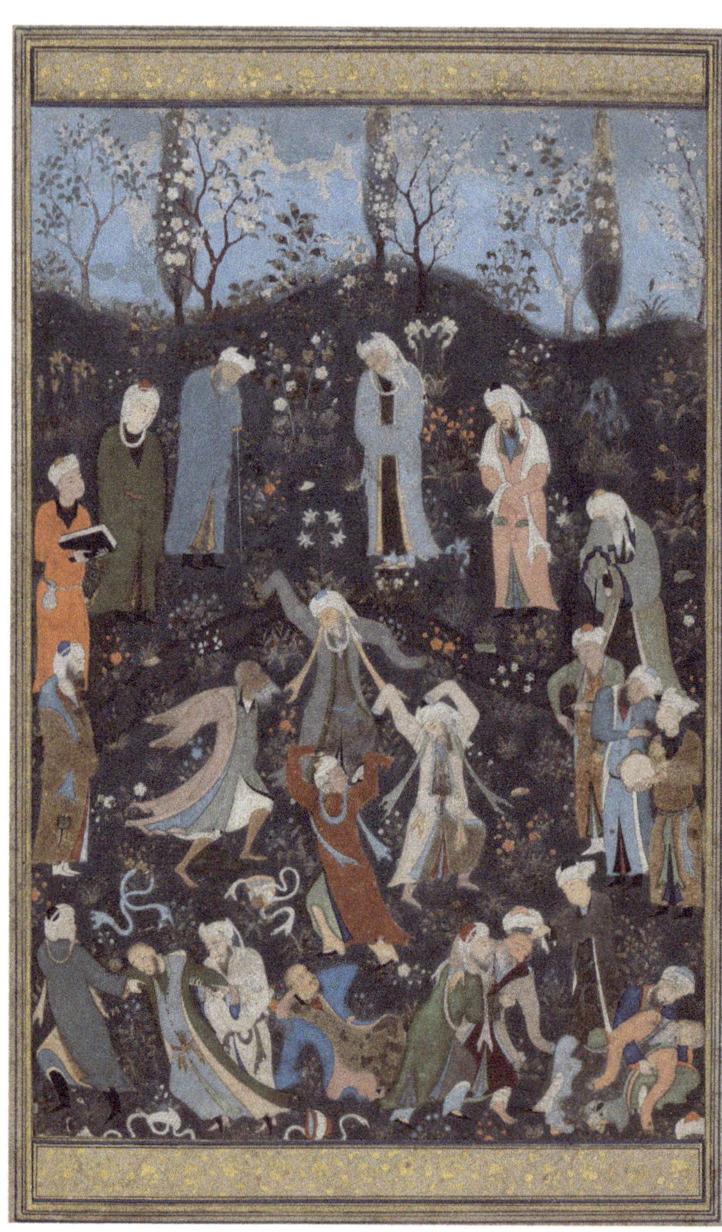

13

NOVEMBER

12 MONDAY

13 TUESDAY

14 WEDNESDAY

15 THURSDAY

16 FRIDAY

17 SATURDAY

18 SUNDAY

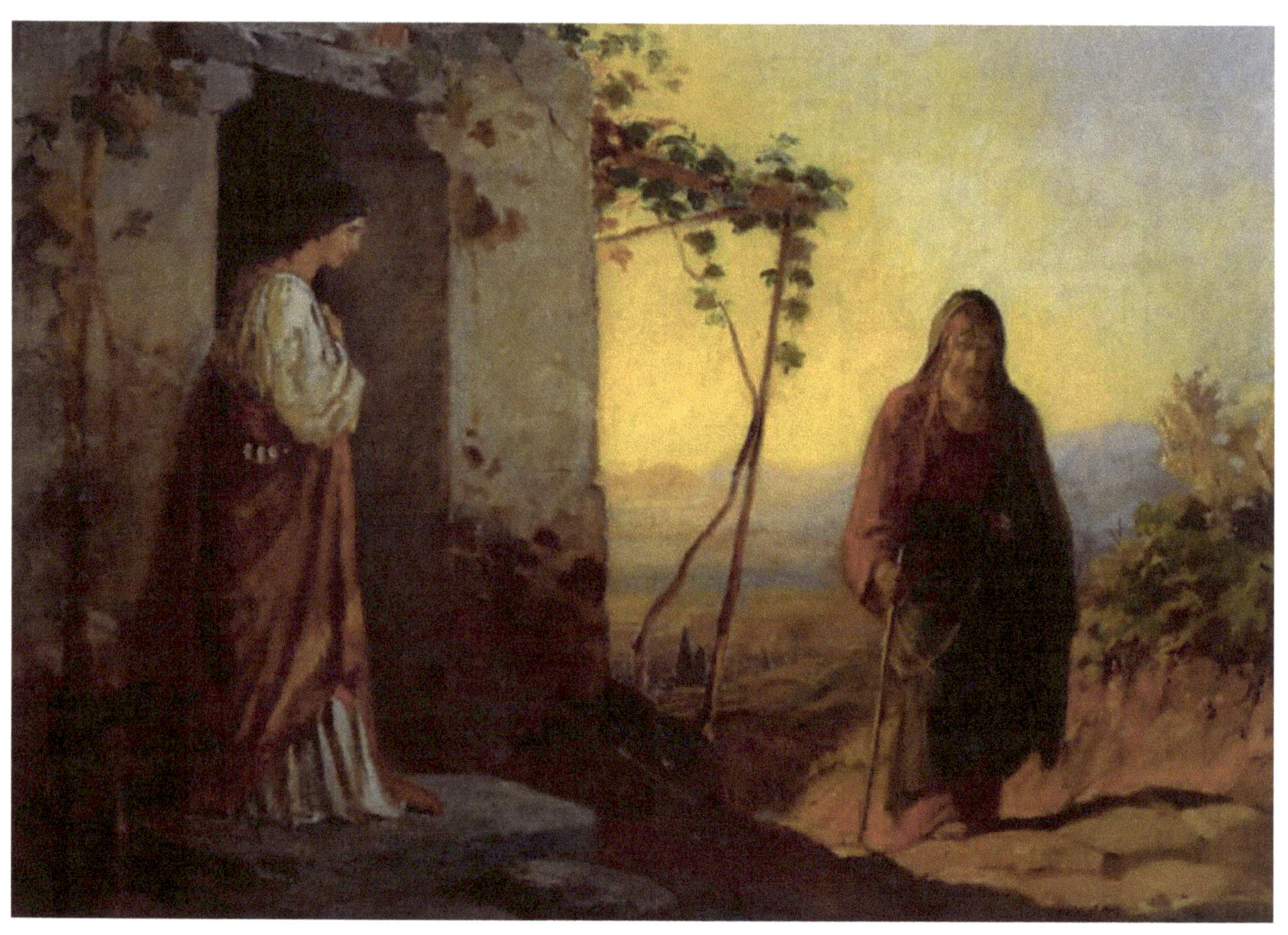

"Maria, sister of Lazarus, meets Jesus who is going to their house", 1864

20

NOVEMBER

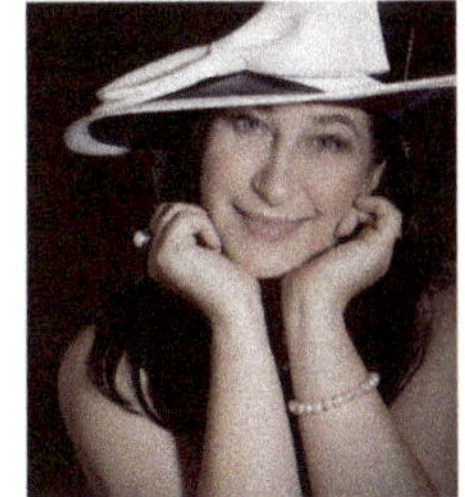

Stations of Life

The stations of life are our shores.
We glide through them like waves over rivers.
From "hello" to a short "bye-bye".
Our lives are full of water.

The stations of life are our frontiers,
Shelters that give us hope,
Oh, how sometimes we sincerely sin,
While afraid to stain our white clothes!

The stations of life are joys and sorrows.
The twining of happy encounters and partings.
We're becoming so hesitant, and what a pity...
There is life in overcoming distances!

21

NOVEMBER

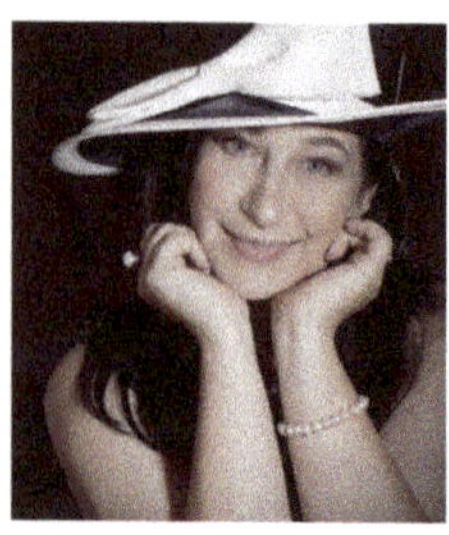

Вокзалы жизни

Вокзалы жизни — наши берега.
Мы в них кочуем как по рекам волны.
От «здравствуй» до короткого «пока»
Жизнь наша протекает полноводно.

Вокзалы жизни — наши рубежи,
Приюты, подарившие надежды,
О! Как порою искренне грешим,
Боясь испачкать белые одежды!

Вокзалы жизни — радость и печаль.
Смешенье счастья встреч и расставаний.
Осёдлость обретаем мы. А жаль...
Жизнь лишь в преодоленье расстояний!

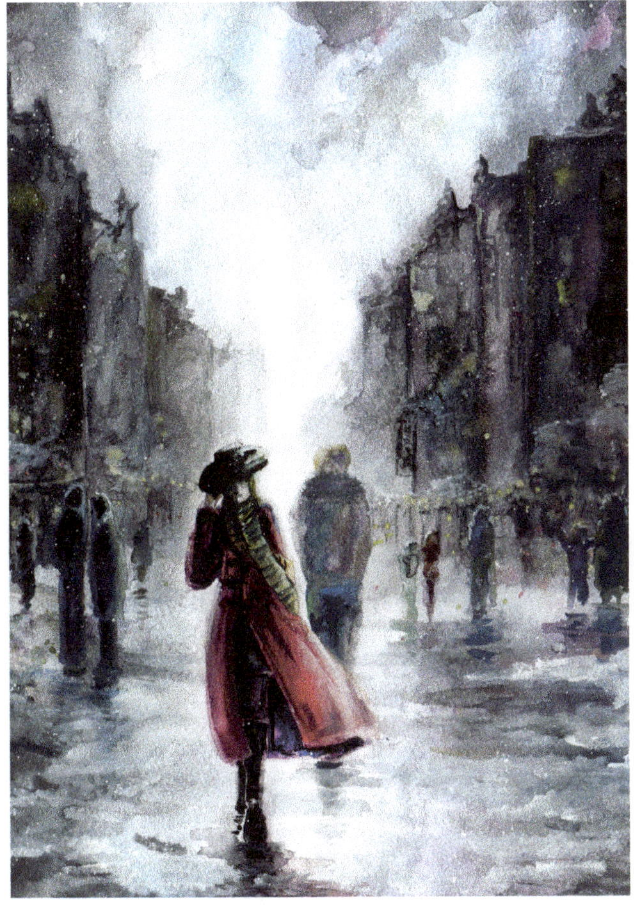

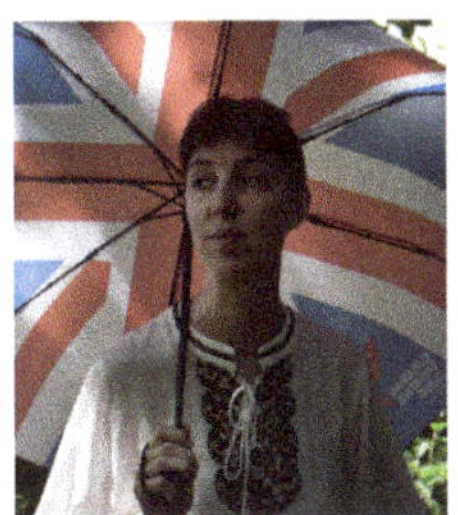

"The last day of the year"

The full title of the painting is "The last day of the year (A love affair that didn't happen)". It is a story about a missed opportunity – two strangers meet in a crowded square on New Year's Eve, but pass by each other. They might have become the happiest couple in the world, but they didn't know about each other, and they never will.

I tried to paint that dull and sleety Moscow winter that had happened a few years ago — slushy, snowless and depressing without any holiday atmosphere. All those lanterns and decorations look a bit out of place in such weather, but children are happy to see them anyway.

Some viewers describe this piece as a story about a broken relationship; others see a heart shape in the sky and interpret it as a love of the city itself – maybe for the heroine in the red coat, maybe for people in general. Anyway, the main idea was a sad story about love, but both characters may still find their happiness, so not all sad stories have a sad end.

23

NOVEMBER

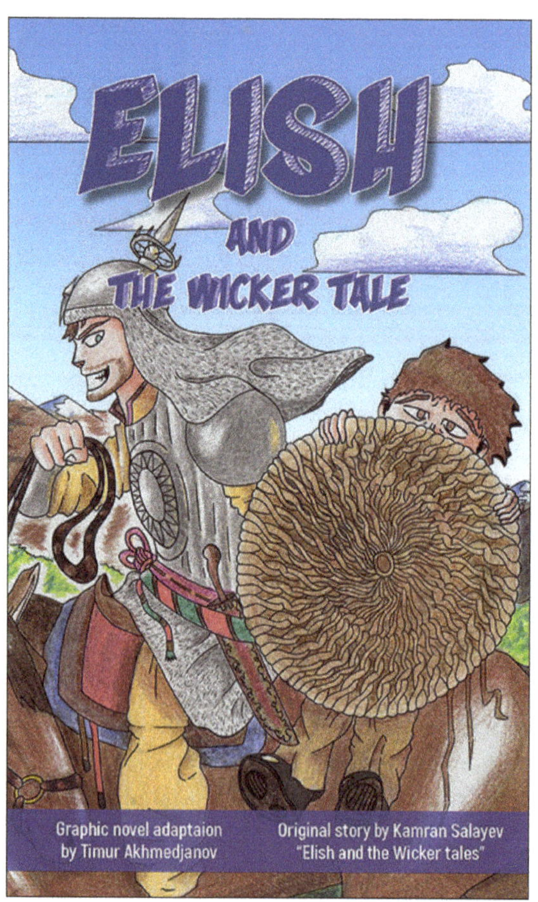

'Elish and the Wicker Tale' is a graphic novel based on the orginal story by Kamran Salayev. It follows the life of Elish, a young boy who has trouble communicating and coping with the world around him. Elish would rather keep to himself, doing what he loves more than anything, crafting wicker artifacts. Once trouble stirs in his world, however, Elish is set on the path of adventure, forced to step outside his comfort zone and confront his fears in order to help those around him. Elish's behavior and insecurities mirror those of children from around the globe who suffer from autism. Just like Elish, children with autism find it hard to understand and relate to people, so they end up devoting their time to something they can understand, usually a hobby or craft such as wicker-making. Kamran Salayev's goal is to promote awareness of this subject through his book and Timur has decided to join him in that endeavor. As of spring 2020, Timur has been working on a comic/graphic novel adaptation of *'Elish and Wicker Tale'*. With support from the crowdfunding campaigns, we are able to publish the graphic novel, allowing children both with and without autism to access this story in a more visual and engaging form. Sales will also contribute to the cause, with 20% of profits going directly to charities and organizations that tackle autism and make the lives of children affected by autism easier and happier.

ISBN: 978-1913356194
RRP: £12.95

25

NOVEMBER

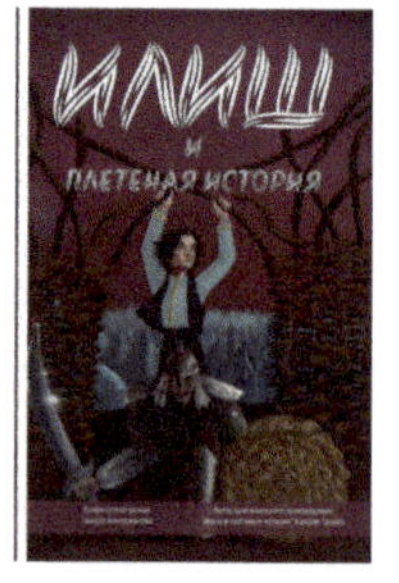

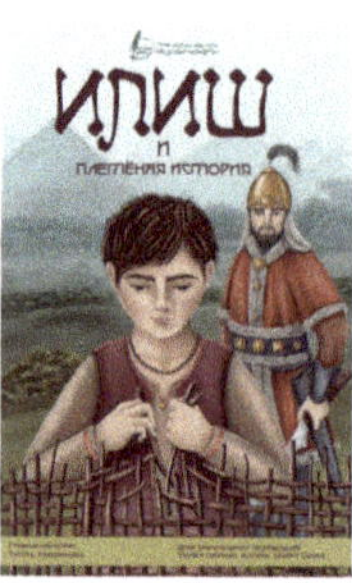

19 MONDAY

20 TUESDAY

21 WEDNESDAY

22 THURSDAY

23 FRIDAY

24 SATURDAY

25 SUNDAY

GAGANENDRANATH TAGORE (INDIA)

"Poet's first flight from London to Paris. 1921

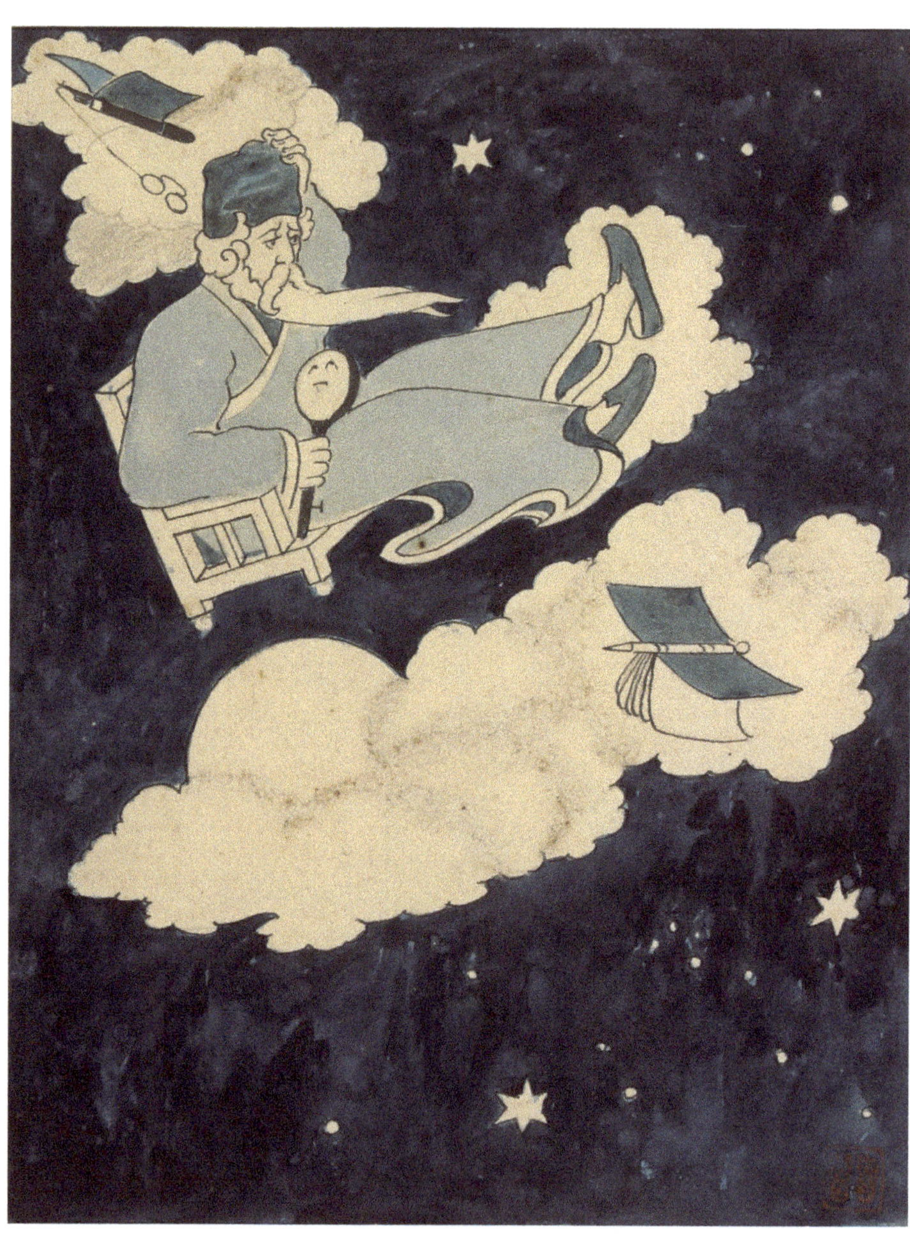

30

NOVEMBER

26 MONDAY

27 TUESDAY

28 WEDNESDAY

29 THURSDAY

30 FRIDAY

01 SATURDAY

02 SUNDAY

"The Quail Shoot", 1775

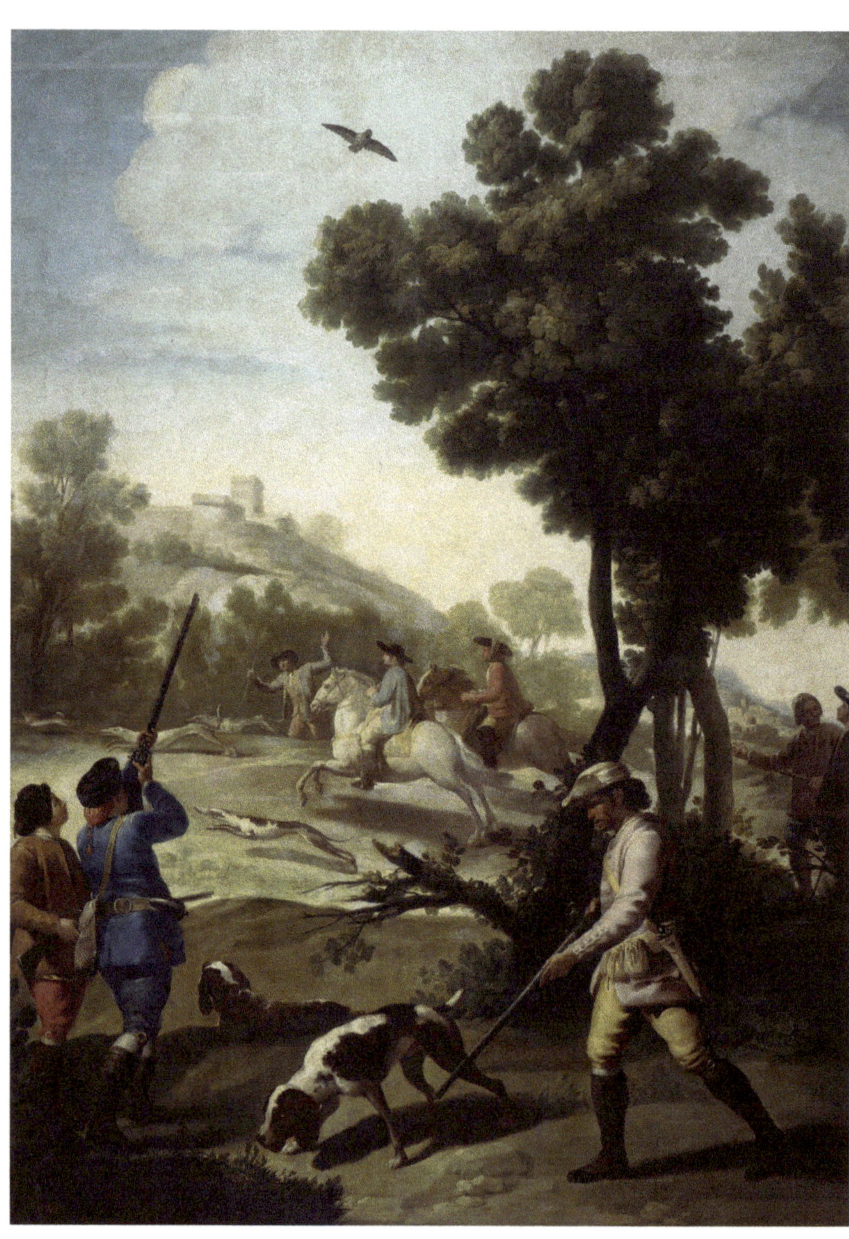

09

DECEMBER

03 MONDAY

04 TUESDAY

05 WEDNESDAY

06 THURSDAY

07 FRIDAY

08 SATURDAY

09 SUNDAY

VLADISLAVA BAYMAGANBETOVA (KAZAKHSTAN)

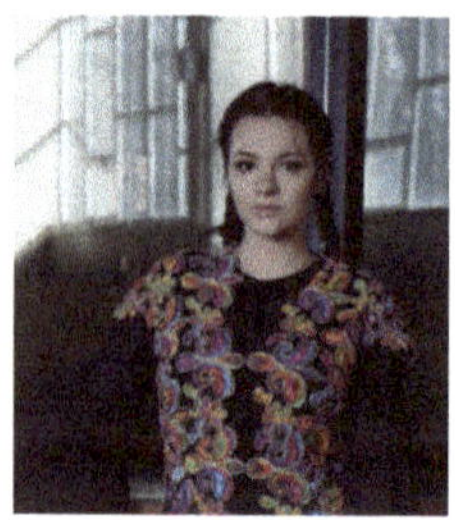

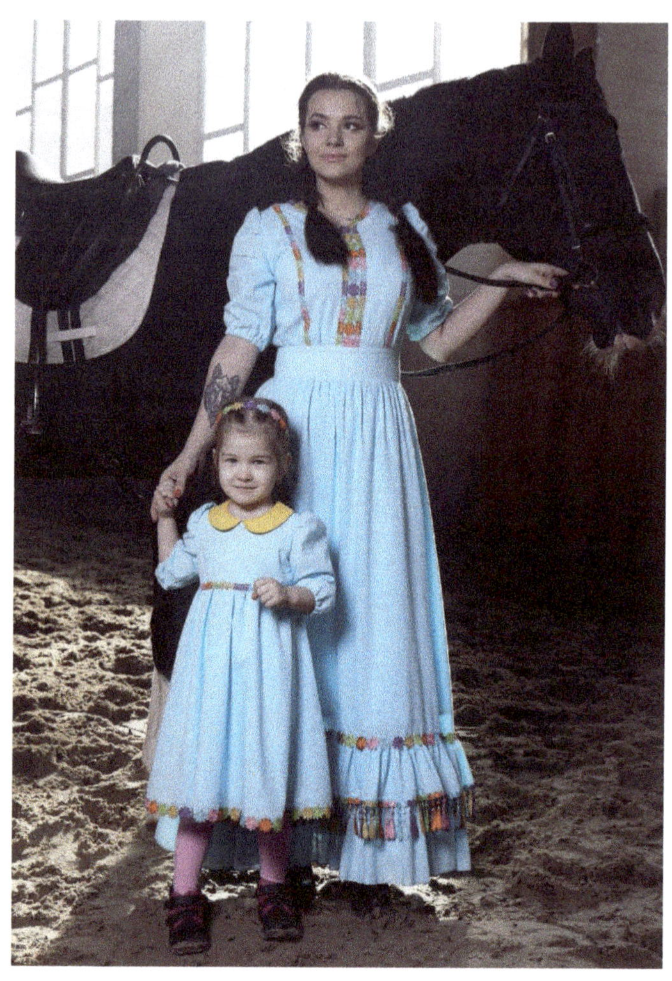

Each nation cherishes its own culture and traditions. The international marriage of my parents influenced my outlook and look, combining elements of the two parts of the world - Europe and Asia. This inspired me to create a collection which tries to reflect the richness of the two cultures, the freedom of choice and harmony.

The collection is an idea of a coherent composition, without the abrupt transitions as in nature between Europe and Asia. Everything is neat and soft but with a claim to be the centre of attention. The decorative surfaces were created with the help of voluminous textile elements, lace and beads. The unconventional cuts and separates make it possible to change the looks by combining different details. Outfits are suitable for festive events, business meetings, and for city everyday life.

16

DECEMBER

The relationship of perception and psychology of color is also reflected. The unity of the opposites of purple and sophisticated black, the predominant blue color - as a symbol of our peaceful sky and the state flag of **independent Kazakhstan**. I wanted to emphasize the combination of modernity and memory of bygone generations in the ethno-dresses. After all, Kazakhstan is a country of nomadic peoples, and a horse has always been an integral part of our ancestors' lives. And one of the most important tasks for every nation is the preservation and maintenance of cultural values.

10 MONDAY

11 TUESDAY

12 WEDNESDAY

13 THURSDAY

14 FRIDAY

15 SATURDAY

16 SUNDAY

"Fergana" Early 20th century

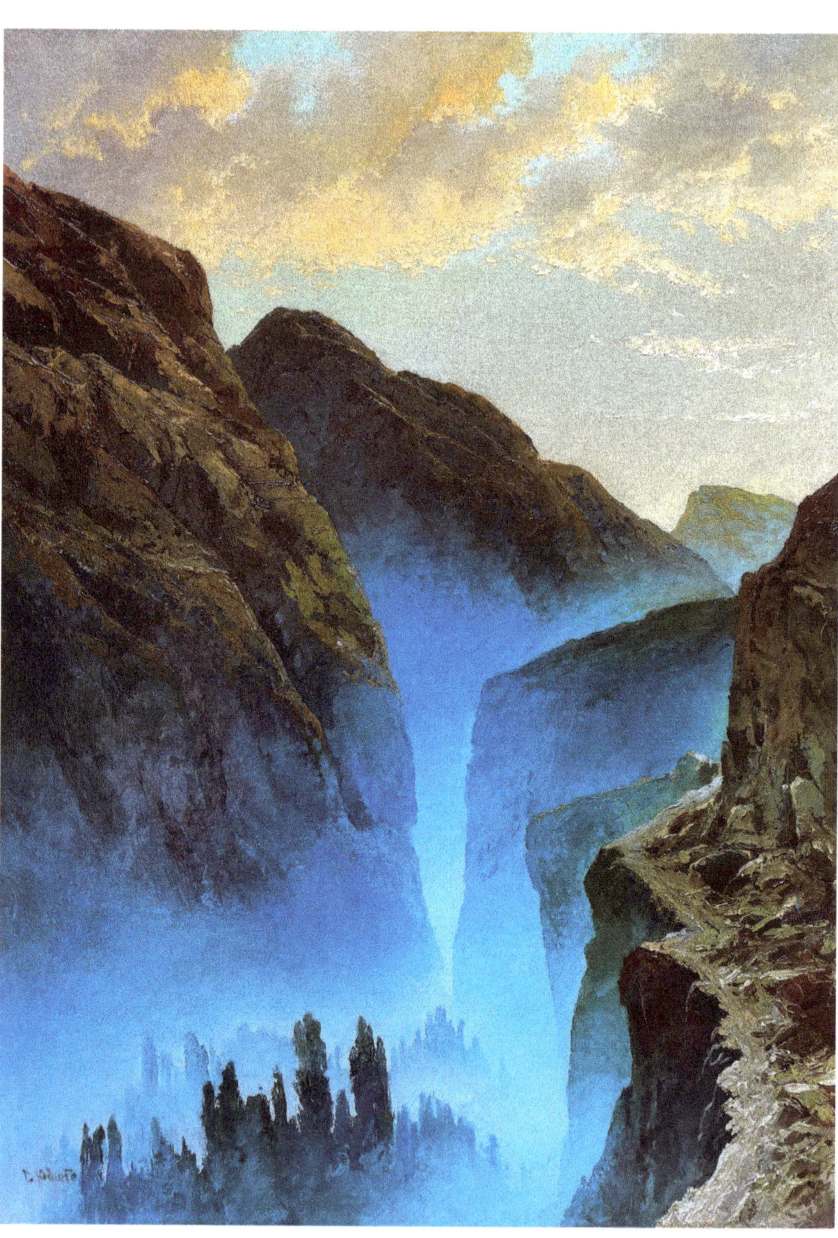

17

DECEMBER

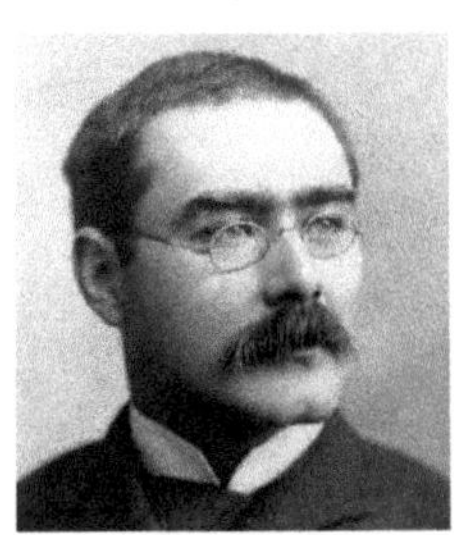

The Queen's Men
"Gloriana"– Rewards and Fairies

Valour and Innocence
Have latterly gone hence
To certain death by certain shame attended.
Envy– ah! even to tears!–
The fortune of their years
Which, though so few, yet so divinely ended.

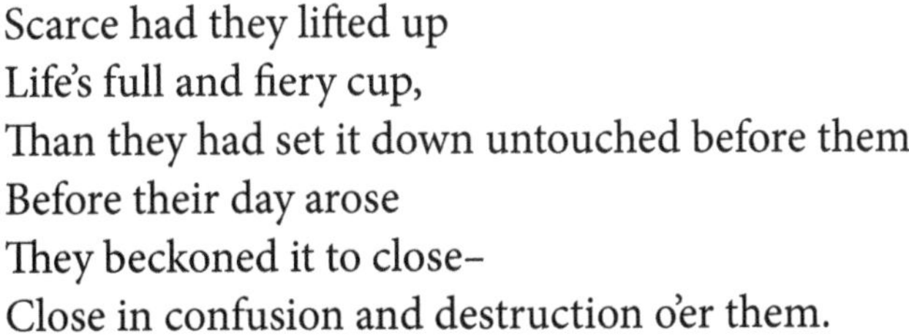

Scarce had they lifted up
Life's full and fiery cup,
Than they had set it down untouched before them.
Before their day arose
They beckoned it to close–
Close in confusion and destruction o'er them.

They did not stay to ask
What prize should crown their task–
Well sure that prize was such as no man strives for;
But passed into eclipse,
Her kiss upon their lips–
Even Belphoebe's, whom they gave their lives for!

18

DECEMBER

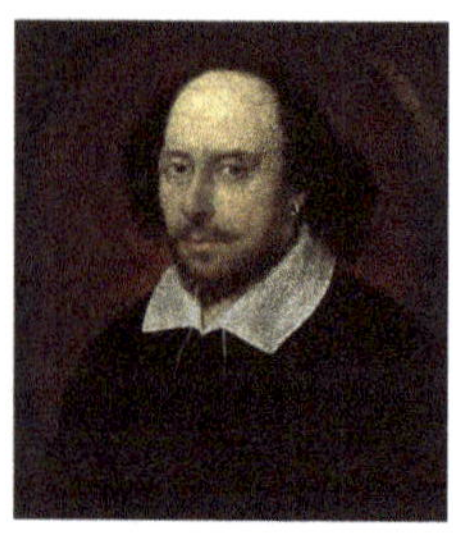

No Longer Mourn For Me...
(From "Sonnets", LXXI)

No longer mourn for me when I am dead
Than you shall hear the surly sullen bell
Give warning to the world that I am fled
From this vile world, with vilest worms to dwell:
Nay, if you read this line , remember not
The hand that writ it; for I love you so,
That I in your sweet thoughts would be forgot,
If thinking on me then should make you woe.
O, if (I say) you look upon this verse,
When I perhaps compounded am with clay,
Do not so much as my poor name rehearse;
But let your love even with my live decay:
Lest the wise world should look into your moan ,
And mock you with me after I am gone.

20

DECEMBER

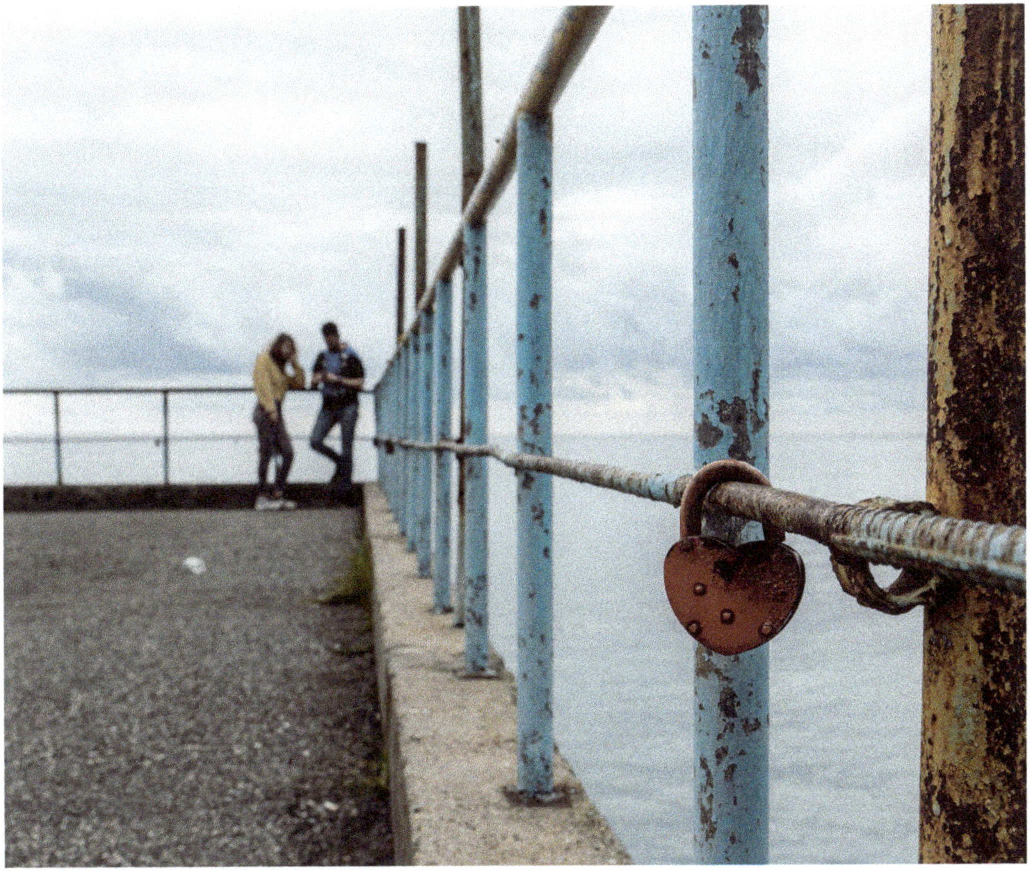

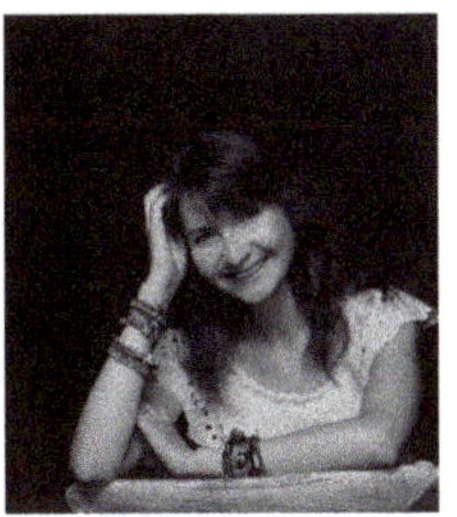

“Signs”
September 2021.
Digital art photography.
Size: 8.65 Mb;
5393x3595.

The photo was taken on a pier jutting into the Black Sea from the beach of Gagra, a small town in Abkhazia.

The pair in the background are my friends with whom we traveled to Abkhazia in the autumn of 2021. They very successfully (and accidentally) settled down at the fence and did not even know what kind of shot I was doing, crouching in front of the red symbolic lock depicted in the foreground of the photo. And, of course, they did not hear my insidious giggle.

21

DECEMBER

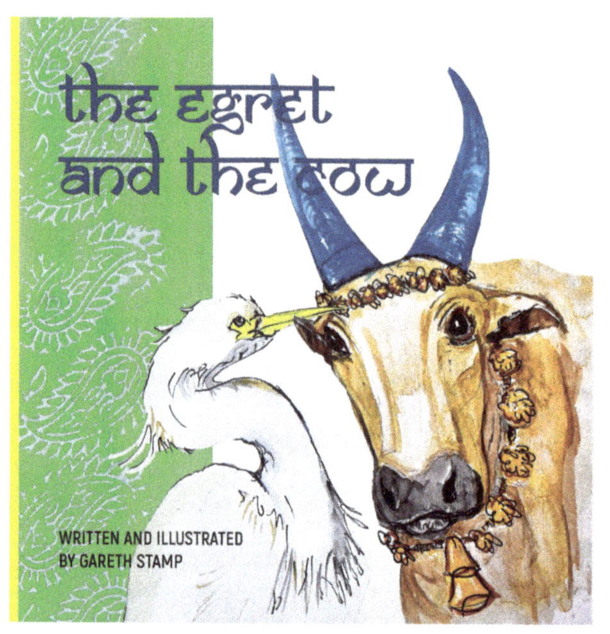

In the flooded fields of Southern India unusual friendships between different animals can be seen - how did they start? Here is one tale that may explain!

ISBN: 978-1913356149
RRP: 9.95

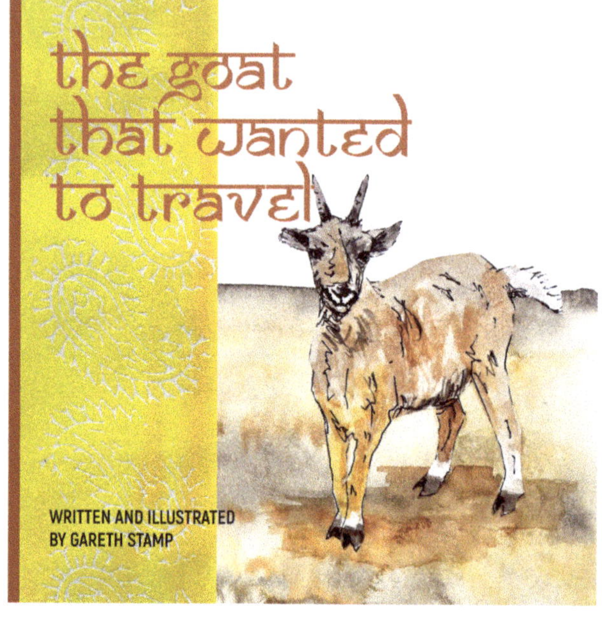

In the bustling Southern city of Bangalore a little goat sets out on his accidental journey - what will he find? And how far will his journey take him?

ISBN: 978-1913356170
RRP: 9.95

23

DECEMBER

17 MONDAY

18 TUESDAY

19 WEDNESDAY

20 THURSDAY

21 FRIDAY

22 SATURDAY

23 SUNDAY

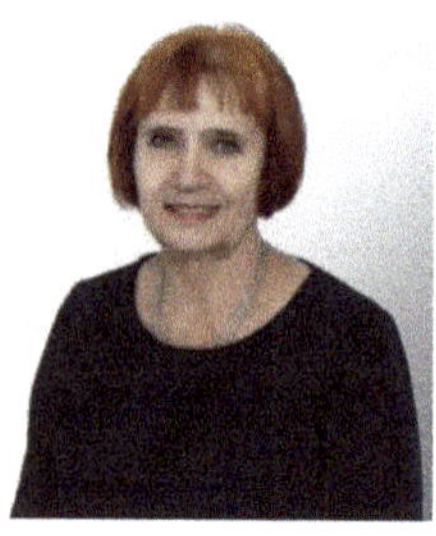

Peaceful Skies

I believe that wise, good hearts
God will unite with a mighty fist.
The invigorating winds will cleanse the conscience,
And scatter like ashes the black smoke of the mountains.
The sky, bottomless, bright and peaceful.
Will embrace the world with motherly love,
With a song of praise,
The fire of love will blaze in our hearts.
The rays of peace in our souls,
Cain's spirit is gone in the wilderness forever.
In thoughts zealous and peaceful aspirations
Judgments unite, like rivers flowing.
Birdsong will fill the air,
The air will be saturated with a fragrant nectar.
The rye field is like the waves on the sea,
For a spiritual feast the bell will ring.

28

DECEMBER

Мірнае неба

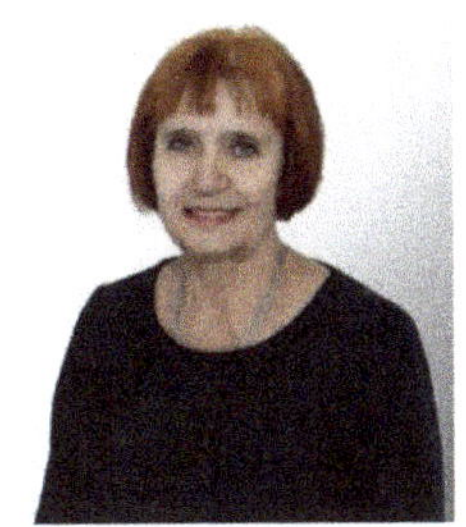

Я веру, што мудрыя, добрыя сэрцы
З`яднае Гасподзь у магутны кулак.
Ачысцяць сумленне бадзёрыя ветры,
Развеяць, як прах, чорны дым у гарах.
Бяздоннае, светлае, мірнае неба
Абдыме з матулінай ласкаю шар,
Аблашчыцца песняй свірэлі хвалебнай,
У сэрцах успыхне любові пажар.
Пасеяць у душах мір светлы прамені,
Дух Каіна кане у нетрах навек.
У мыслях руплівых, і мірных памкненнях
З`яднаюцца думкі, як плыні у рэк.
Птушыныя спевы напоўняць прасторы,
Паветра насыціць духмяны нектар.
Жытнёвае поле, як хвалі на моры,
На свята духоўнае скліча званар…

29

DECEMBER

Follow Steve Mile, a teenager with a dangerously short temper and his best friend John, as they join a summer camp called "Jack's Wood". But after just a few hours there, it becomes clear that Jack's Wood is understaffed and is really only running from the Enthusiasm from it's founder and camp Leader; Mr Chang! And the more time they spend there, the more it is clear that Jack's Wood isn't just filled with strangest people on earth, but also Jack's Wood isn't everything it seems.

Volume One is a big introduction to the larger story that establishes most of the characters' personalities and the different tones the story dwells into from a jokey fun ride through the activities, as well as the darker tone inside the forest. Also I think the ending is a perfect way to set up the real action of this bigger narrative.

ISBN: 978-1-913356-18-7
RRP: £12.95

30

DECEMBER

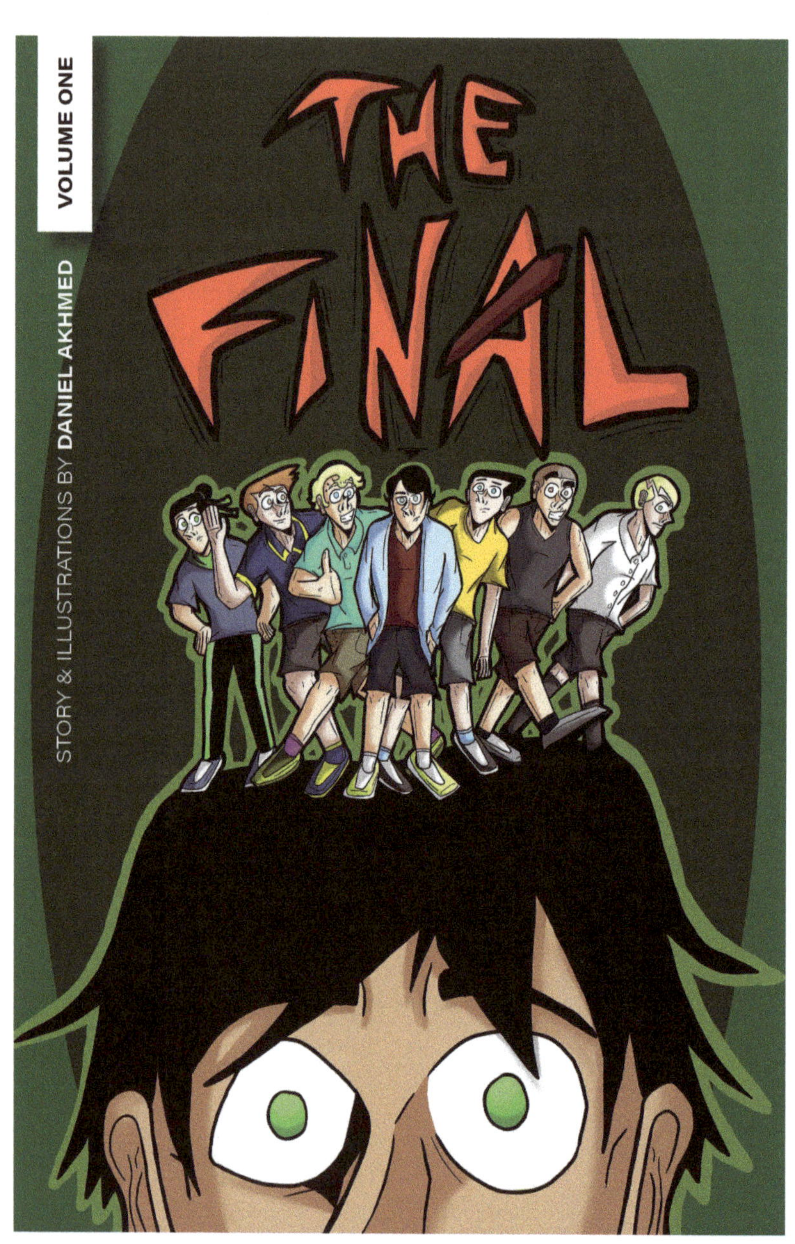

24 MONDAY

25 TUESDAY

26 WEDNESDAY

27 THURSDAY

28 FRIDAY

29 SATURDAY

30 SUNDAY

TAINA KAUNIS (RUSSIA)

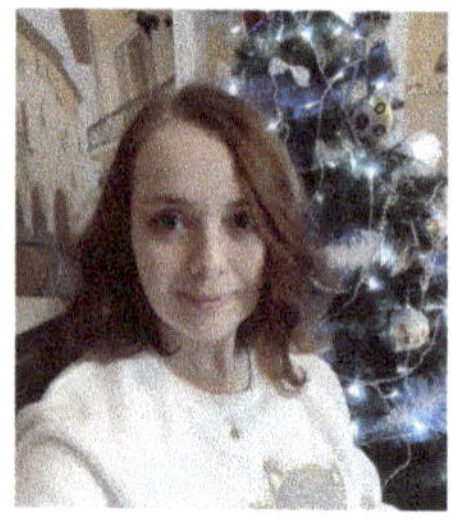

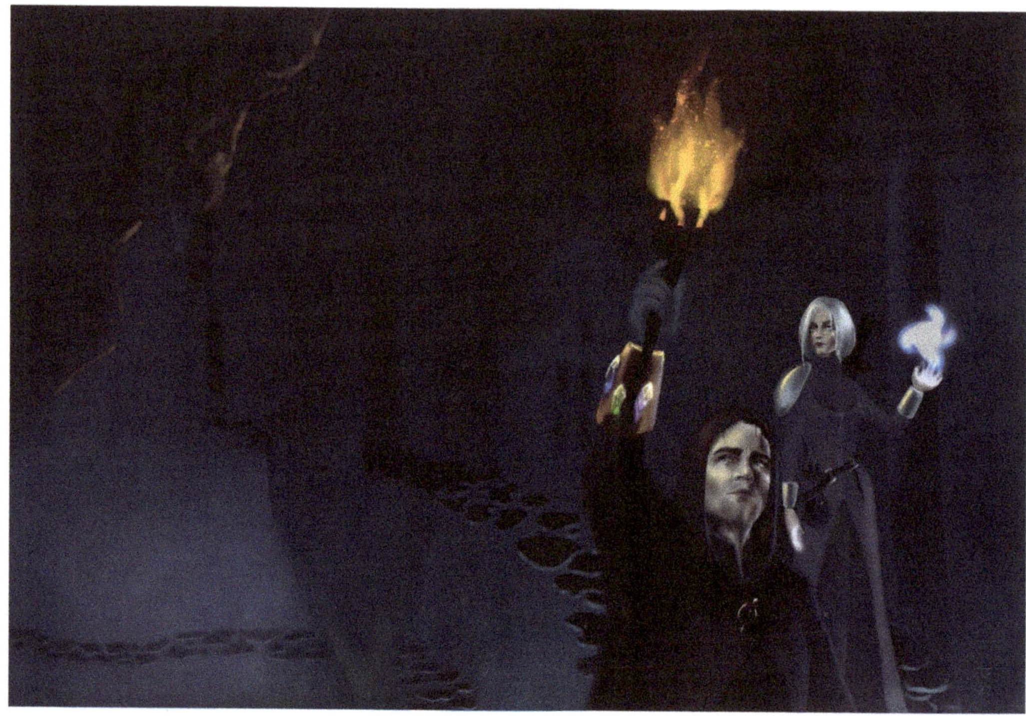

"Under the Veil"
Say that spell "Close your eyes, I'll tell you a story. Once upon a time...", and let the magic begin.

31

DECEMBER

31 MONDAY

01 TUESDAY

02 WEDNESDAY

03 THURSDAY

04 FRIDAY

05 SATURDAY

06 SUNDAY

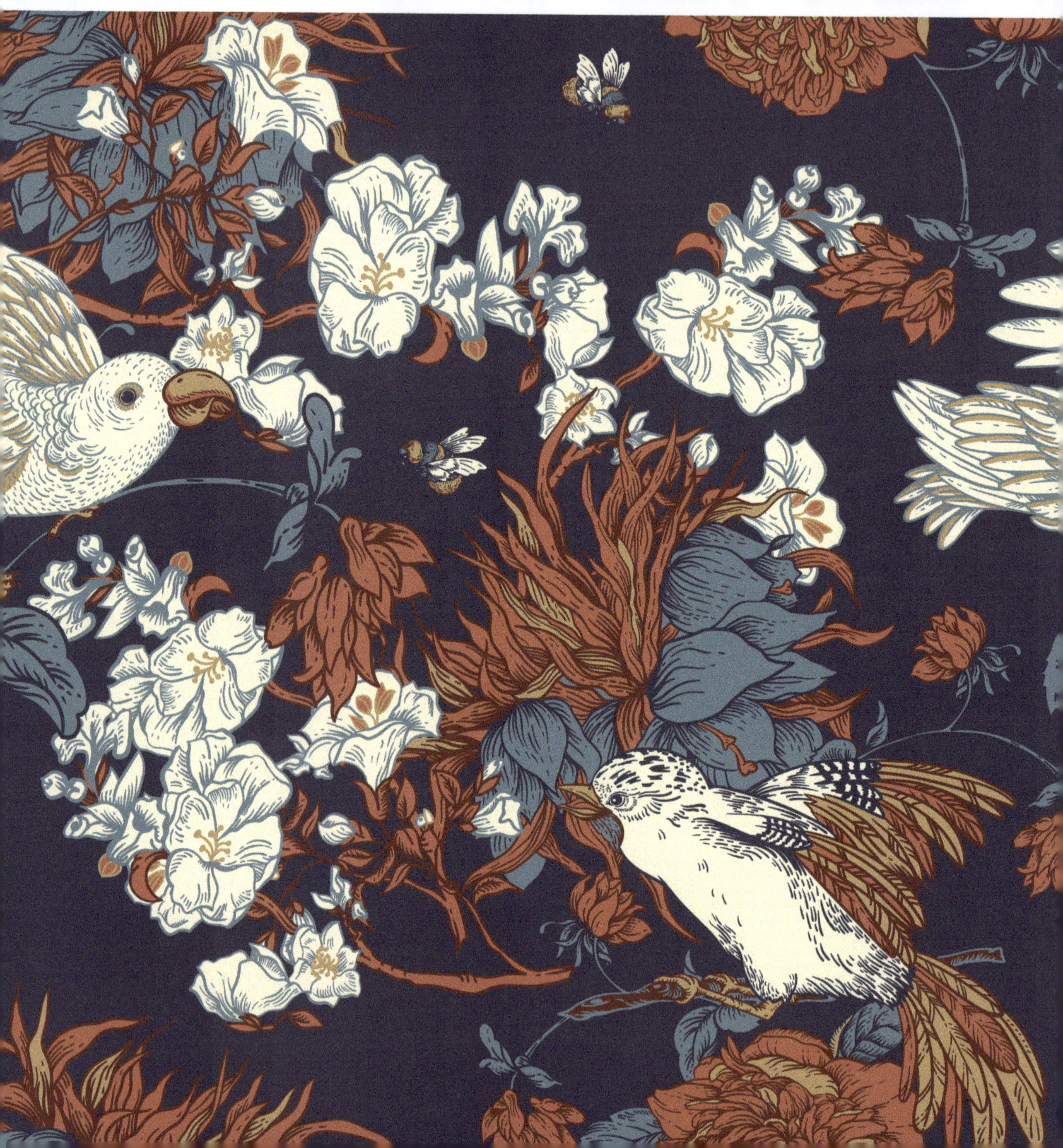

CALENDAR 2024

January

S	M	T	W	T	F	S
	1	2	3	4	5	6
7	8	9	10	11	12	13
14	15	16	17	18	19	20
21	22	23	24	25	26	27
28	29	30	31			

February

S	M	T	W	T	F	S
				1	2	3
4	5	6	7	8	9	10
11	12	13	14	15	16	17
18	19	20	21	22	23	24
25	26	27	28	29		

March

S	M	T	W	T	F	S
					1	2
3	4	5	6	7	8	9
10	11	12	13	14	15	16
17	18	19	20	21	22	23
24	25	26	27	28	29	30
31						

April

S	M	T	W	T	F	S
	1	2	3	4	5	6
7	8	9	10	11	12	13
14	15	16	17	18	19	20
21	22	23	24	25	26	27
28	29	30				

May

S	M	T	W	T	F	S
			1	2	3	4
5	6	7	8	9	10	11
12	13	14	15	16	17	18
19	20	21	22	23	24	25
26	27	28	29	30	31	

June

S	M	T	W	T	F	S
						1
2	3	4	5	6	7	8
9	10	11	12	13	14	15
16	17	18	19	20	21	22
23	24	25	26	27	28	29
30						

July

S	M	T	W	T	F	S
	1	2	3	4	5	6
7	8	9	10	11	12	13
14	15	16	17	18	19	20
21	22	23	24	25	26	27
28	29	30	31			

August

S	M	T	W	T	F	S
				1	2	3
4	5	6	7	8	9	10
11	12	13	14	15	16	17
18	19	20	21	22	23	24
25	26	27	28	29	30	31

September

S	M	T	W	T	F	S
1	2	3	4	5	6	7
8	9	10	11	12	13	14
15	16	17	18	19	20	21
22	23	24	25	26	27	28
29	30					

October

S	M	T	W	T	F	S
		1	2	3	4	5
6	7	8	9	10	11	12
13	14	15	16	17	18	19
20	21	22	23	24	25	26
27	28	29	30	31		

November

S	M	T	W	T	F	S
					1	2
3	4	5	6	7	8	9
10	11	12	13	14	15	16
17	18	19	20	21	22	23
24	25	26	27	28	29	30

December

S	M	T	W	T	F	S
1	2	3	4	5	6	7
8	9	10	11	12	13	14
15	16	17	18	19	20	21
22	23	24	25	26	27	28
29	30	31				

CONTENTS

ALMANAC VOICES OF FRIENDS: POETRY AND ART 2023

www.ingramcontent.com/pod-product-compliance
Lightning Source LLC
LaVergne TN
LVHW060601110826
845154LV00004B/102
9781913356590